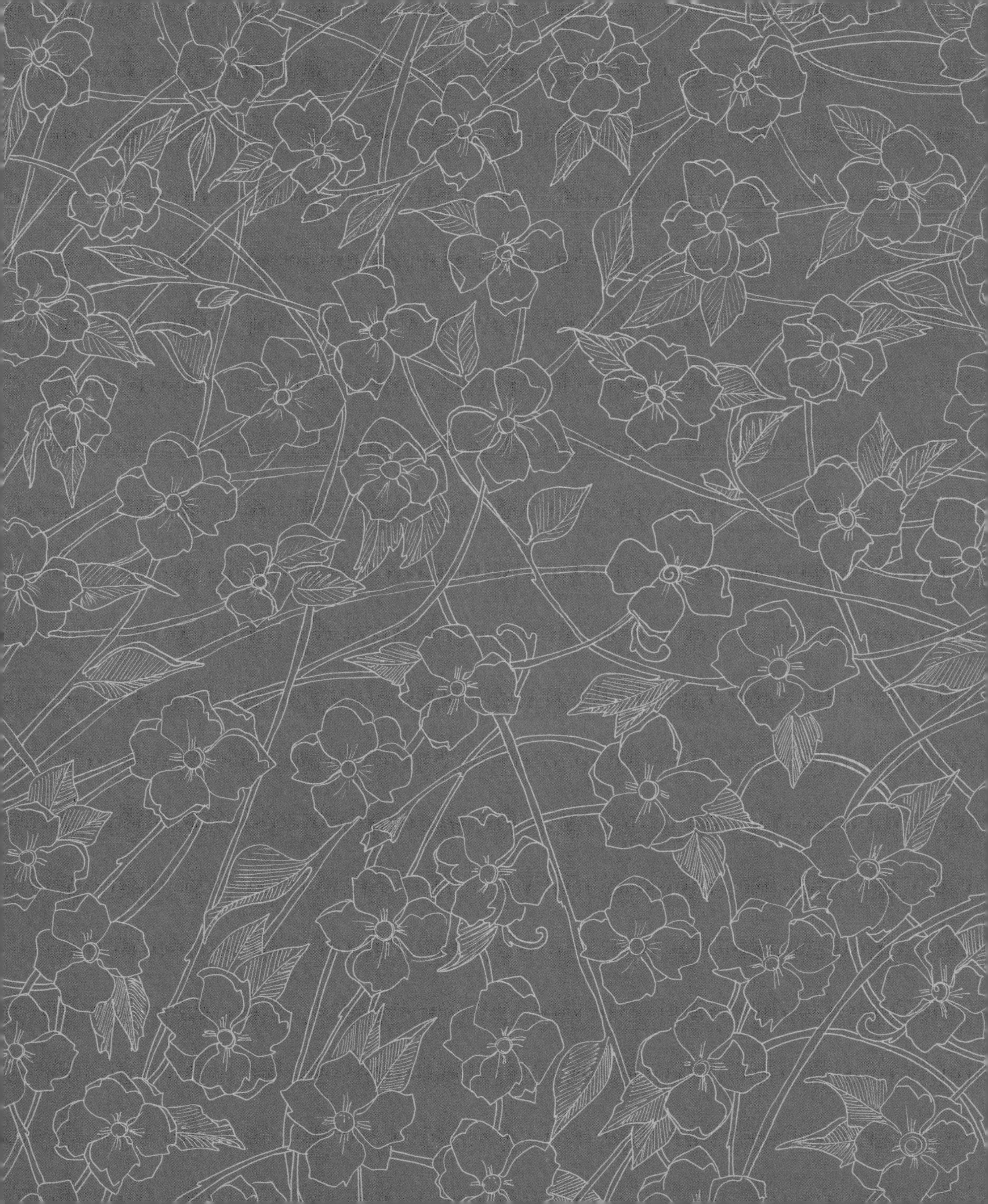

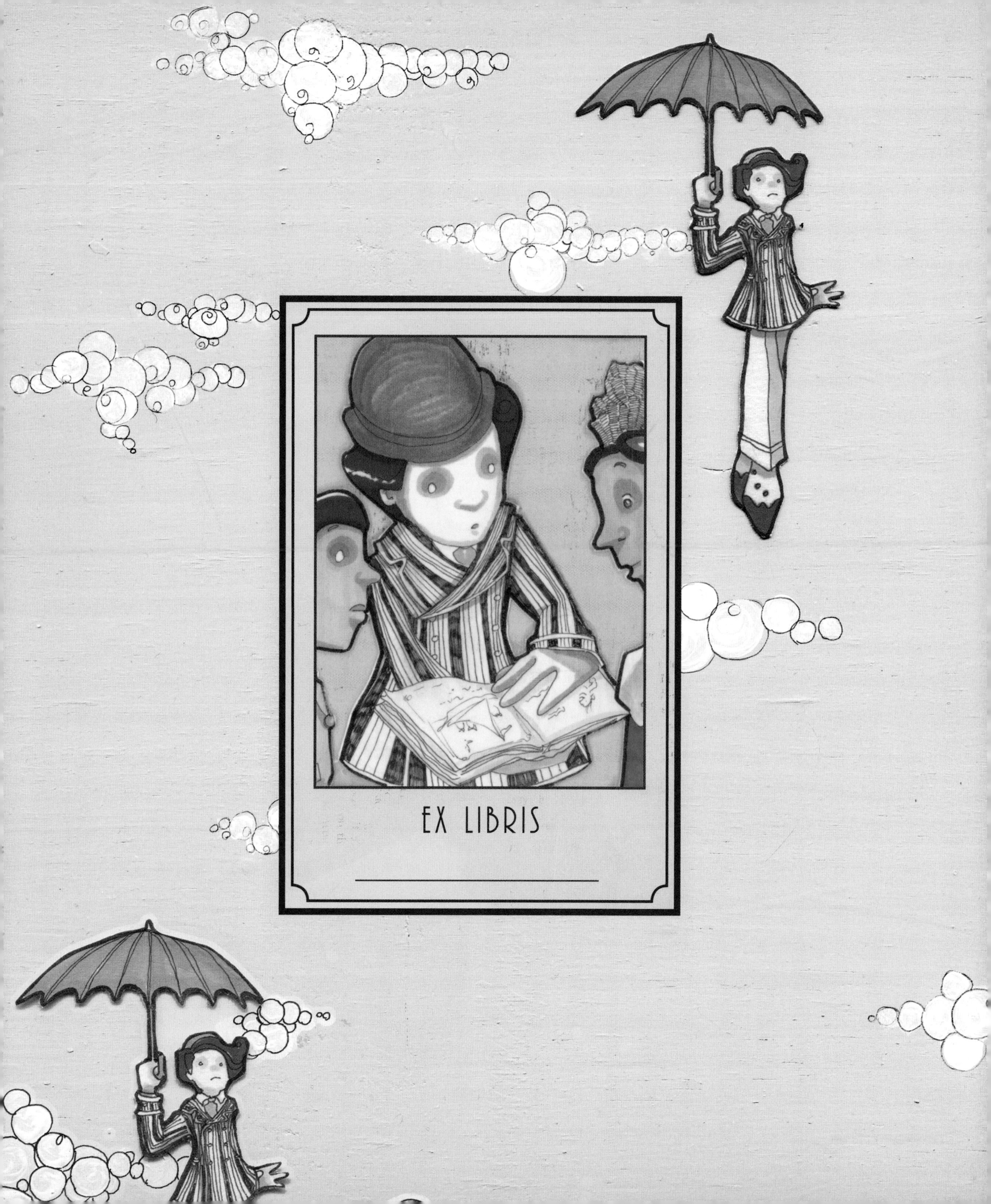
EX LIBRIS

RETURN OF THE

DAPPER MEN

WRITTEN BY

JIM McCANN

ART BY

JANET LEE

LETTERED BY
DAVE LANPHEAR

ORIGINALLY EDITED BY
STEPHEN CHRISTY

TOP SHELF EDITION EDITED BY
CHRIS STAROS & LEIGH WALTON

DESIGNED BY
ERIC SKILLMAN

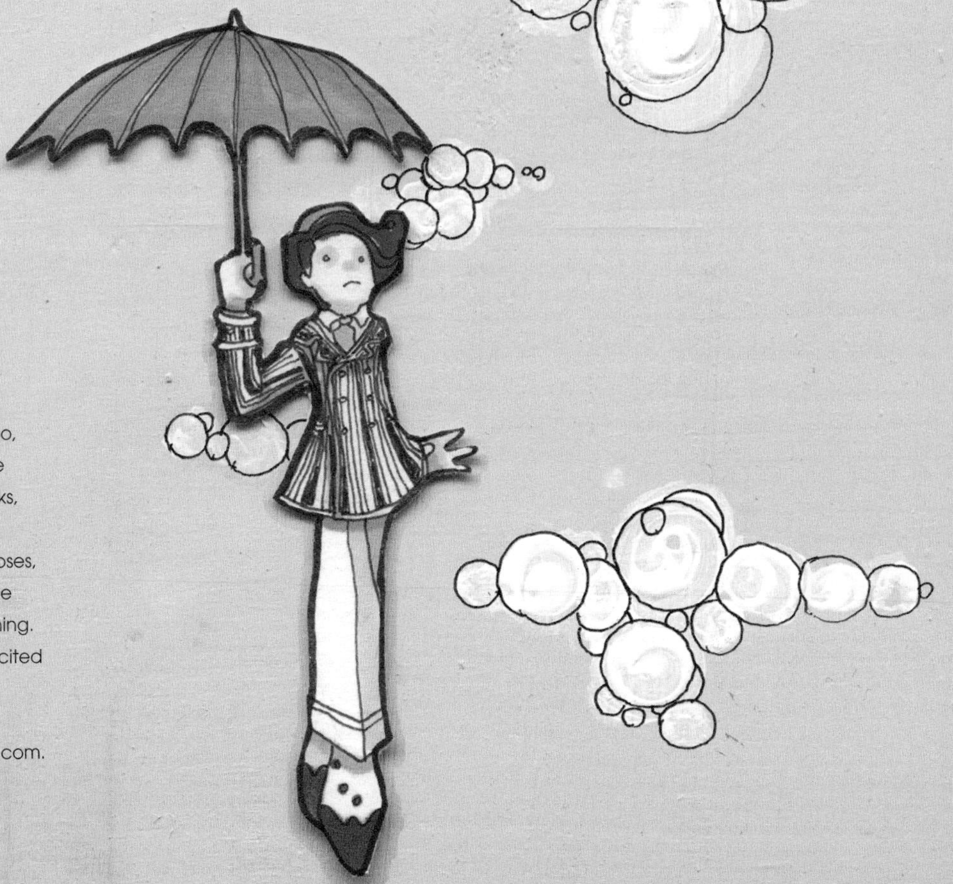

Return of the Dapper Men: Deluxe Edition

Published by
Top Shelf Productions
PO Box 1282
Marietta, GA 30061-1282
USA

Editor-in-Chief: Chris Staros

Top Shelf Productions is an imprint of IDW Publishing, a division of Idea and Design Works, LLC. Offices: 2765 Truxtun Road, San Diego, CA 92106. Top Shelf Productions®, the Top Shelf logo, Idea and Design Works®, and the IDW logo are registered trademarks of Idea and Design Works, LLC.

Visit our online catalog at www.topshelfcomix.com.

ISBN 978-1-60309-413-9

Printed in China.

21 20 19 18 17 1 2 3 4 5

FOR ALL THE PEOPLE AND STORIES OF
YESTERDAY WHO INSPIRE US TODAY TO
DREAM OF TOMORROW.

— JIM AND JANET

SPECIAL THANKS TO:

Graphic genius Jeremy Brody, lifesaver Scott Newman, master designer Todd
Klein, the original dapper man Tim Gunn, the ever fabulous Gulag Boy,
Rebecca Taylor, the fine folks at Chromatics, composer Jonathan Gjertsen,
our incredibly patient and supportive friends and families, and the writers &
artists whose works continue to inspire our imaginations every day.

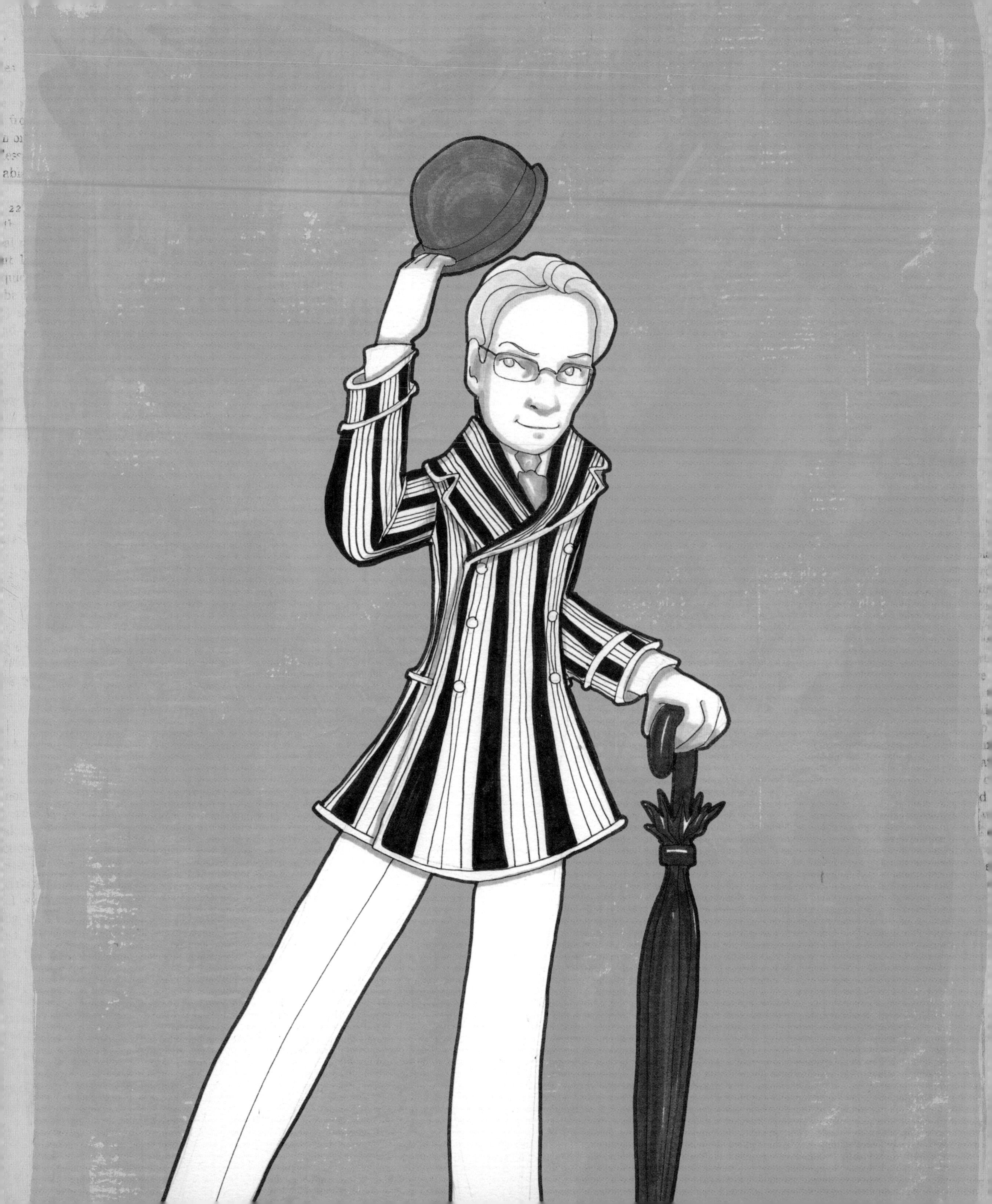

INTRODUCTION
by
TIM GUNN

I am an avid reader and I love a good story. I'm especially fond of tales that disorient the reader and cause one to question what's real and what isn't. I find stories of this kind to recalibrate my thinking about my place in the world; think *Alice in Wonderland, Through the Looking Glass, The Wizard of Oz,* or even *Pinocchio.*

Accordingly, I am a huge fan of the work of Jim McCann. In my opinion, he is the *ne plus ultra* storyteller — wildly inventive, intelligent, research driven, sharp witted, and he shuns the mundane.

Return of the Dapper Men is a transformational experience, a morality tale that is certain to become an instant contemporary classic. The narrative is instantly captivating and always multi-dimensional. The reader will find puzzles, riddles, and anagrams that serve as catalysts for further investigation and research. Be armed with Google and Merriam-Webster.com in order to enjoy the full-tilt experience of this wondrous read. Furthermore, you'll fall in love with the story's two main characters, Ayden and Zoe, who are part Hansel and Gretel and part Tristan and Isolde.

Then there is the remarkable, breathtaking artwork of Janet Lee. I read Jim's story before seeing Janet's artwork for the book. I found Jim's words to be so vividly visual that it was easy for me to imagine the Big Bang, the topsy-turvy land of Anorev, the visage of Ayden and Zoe, and the Clockwork Angel, which figures prominently and mysteriously in the story. Accordingly, I was apprehensive about seeing Janet's work for fear of disappointment. Au contraire; I was rendered speechless by her illustrations — rich and evocative with great depth of surface.

Be prepared to take a fantastic journey. If you're even remotely like me, then you will be permanently altered.

Tim Gunn is an American fashion consultant and Emmy-winning television personality, best known as co-host and mentor for the reality show *Project Runway.* He has also been the chair of the fashion department at Parsons School of Design, fashion dean at Fifth & Pacific, chief creative officer at Liz Claiborne, and the author of several books.

To anyone who ever
fell down a rabbit hole,
walked to the sidewalk's end,
danced a wild rumpus,
or followed the
second star to the right,
may you find
adventure, wonder,
and a little something
from which dreams are made
in these pages.

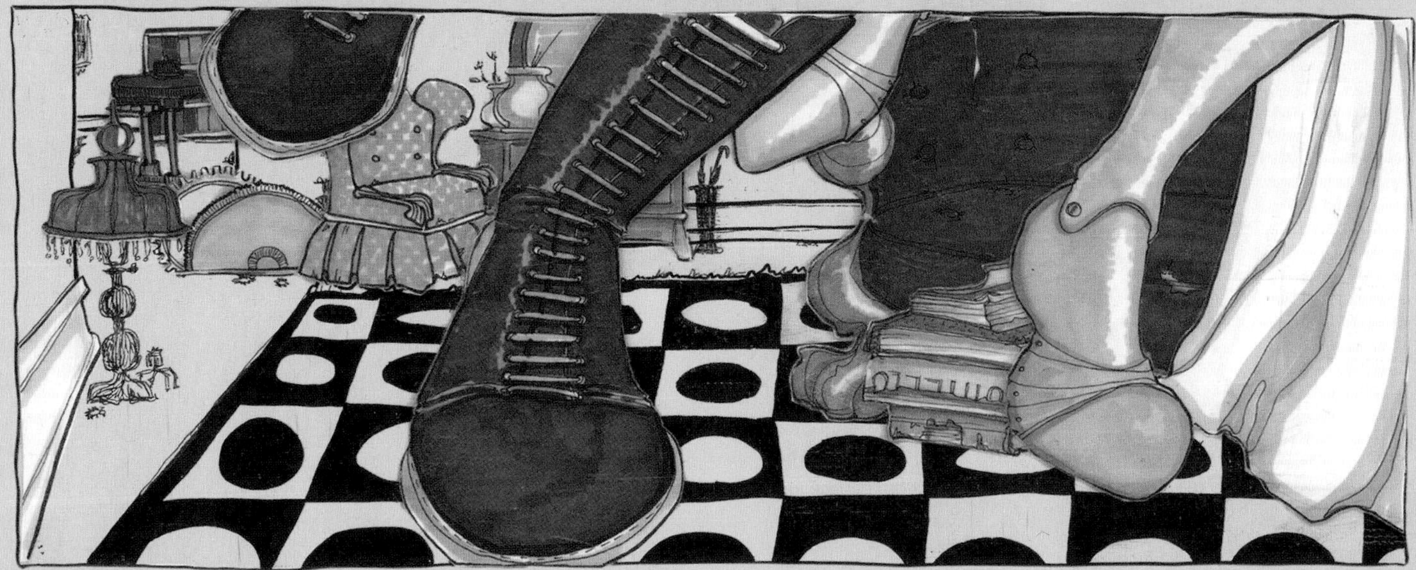

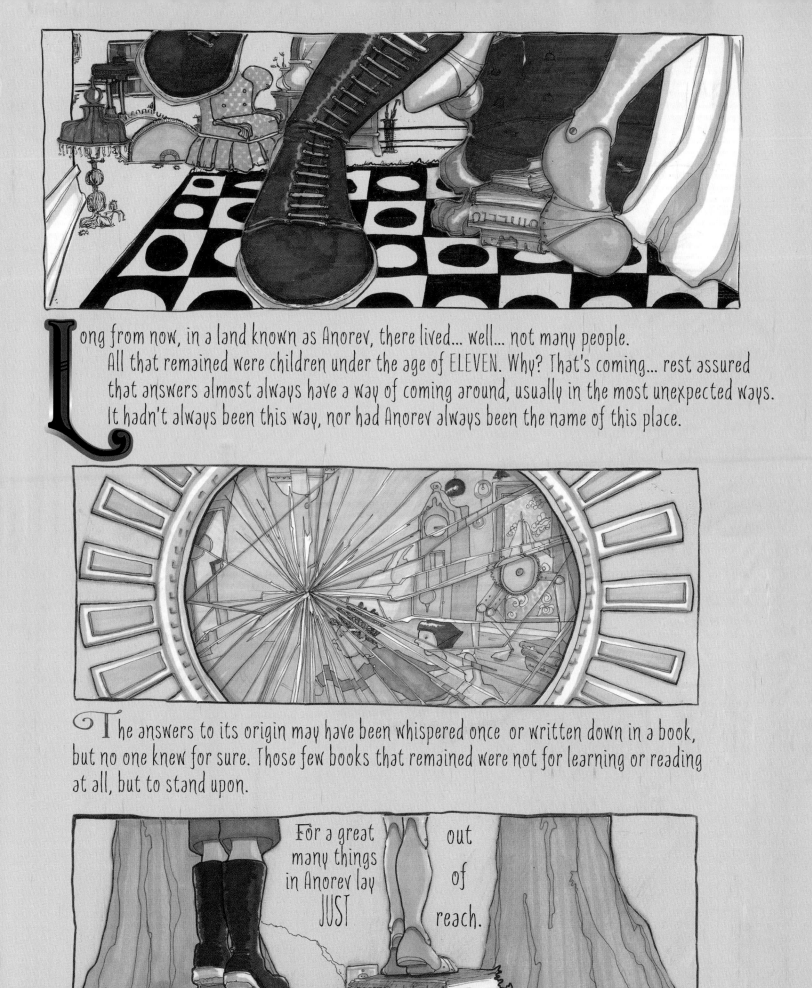

Long from now, in a land known as Anorev, there lived... well... not many people.

All that remained were children under the age of ELEVEN. Why? That's coming... rest assured that answers almost always have a way of coming around, usually in the most unexpected ways. It hadn't always been this way, nor had Anorev always been the name of this place.

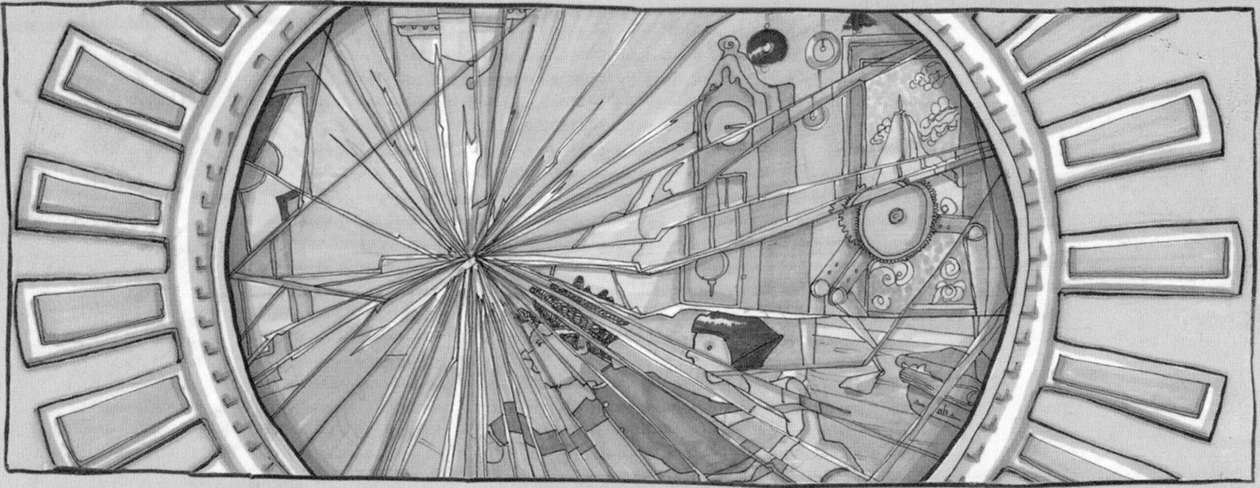

The answers to its origin may have been whispered once or written down in a book, but no one knew for sure. Those few books that remained were not for learning or reading at all, but to stand upon.

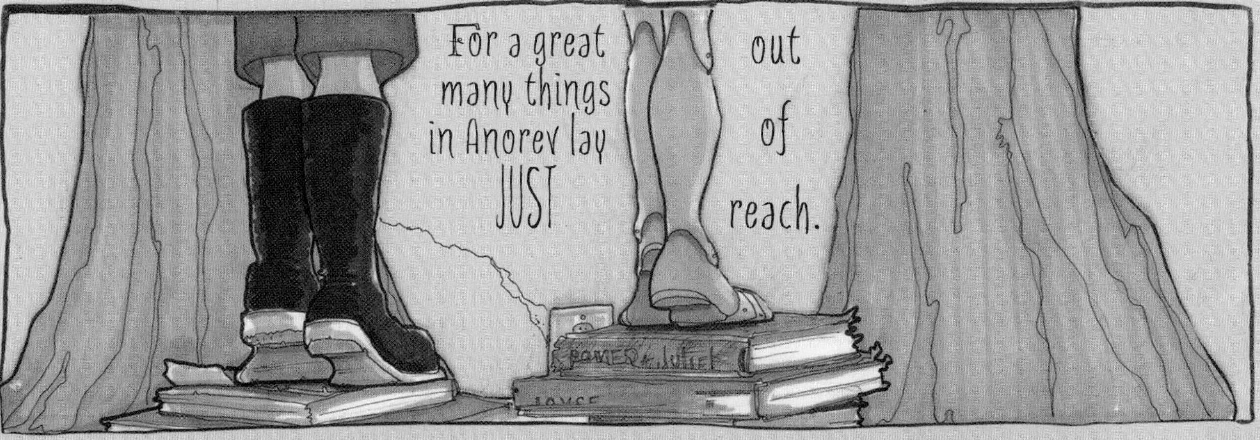
For a great many things in Anorev lay JUST
out of reach.

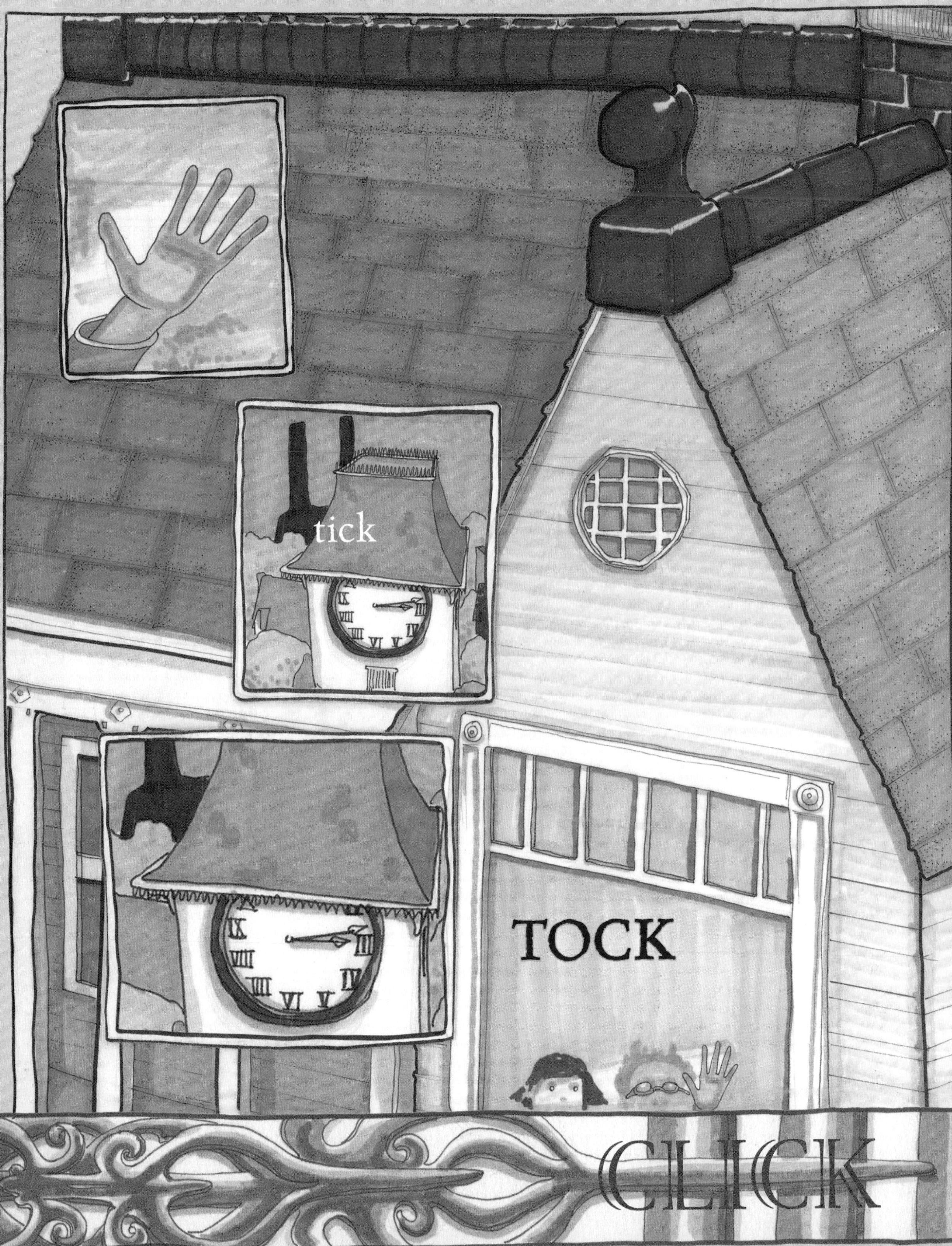
tick
TOCK
CLICK

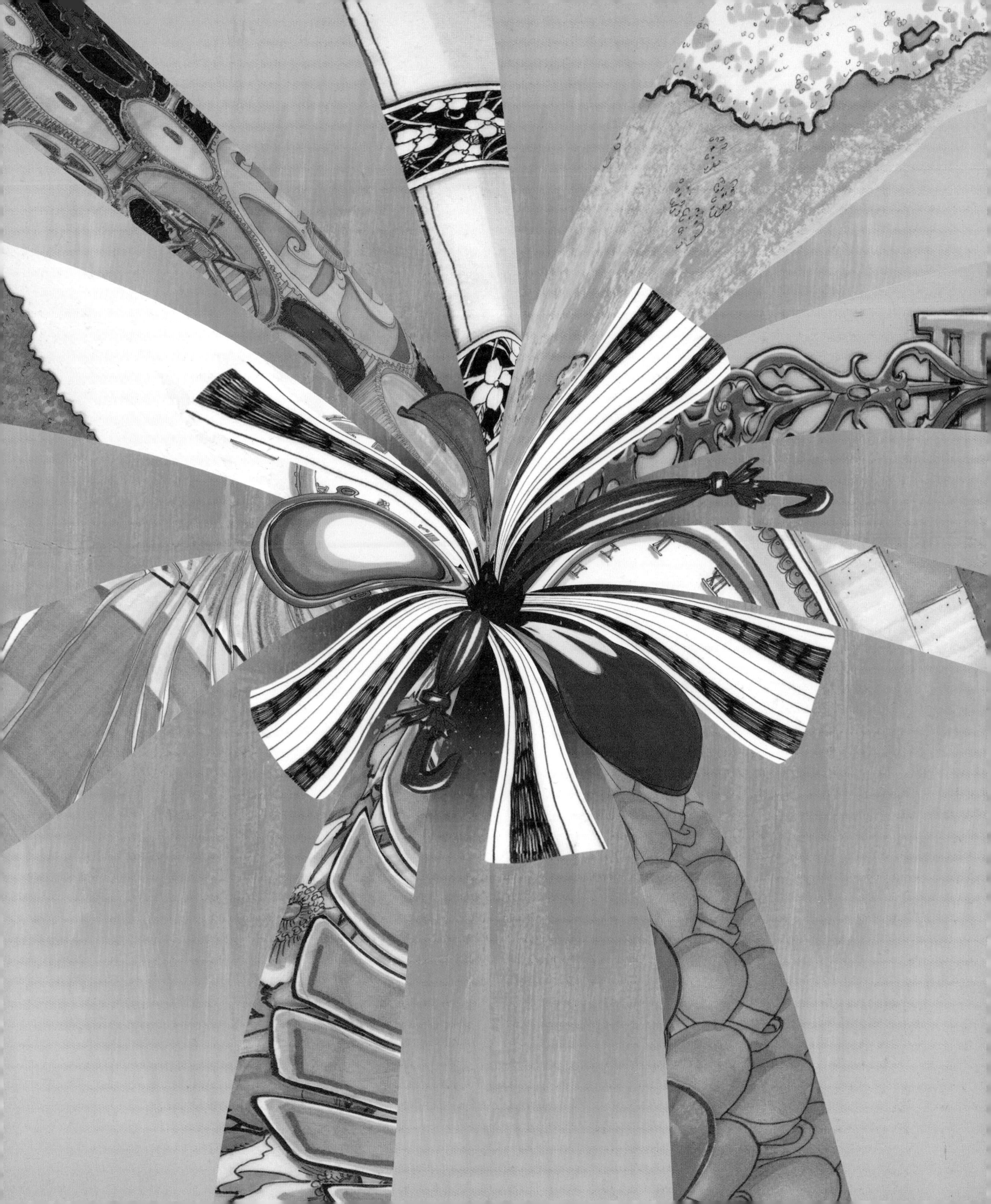

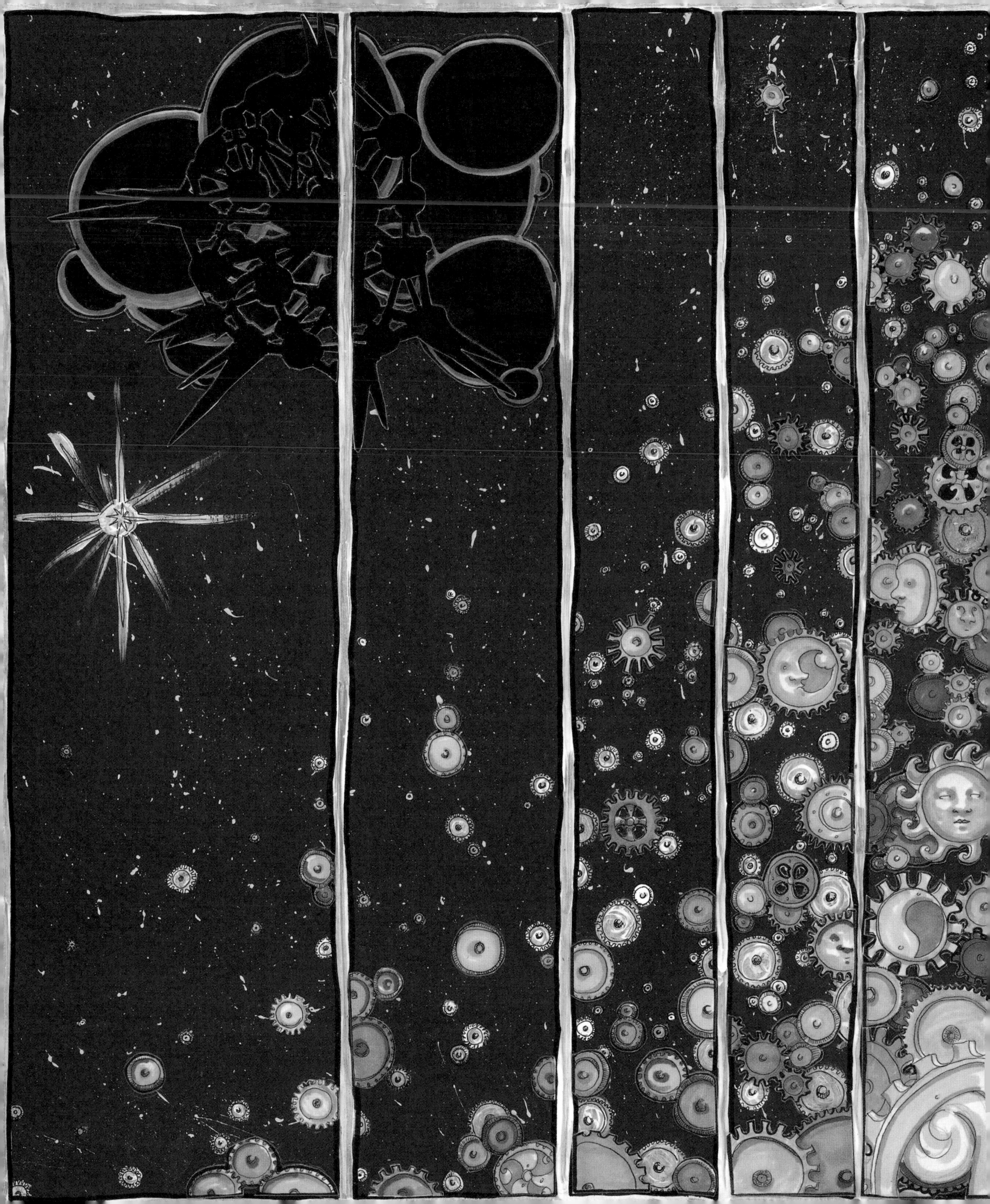

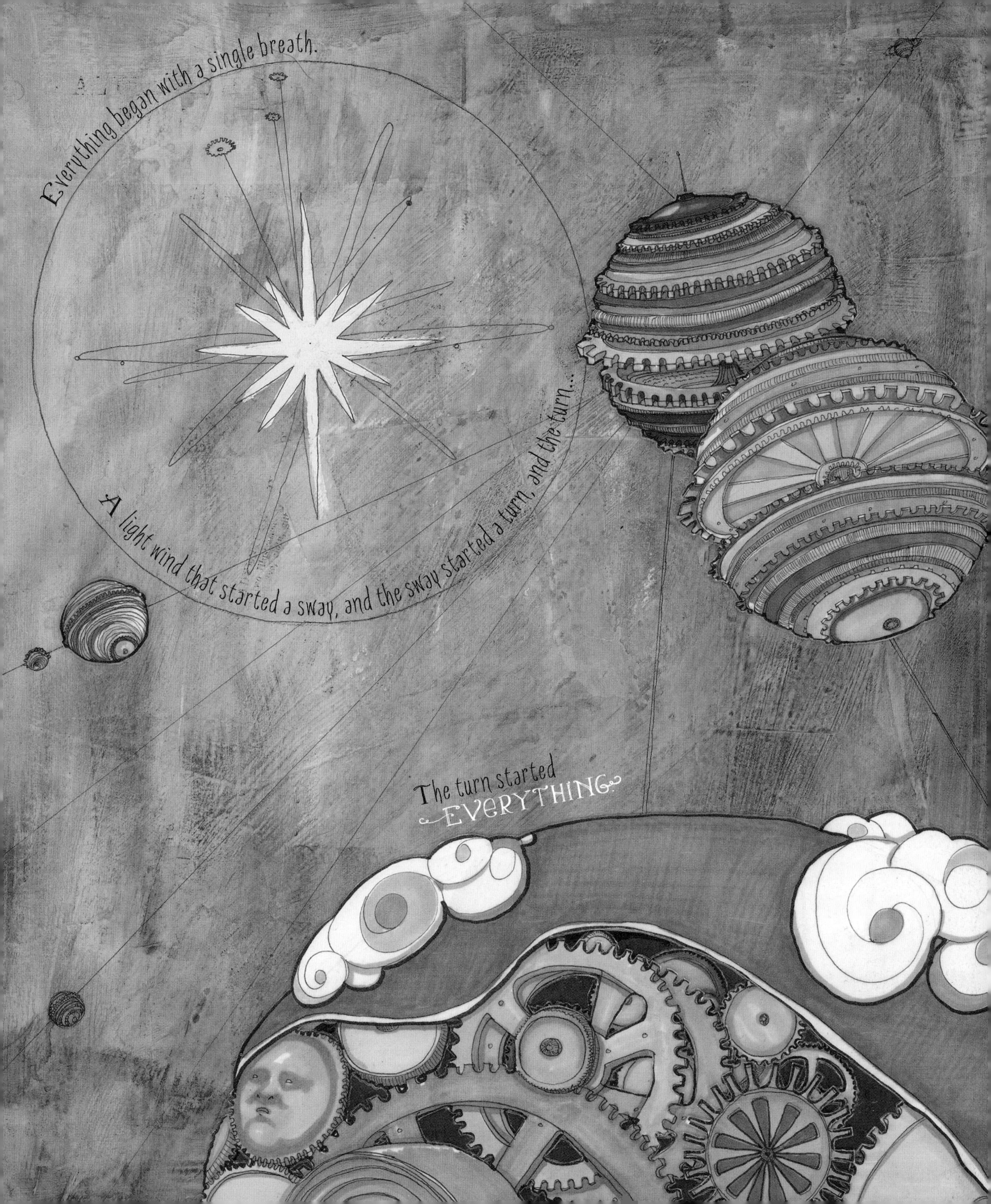
Everything began with a single breath.
A light wind that started a sway, and the sway started a turn, and the turn...
The turn started EVERYTHING.

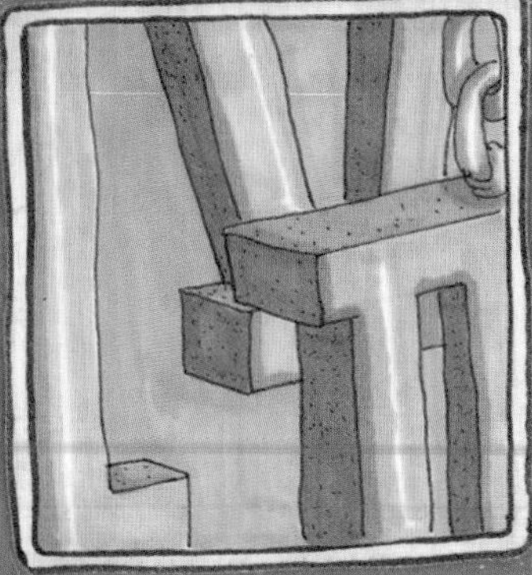

Everything grew and soon needed Time.

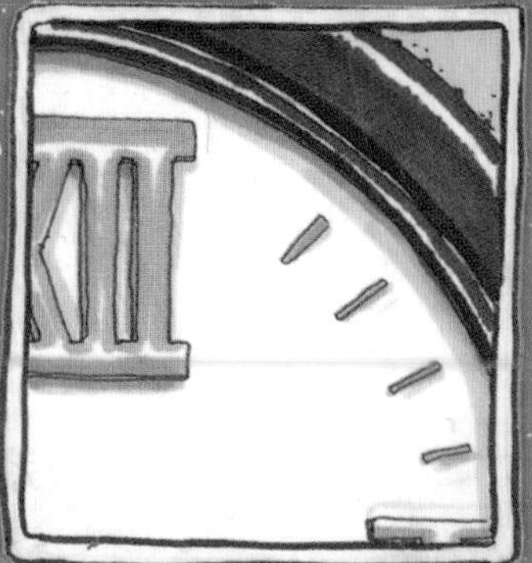

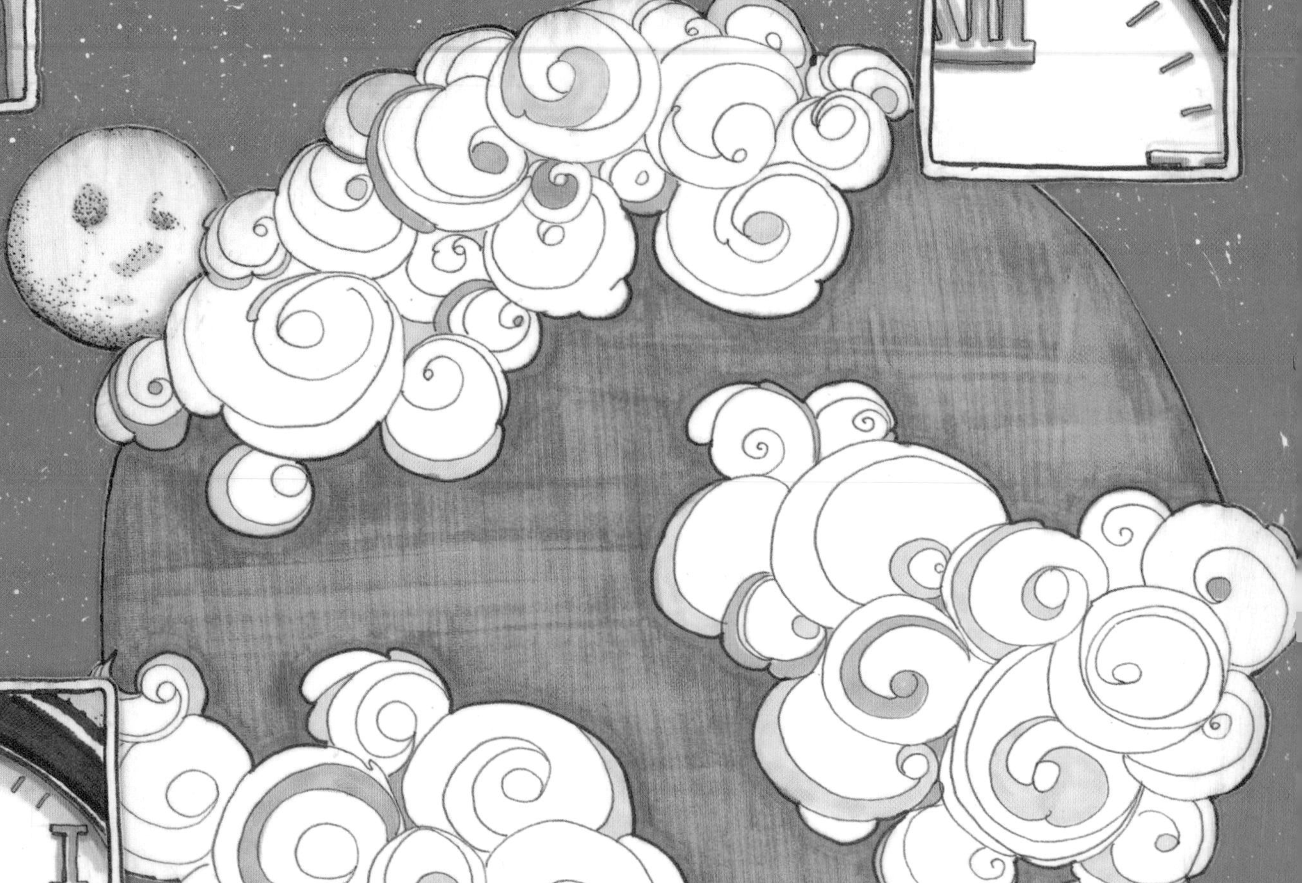

Numbers to mark the progress that had been made.

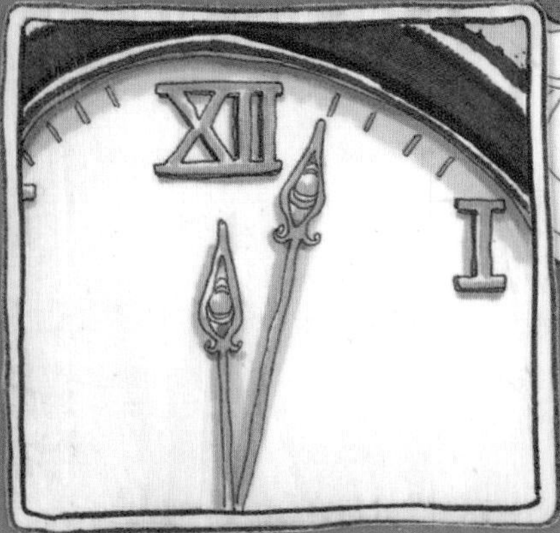

For much had been built and created.

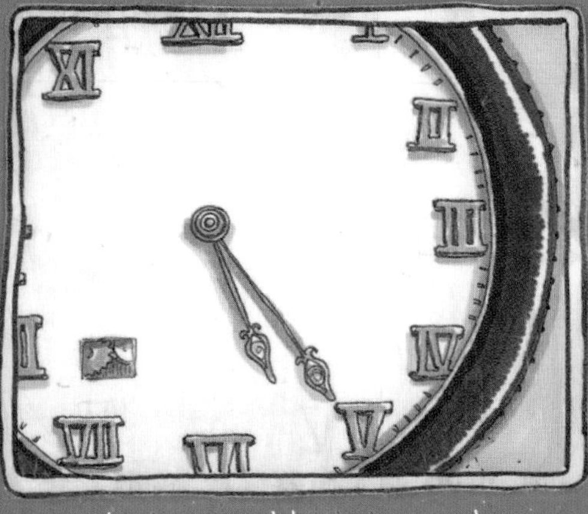

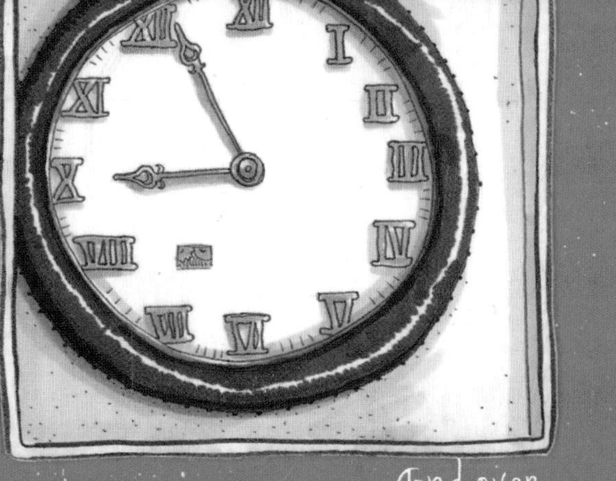

And much had been turned over.

And over.

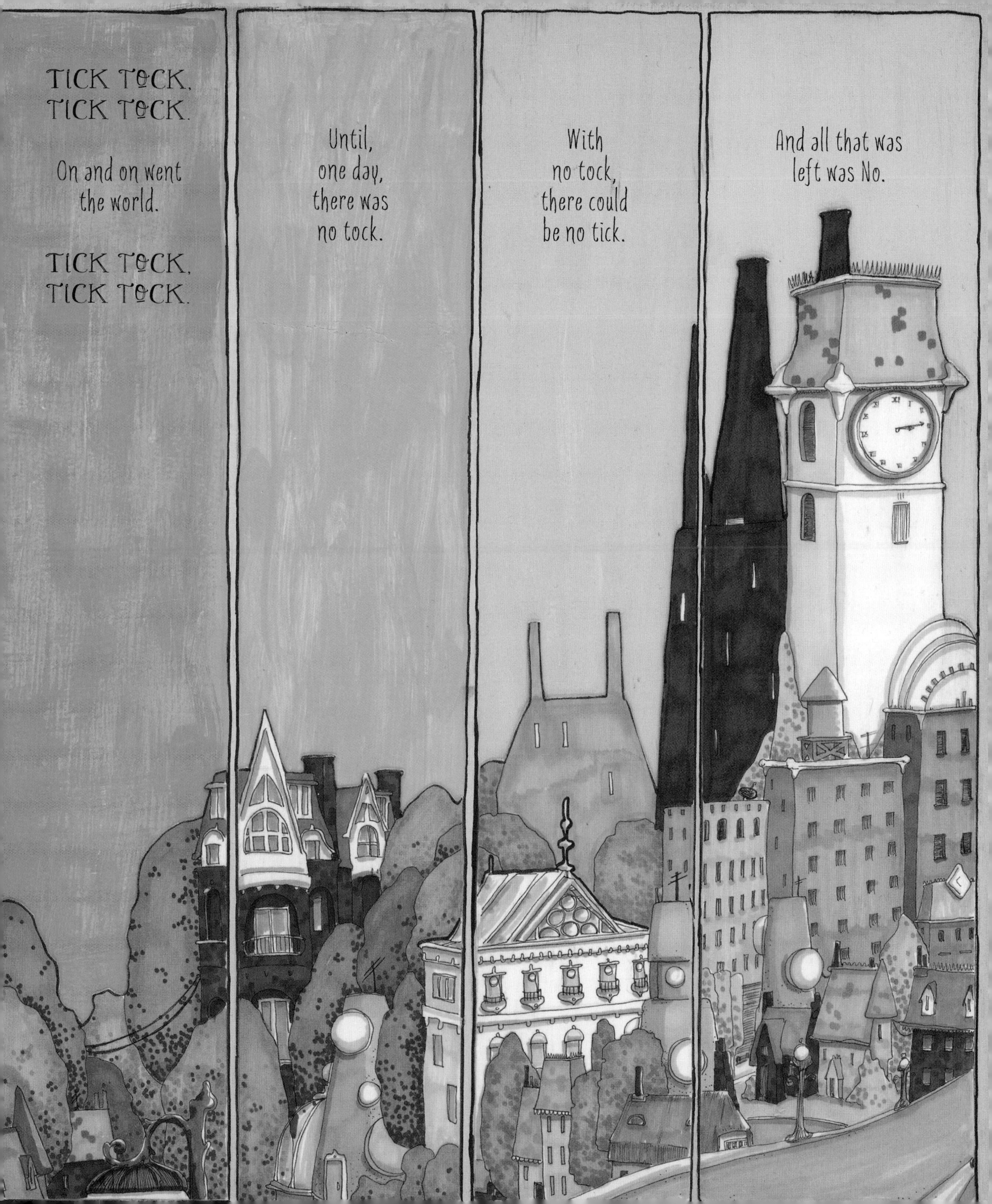
TICK TOCK,
TICK TOCK.
On and on went the world.
TICK TOCK,
TICK TOCK.
Until, one day, there was no tock.
With no tock, there could be no tick.
And all that was left was No.

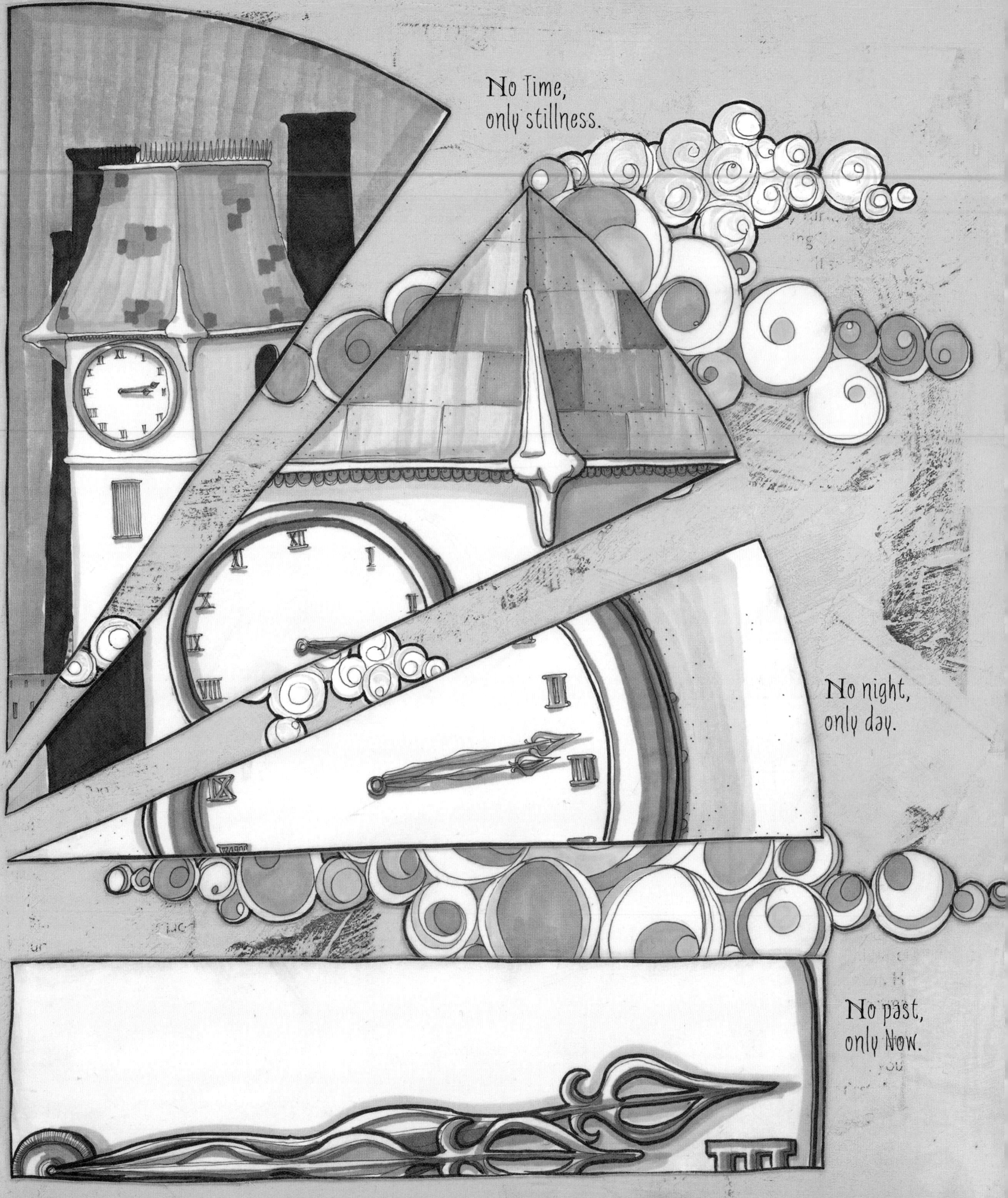
No Time,
only stillness.
No night,
only day.
No past,
only Now.

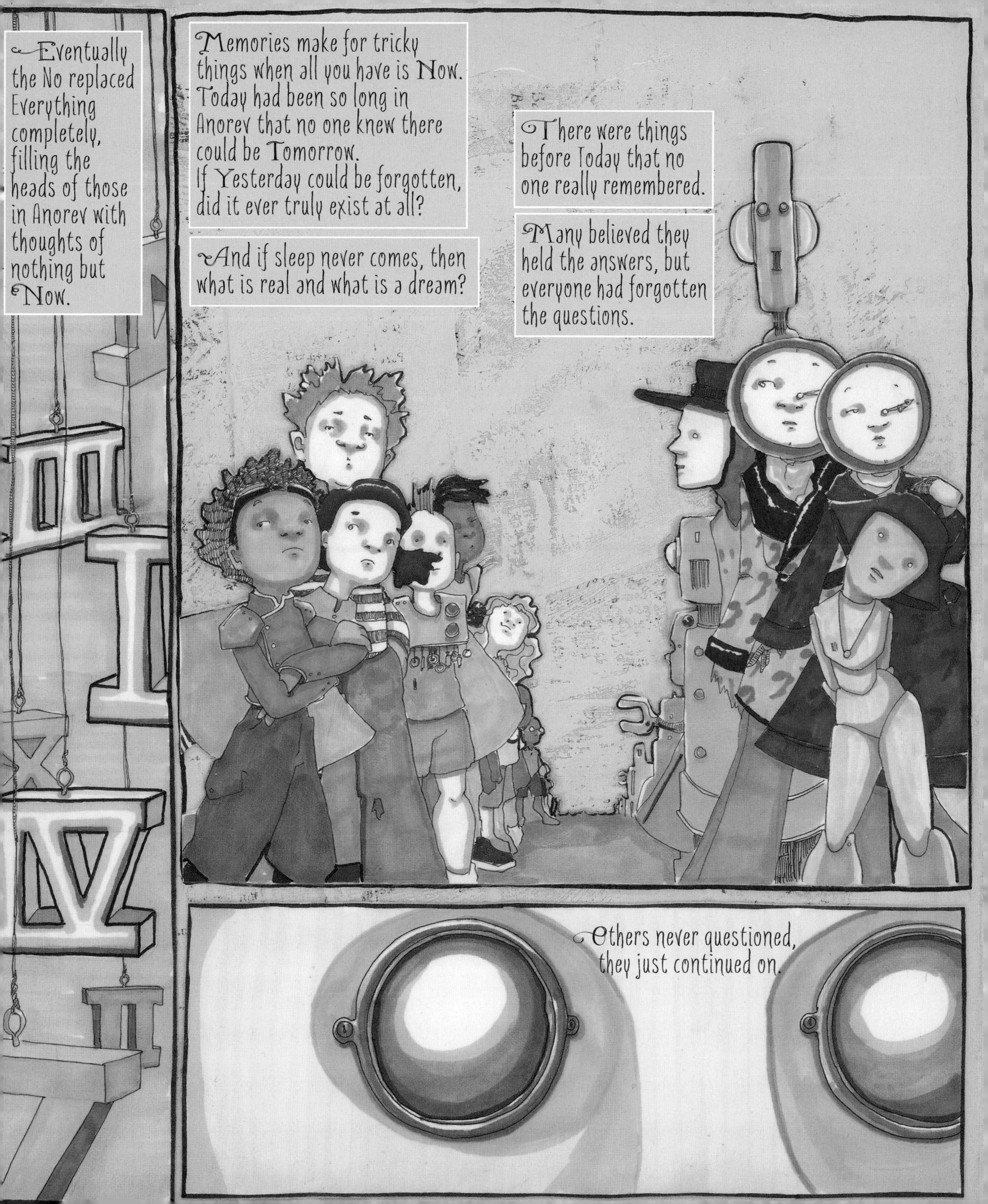
Eventually the No replaced Everything completely, filling the heads of those in Anorev with thoughts of nothing but Now.
Memories make for tricky things when all you have is Now. Today had been so long in Anorev that no one knew there could be Tomorrow. If Yesterday could be forgotten, did it ever truly exist at all?
And if sleep never comes, then what is real and what is a dream?
There were things before Today that no one really remembered.
Many believed they held the answers, but everyone had forgotten the questions.
Others never questioned, they just continued on.

There were whispers of Darkness and Time.

But no one knew what those words meant any more than they understood why the land stopped and the sky began.

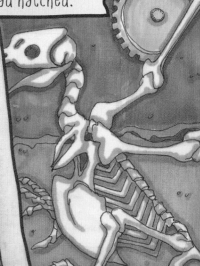

Or what was really in an egg, for none had hatched.

This was a land of children and machines. Neither knew who made the other and both claimed to be the First.

The children cared for playing and the machines for working--which is how it should be. But with no one to tell them to settle down or stop working, both continued along. And continued. And continued.

And continued.

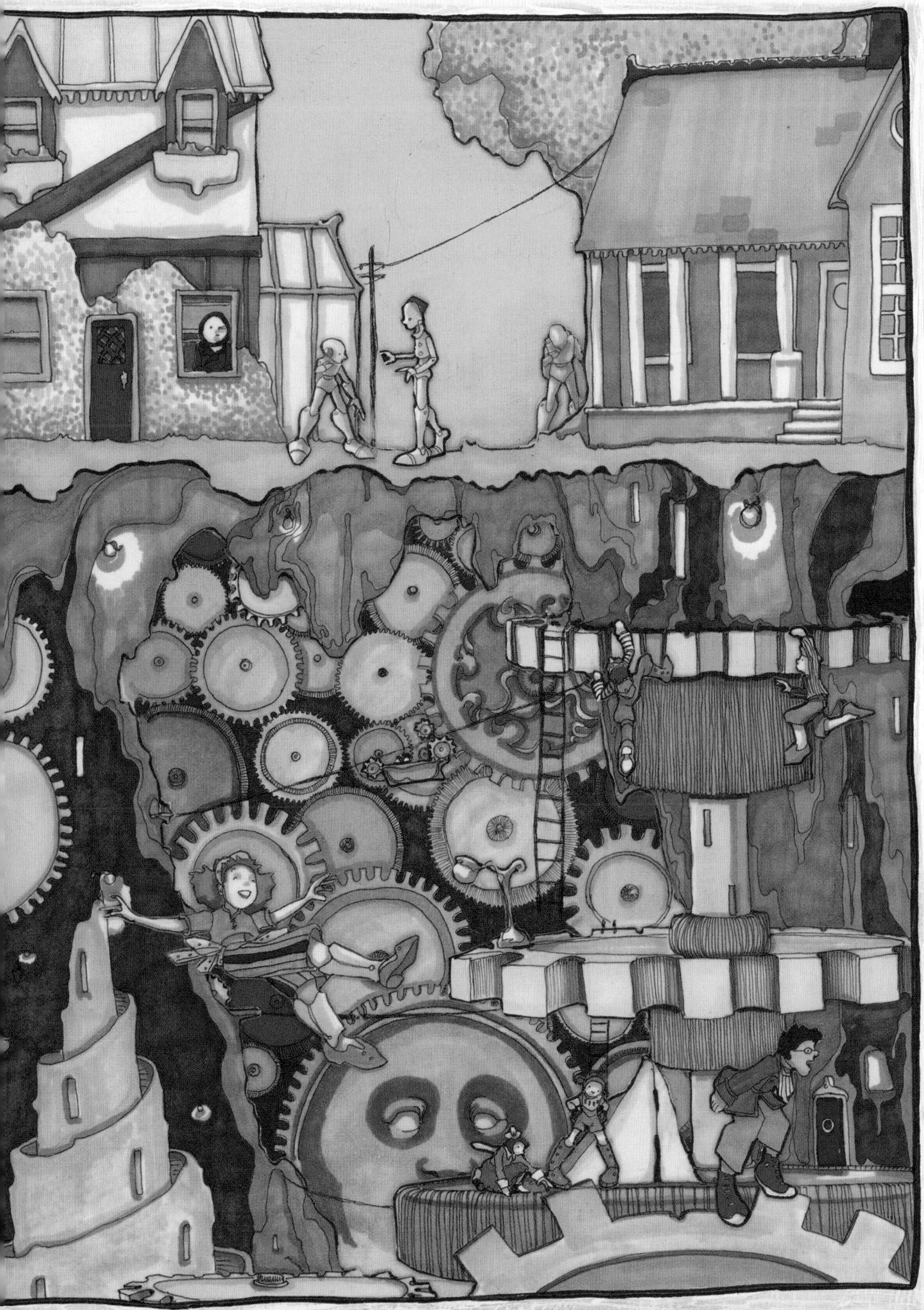

Soon, neither children nor machines knew which was work nor what was play, and neither seemed to be of any fun or any use.

Purpose was lost and both the children and the machines retreated to themselves. The children built a life among the gears of the world and ignored what was above, while the machines lived quietly in homes long abandoned.

They didn't share their knowledge or wisdom nor did they speak of the past, all of which is what makes history.

So that is why what was to come would take them all by surprise.

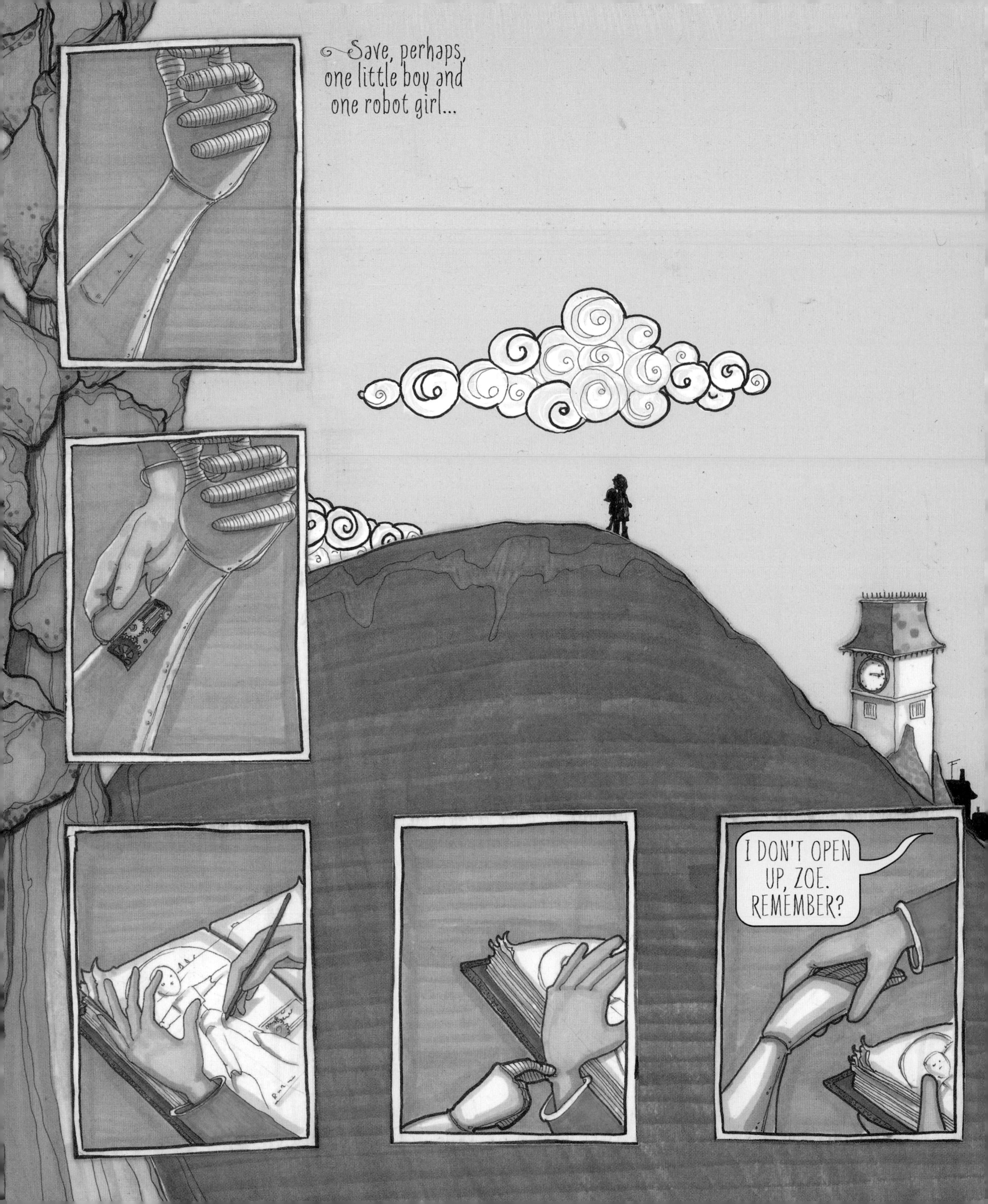
Save, perhaps, one little boy and one robot girl...
I DON'T OPEN UP, ZOE. REMEMBER?

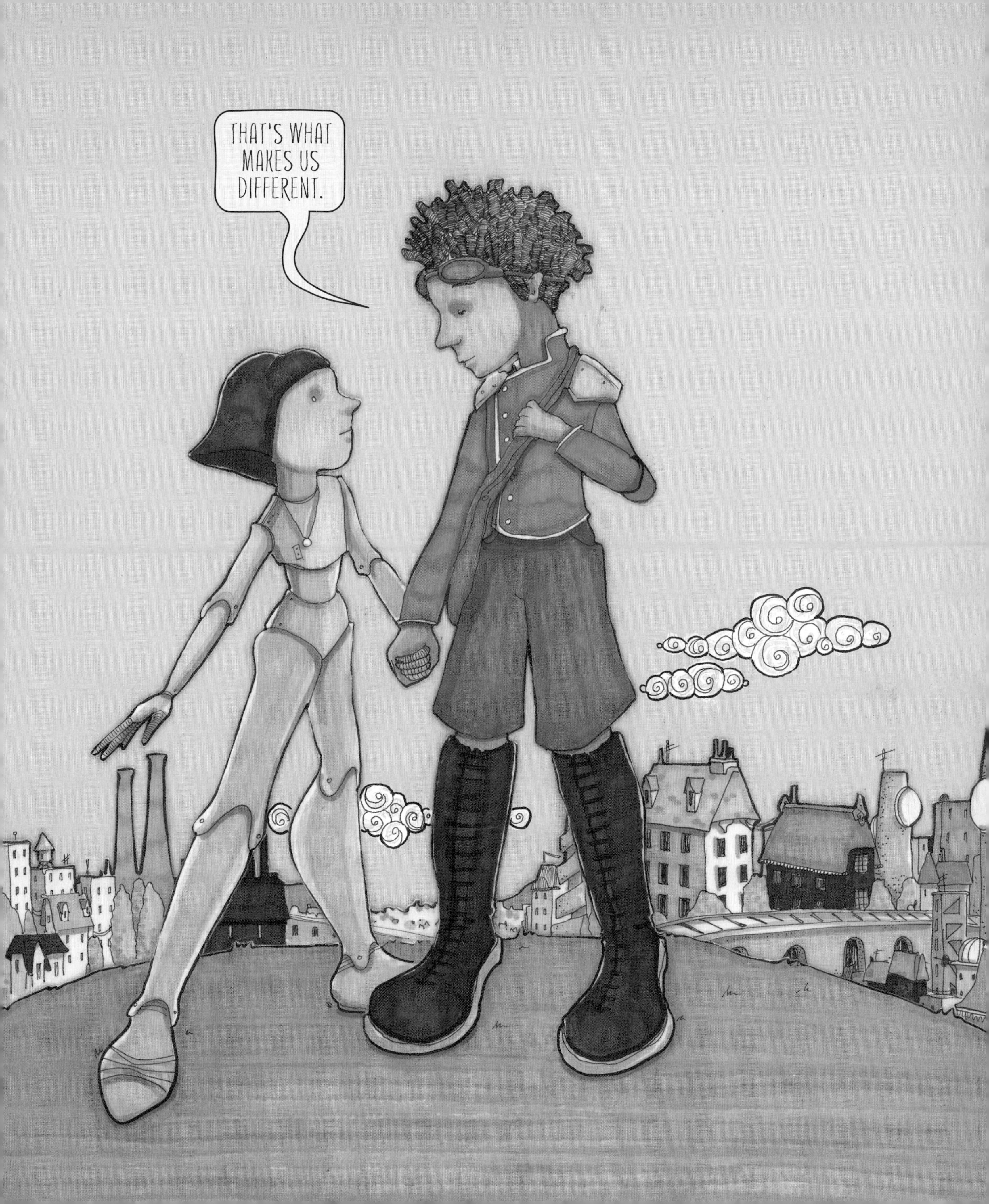
THAT'S WHAT MAKES US DIFFERENT.

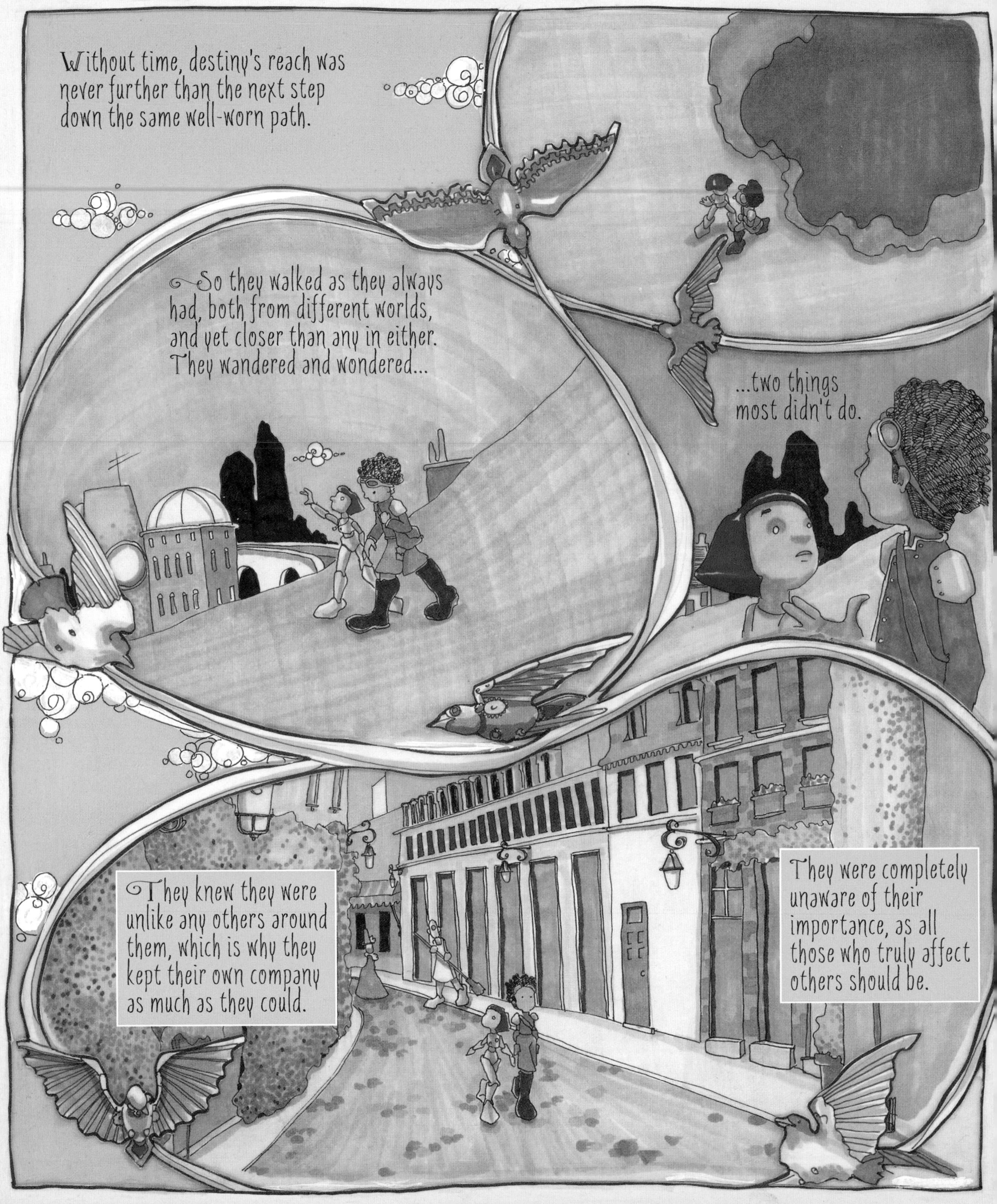

Without time, destiny's reach was never further than the next step down the same well-worn path.
So they walked as they always had, both from different worlds, and yet closer than any in either. They wandered and wondered...
...two things most didn't do.
They knew they were unlike any others around them, which is why they kept their own company as much as they could.
They were completely unaware of their importance, as all those who truly affect others should be.

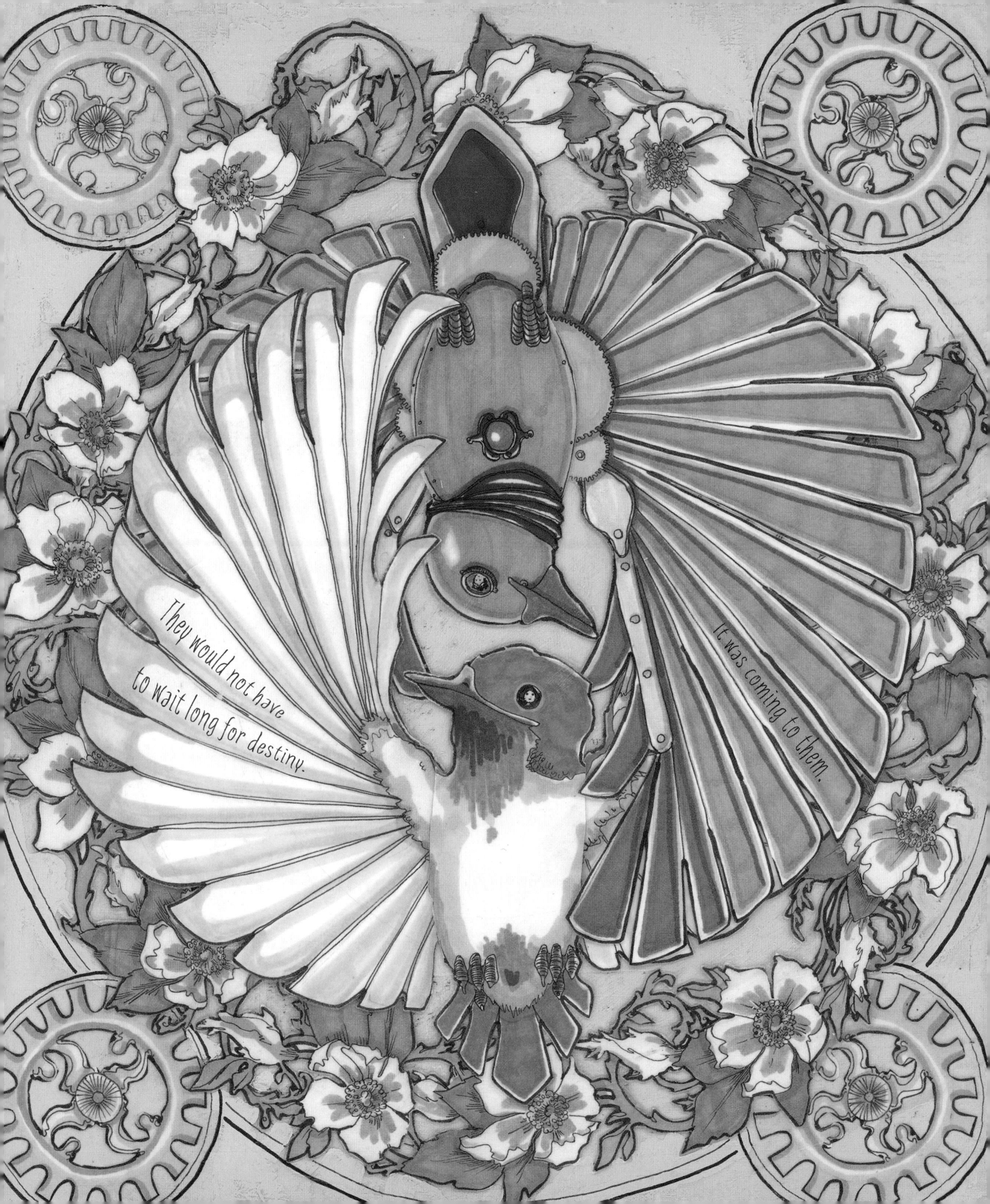
They would not have
to wait long for destiny.
It was coming to them.

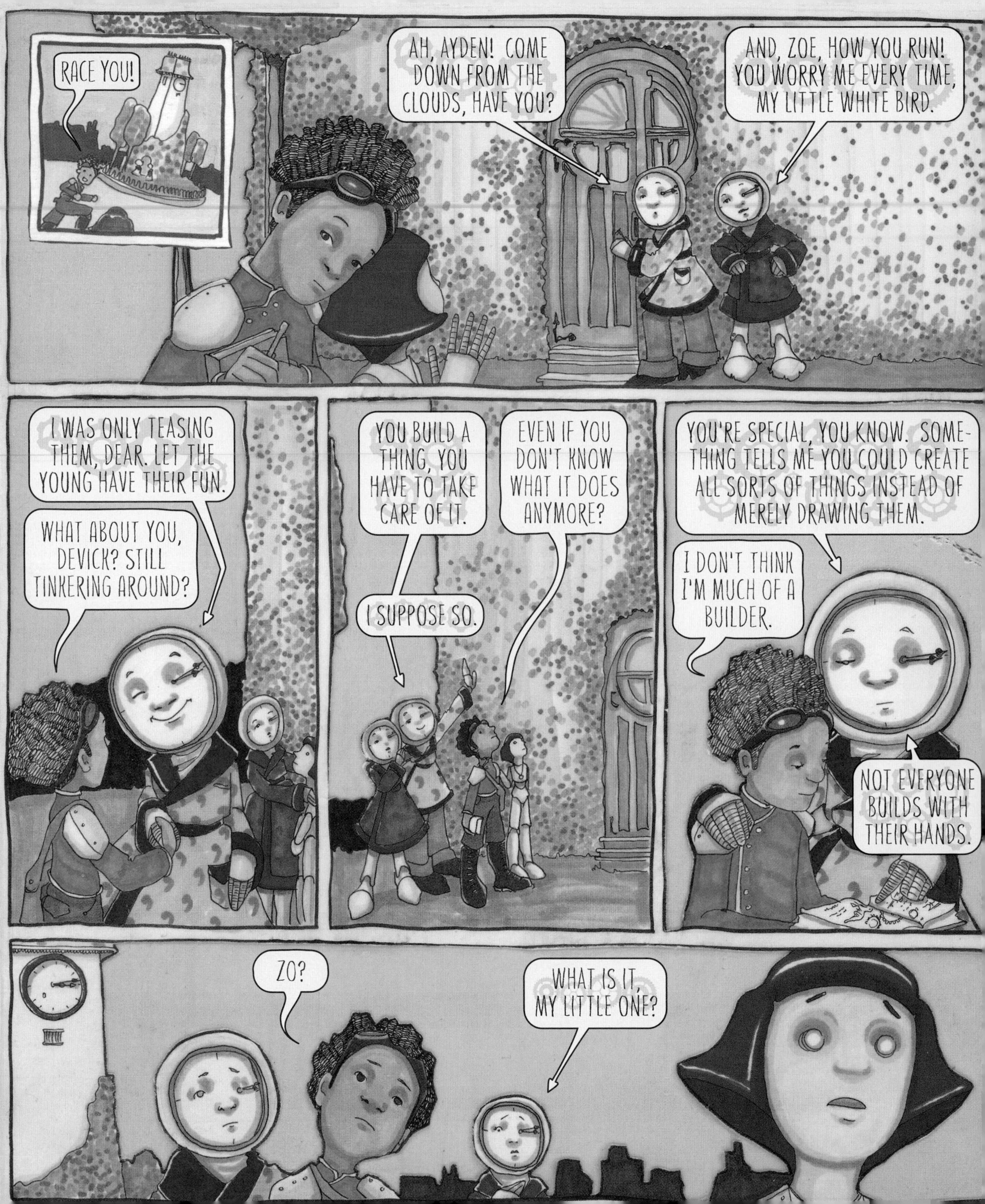

RACE YOU!
AH, AYDEN! COME DOWN FROM THE CLOUDS, HAVE YOU?
AND, ZOE, HOW YOU RUN! YOU WORRY ME EVERY TIME, MY LITTLE WHITE BIRD.
I WAS ONLY TEASING THEM, DEAR. LET THE YOUNG HAVE THEIR FUN.
WHAT ABOUT YOU, DEVICK? STILL TINKERING AROUND?
YOU BUILD A THING, YOU HAVE TO TAKE CARE OF IT.
I SUPPOSE SO.
EVEN IF YOU DON'T KNOW WHAT IT DOES ANYMORE?
YOU'RE SPECIAL, YOU KNOW. SOMETHING TELLS ME YOU COULD CREATE ALL SORTS OF THINGS INSTEAD OF MERELY DRAWING THEM.
I DON'T THINK I'M MUCH OF A BUILDER.
NOT EVERYONE BUILDS WITH THEIR HANDS.
ZO?
WHAT IS IT, MY LITTLE ONE?

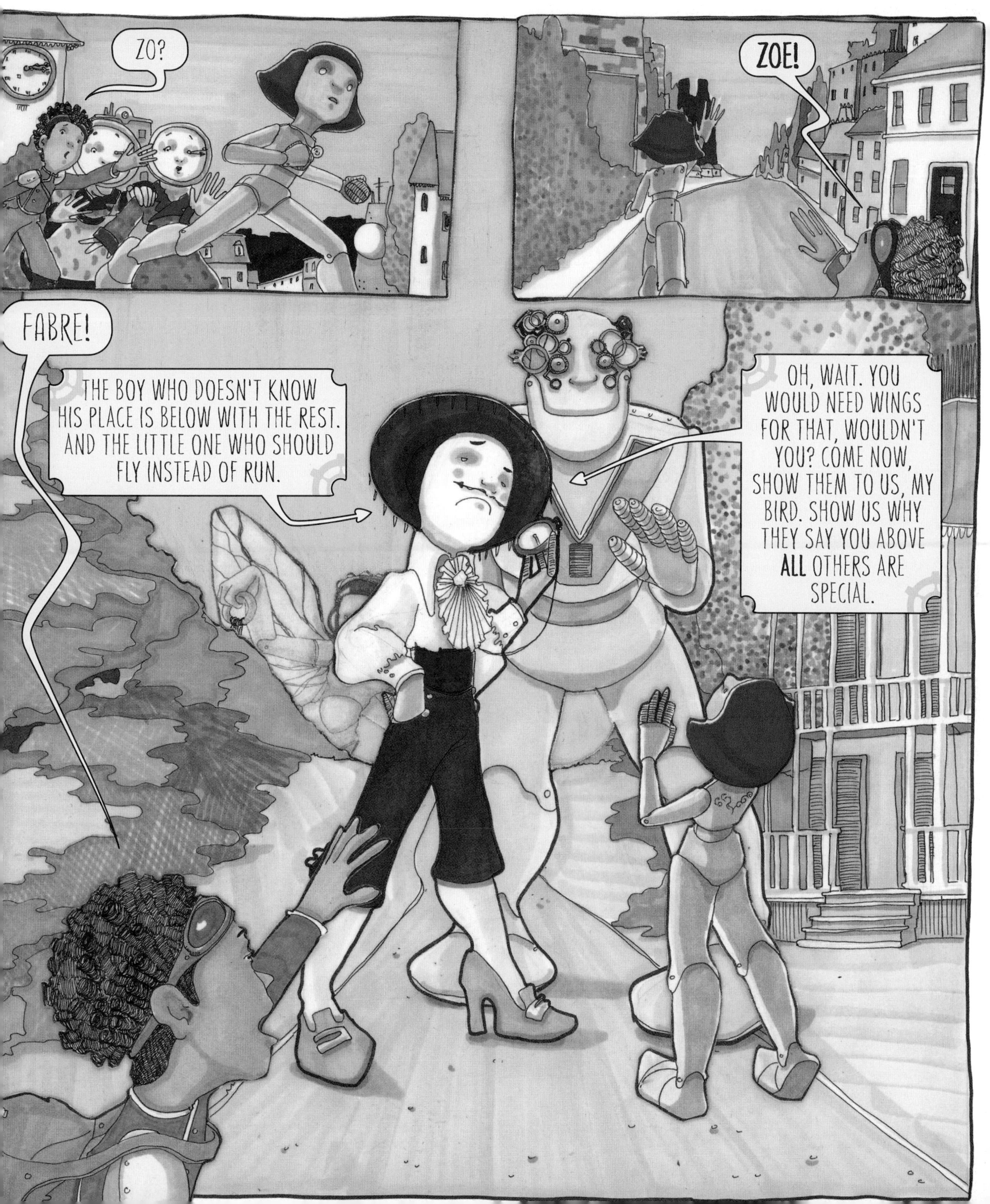
ZO?
ZOE!
FABRE!
THE BOY WHO DOESN'T KNOW HIS PLACE IS BELOW WITH THE REST. AND THE LITTLE ONE WHO SHOULD FLY INSTEAD OF RUN.
OH, WAIT. YOU WOULD NEED WINGS FOR THAT, WOULDN'T YOU? COME NOW, SHOW THEM TO US, MY BIRD. SHOW US WHY THEY SAY YOU ABOVE **ALL** OTHERS ARE SPECIAL.

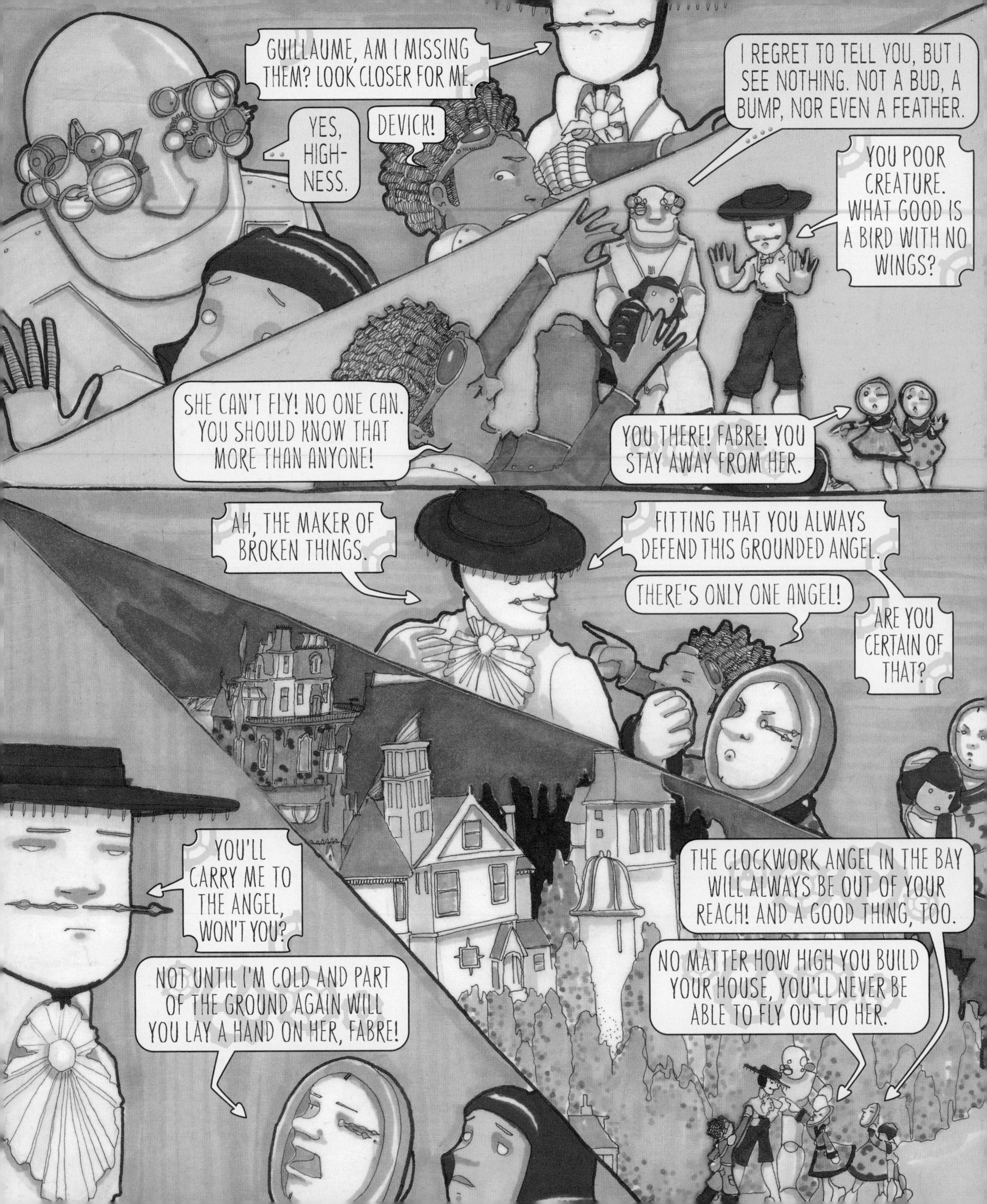
GUILLAUME, AM I MISSING THEM? LOOK CLOSER FOR ME.
YES, HIGH-NESS.
DEVICK!
I REGRET TO TELL YOU, BUT I SEE NOTHING. NOT A BUD, A BUMP, NOR EVEN A FEATHER.
YOU POOR CREATURE. WHAT GOOD IS A BIRD WITH NO WINGS?
SHE CAN'T FLY! NO ONE CAN. YOU SHOULD KNOW THAT MORE THAN ANYONE!
YOU THERE! FABRE! YOU STAY AWAY FROM HER.
AH, THE MAKER OF BROKEN THINGS.
FITTING THAT YOU ALWAYS DEFEND THIS GROUNDED ANGEL.
THERE'S ONLY ONE ANGEL!
ARE YOU CERTAIN OF THAT?
YOU'LL CARRY ME TO THE ANGEL, WON'T YOU?
NOT UNTIL I'M COLD AND PART OF THE GROUND AGAIN WILL YOU LAY A HAND ON HER, FABRE!
THE CLOCKWORK ANGEL IN THE BAY WILL ALWAYS BE OUT OF YOUR REACH! AND A GOOD THING, TOO.
NO MATTER HOW HIGH YOU BUILD YOUR HOUSE, YOU'LL NEVER BE ABLE TO FLY OUT TO HER.

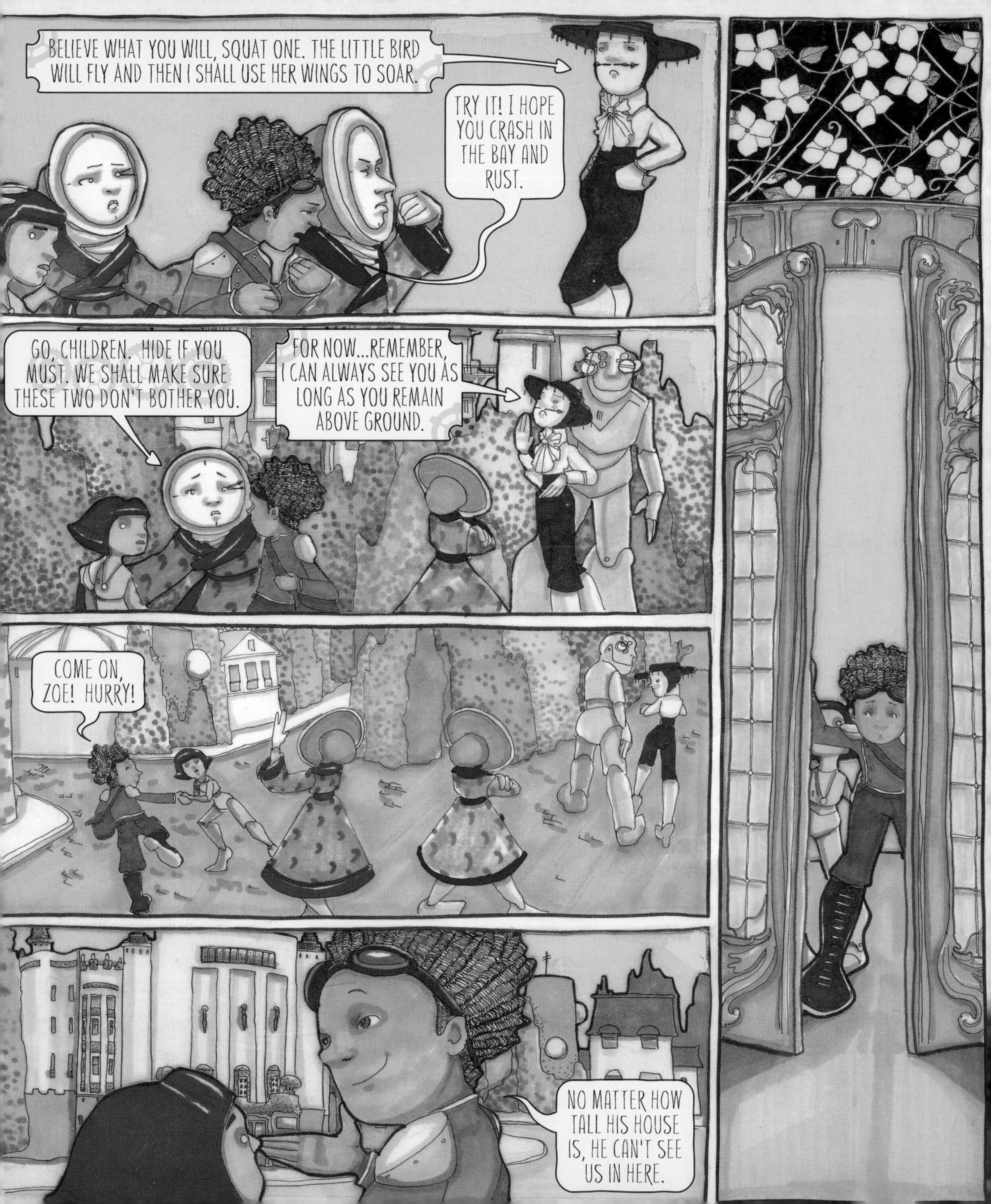
BELIEVE WHAT YOU WILL, SQUAT ONE. THE LITTLE BIRD WILL FLY AND THEN I SHALL USE HER WINGS TO SOAR.
TRY IT! I HOPE YOU CRASH IN THE BAY AND RUST.
GO, CHILDREN. HIDE IF YOU MUST. WE SHALL MAKE SURE THESE TWO DON'T BOTHER YOU.
FOR NOW...REMEMBER, I CAN ALWAYS SEE YOU AS LONG AS YOU REMAIN ABOVE GROUND.
COME ON, ZOE! HURRY!
NO MATTER HOW TALL HIS HOUSE IS, HE CAN'T SEE US IN HERE.

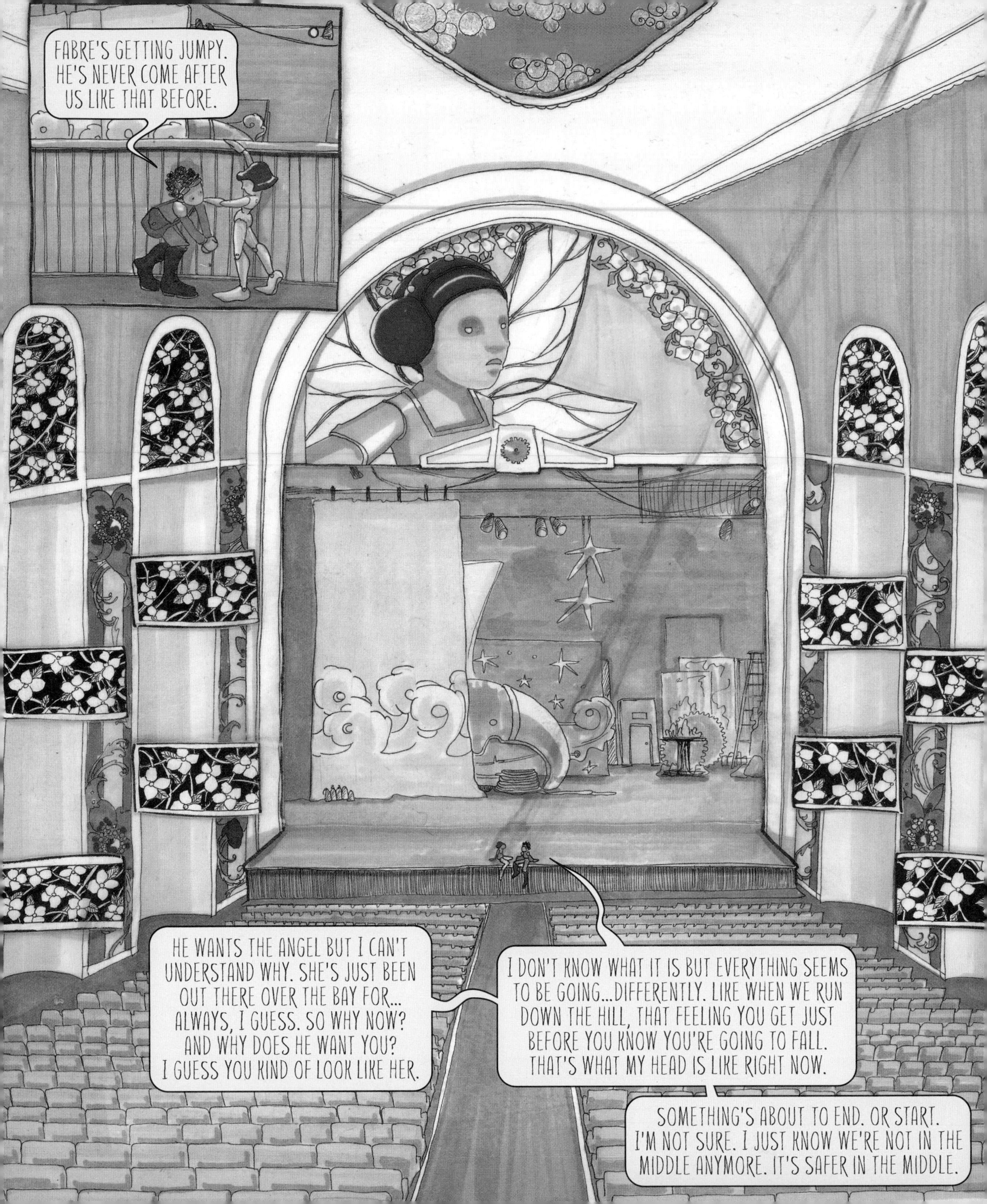
FABRE'S GETTING JUMPY. HE'S NEVER COME AFTER US LIKE THAT BEFORE.
HE WANTS THE ANGEL BUT I CAN'T UNDERSTAND WHY. SHE'S JUST BEEN OUT THERE OVER THE BAY FOR... ALWAYS, I GUESS. SO WHY NOW? AND WHY DOES HE WANT YOU? I GUESS YOU KIND OF LOOK LIKE HER.
I DON'T KNOW WHAT IT IS BUT EVERYTHING SEEMS TO BE GOING...DIFFERENTLY. LIKE WHEN WE RUN DOWN THE HILL, THAT FEELING YOU GET JUST BEFORE YOU KNOW YOU'RE GOING TO FALL. THAT'S WHAT MY HEAD IS LIKE RIGHT NOW.
SOMETHING'S ABOUT TO END. OR START. I'M NOT SURE. I JUST KNOW WE'RE NOT IN THE MIDDLE ANYMORE. IT'S SAFER IN THE MIDDLE.

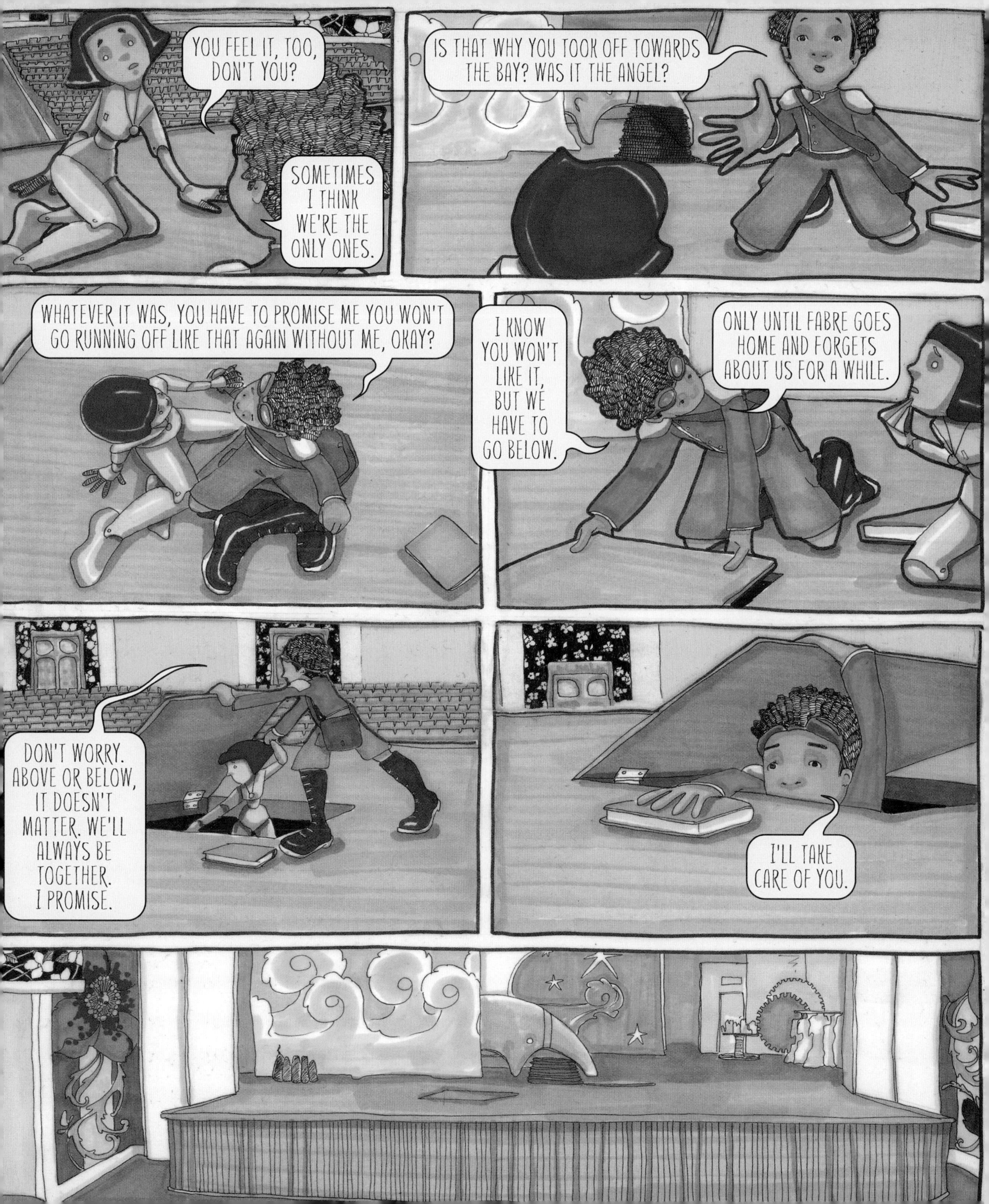
YOU FEEL IT, TOO, DON'T YOU?
SOMETIMES I THINK WE'RE THE ONLY ONES.
IS THAT WHY YOU TOOK OFF TOWARDS THE BAY? WAS IT THE ANGEL?
WHATEVER IT WAS, YOU HAVE TO PROMISE ME YOU WON'T GO RUNNING OFF LIKE THAT AGAIN WITHOUT ME, OKAY?
I KNOW YOU WON'T LIKE IT, BUT WE HAVE TO GO BELOW.
ONLY UNTIL FABRE GOES HOME AND FORGETS ABOUT US FOR A WHILE.
DON'T WORRY. ABOVE OR BELOW, IT DOESN'T MATTER. WE'LL ALWAYS BE TOGETHER. I PROMISE.
I'LL TAKE CARE OF YOU.

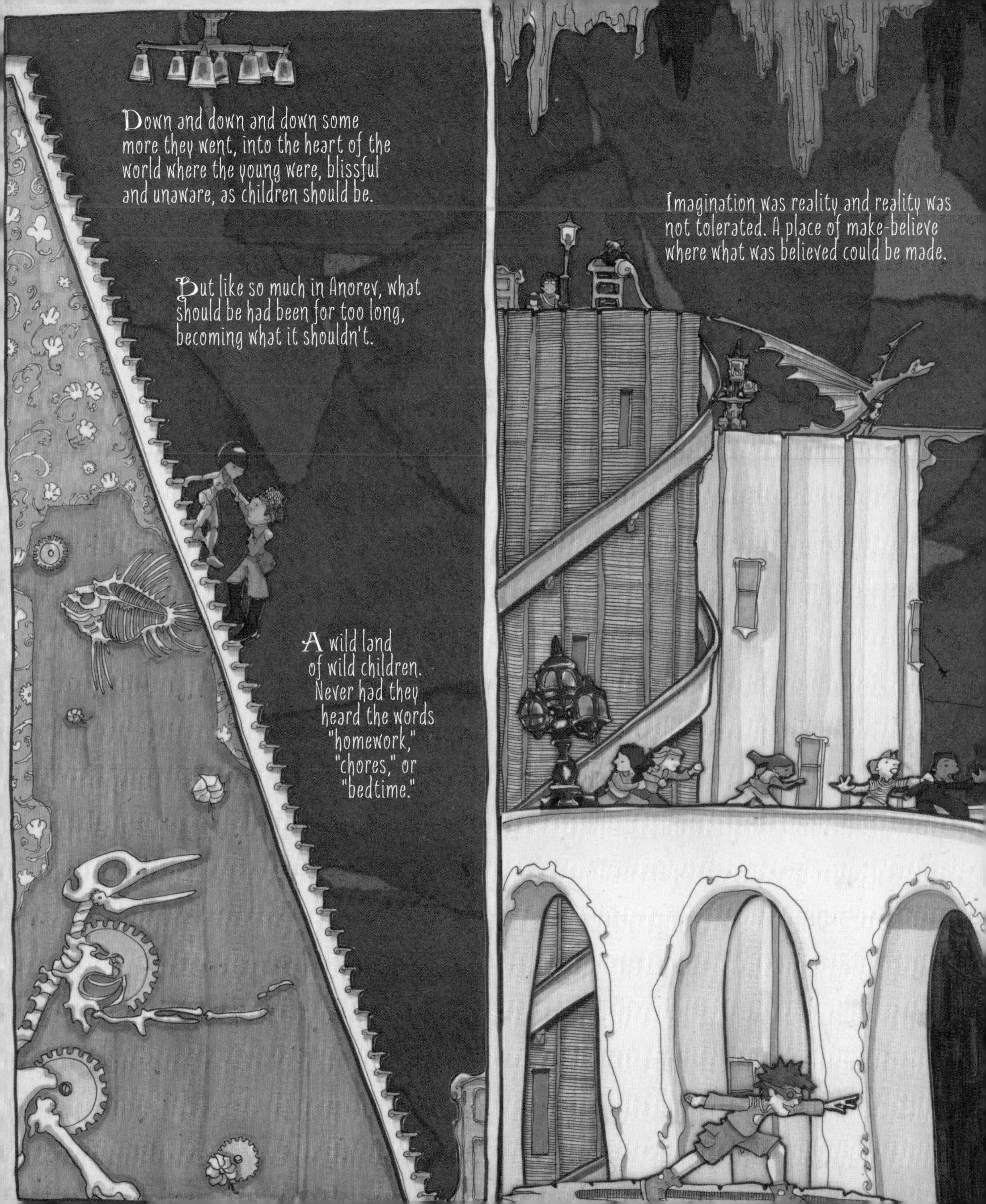
Down and down and down some more they went, into the heart of the world where the young were, blissful and unaware, as children should be.
But like so much in Anorev, what should be had been for too long, becoming what it shouldn't.
A wild land of wild children. Never had they heard the words "homework," "chores," or "bedtime."
Imagination was reality and reality was not tolerated. A place of make-believe where what was believed could be made.

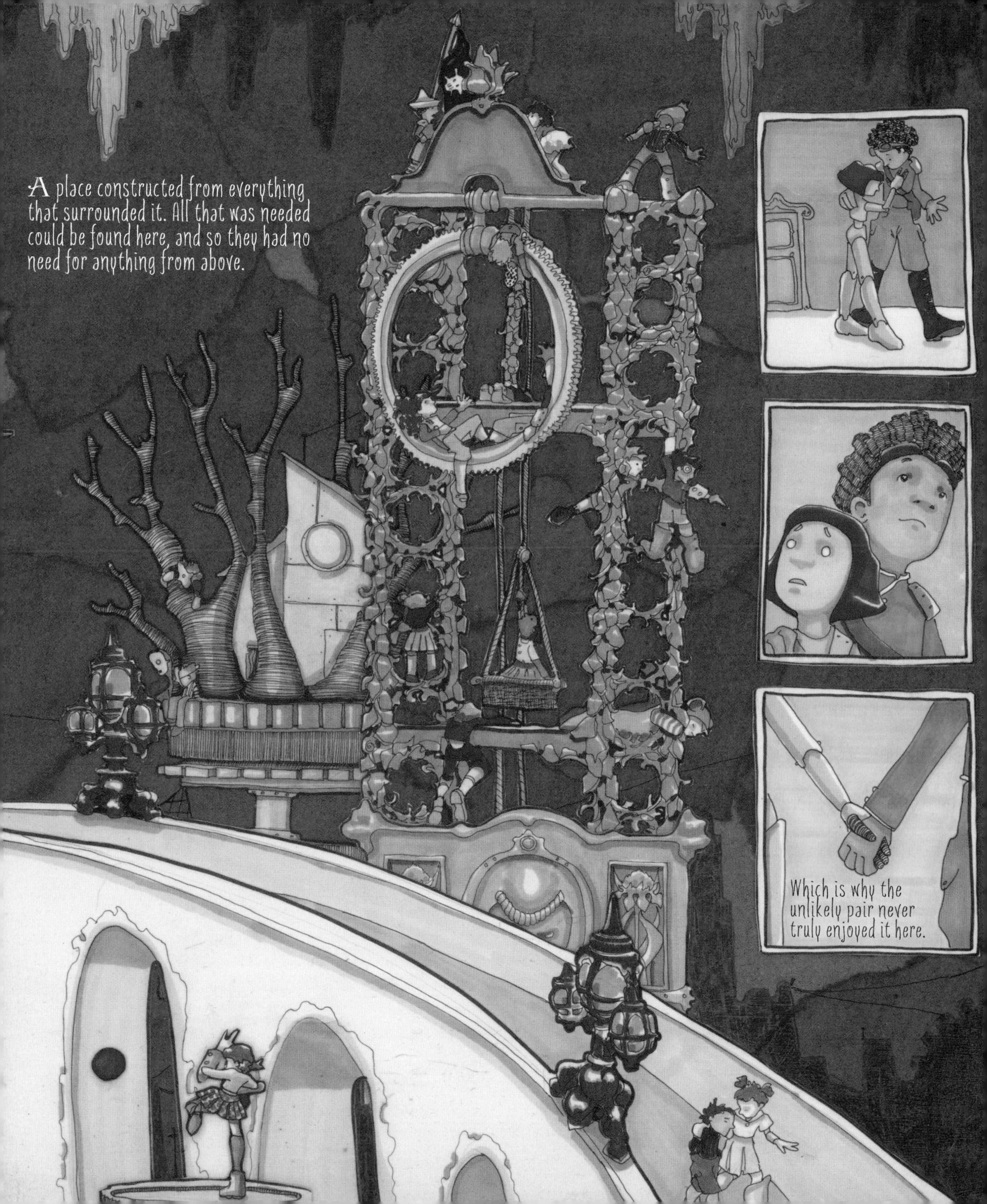
A place constructed from everything that surrounded it. All that was needed could be found here, and so they had no need for anything from above.
Which is why the unlikely pair never truly enjoyed it here.

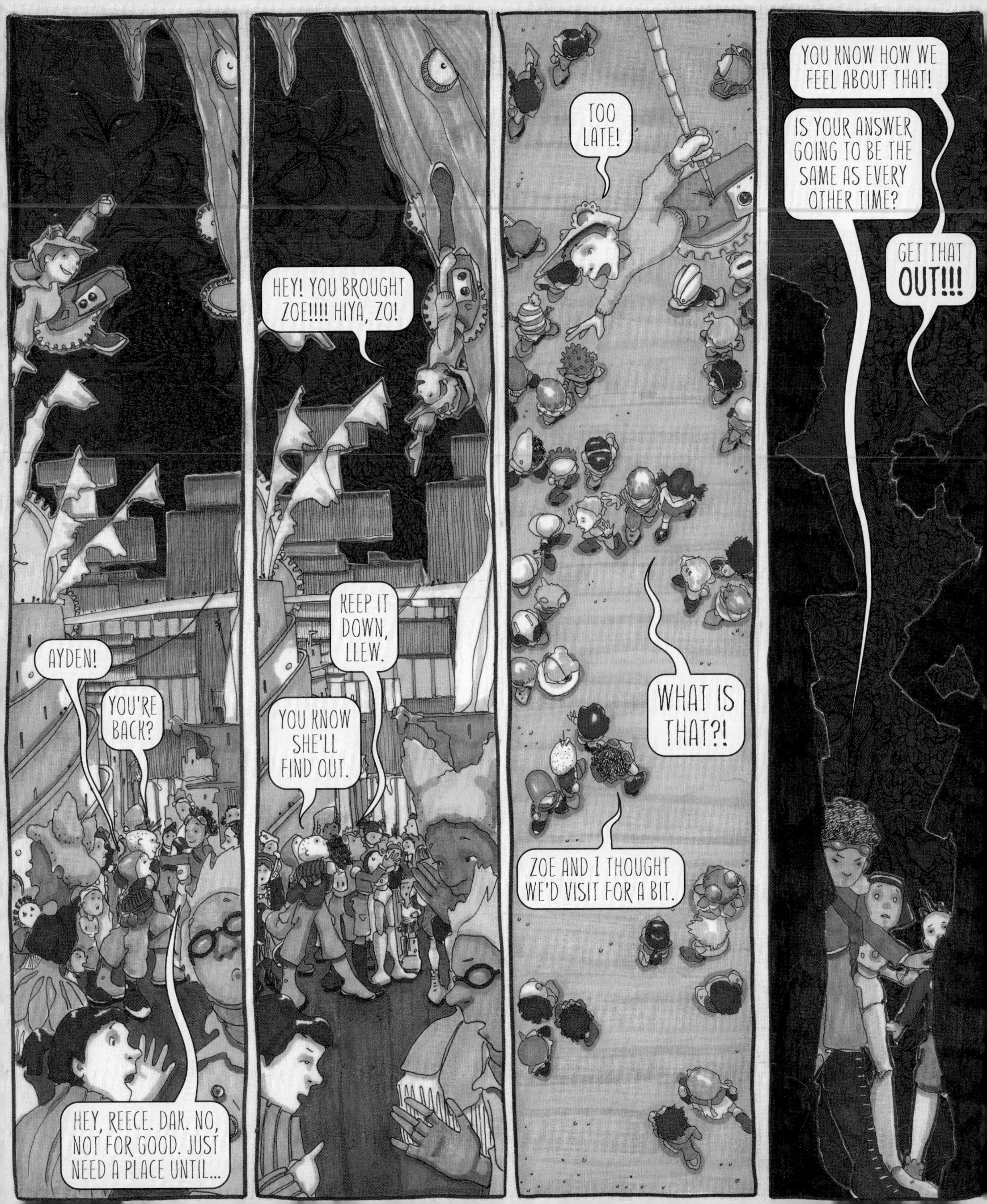
AYDEN!
YOU'RE BACK?
HEY, REECE. DAK. NO, NOT FOR GOOD. JUST NEED A PLACE UNTIL...
HEY! YOU BROUGHT ZOE!!!! HIYA, ZO!
KEEP IT DOWN, LLEW.
YOU KNOW SHE'LL FIND OUT.
TOO LATE!
WHAT IS THAT?!
ZOE AND I THOUGHT WE'D VISIT FOR A BIT.
YOU KNOW HOW WE FEEL ABOUT THAT!
IS YOUR ANSWER GOING TO BE THE SAME AS EVERY OTHER TIME?
GET THAT OUT!!!

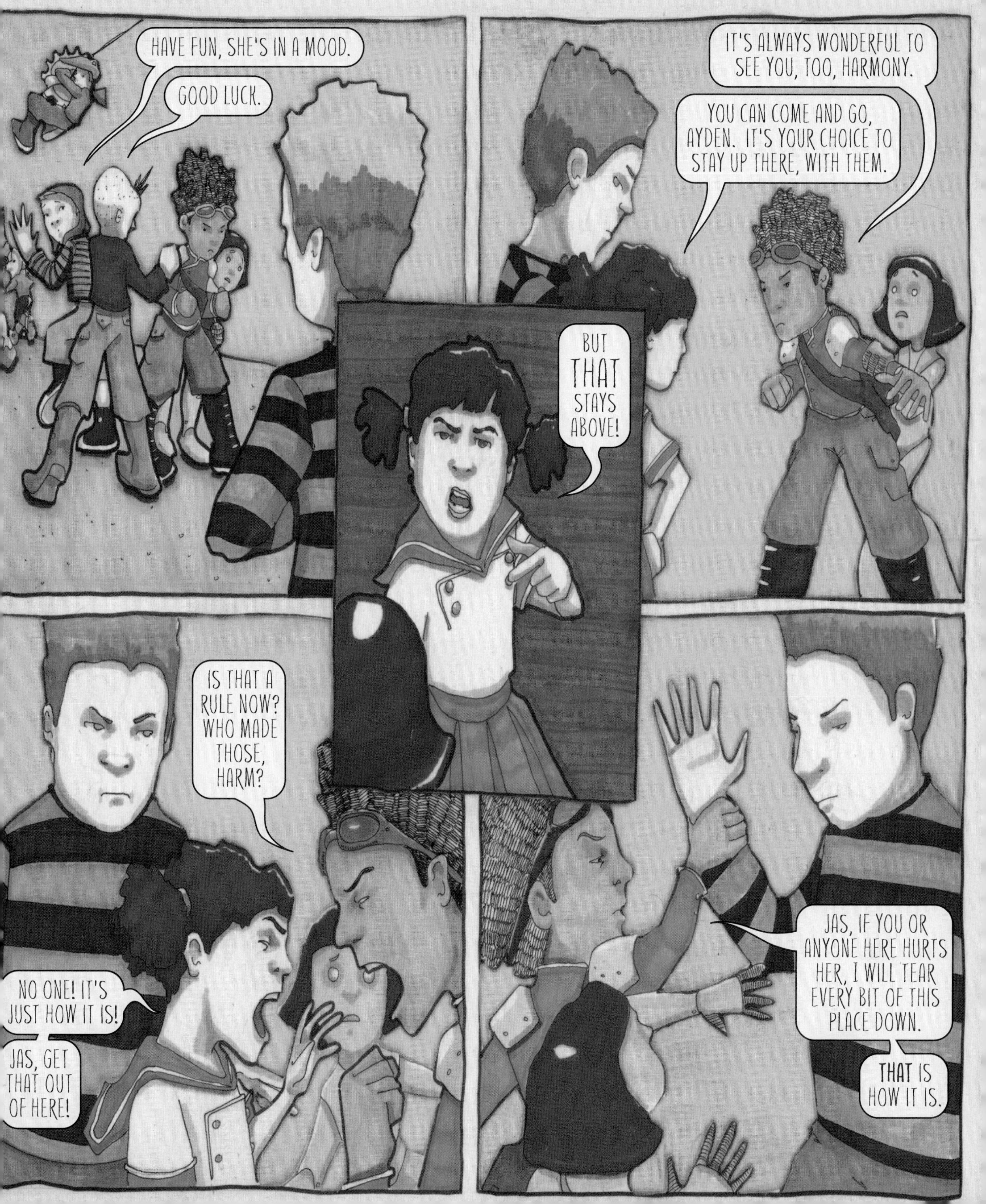
HAVE FUN, SHE'S IN A MOOD.
GOOD LUCK.
IT'S ALWAYS WONDERFUL TO SEE YOU, TOO, HARMONY.
YOU CAN COME AND GO, AYDEN. IT'S YOUR CHOICE TO STAY UP THERE, WITH THEM.
BUT THAT STAYS ABOVE!
IS THAT A RULE NOW? WHO MADE THOSE, HARM?
NO ONE! IT'S JUST HOW IT IS!
JAS, GET THAT OUT OF HERE!
JAS, IF YOU OR ANYONE HERE HURTS HER, I WILL TEAR EVERY BIT OF THIS PLACE DOWN.
THAT IS HOW IT IS.

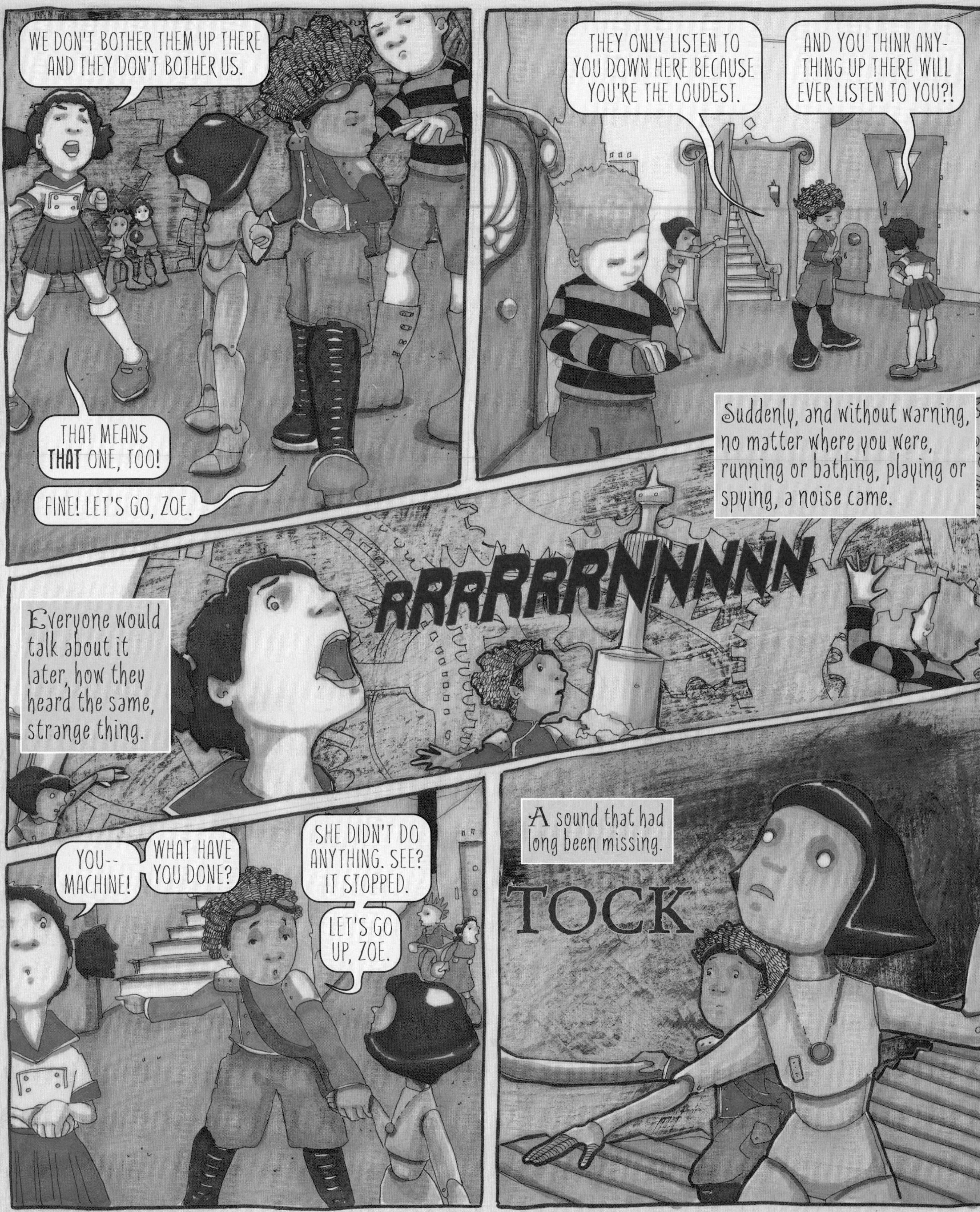

WE DON'T BOTHER THEM UP THERE AND THEY DON'T BOTHER US.
THAT MEANS **THAT** ONE, TOO!
FINE! LET'S GO, ZOE.
THEY ONLY LISTEN TO YOU DOWN HERE BECAUSE YOU'RE THE LOUDEST.
AND YOU THINK ANY-THING UP THERE WILL EVER LISTEN TO YOU?!
Suddenly, and without warning, no matter where you were, running or bathing, playing or spying, a noise came.
Everyone would talk about it later, how they heard the same, strange thing.
RRRRRRNNNNNN
YOU-- MACHINE!
WHAT HAVE YOU DONE?
SHE DIDN'T DO ANYTHING. SEE? IT STOPPED.
LET'S GO UP, ZOE.
A sound that had long been missing.
TOCK

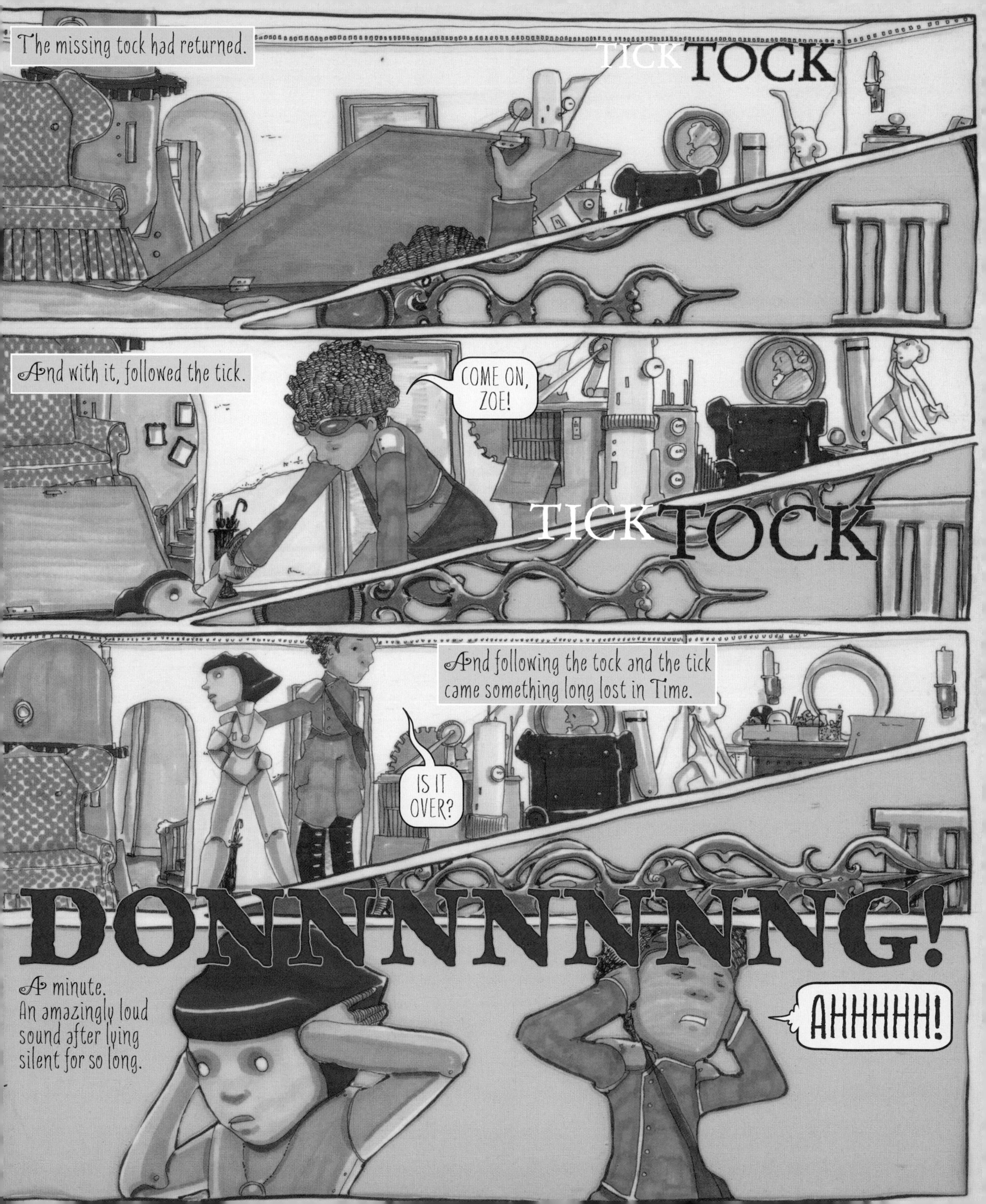
The missing tock had returned.
TICK TOCK
And with it, followed the tick.
COME ON, ZOE!
TICK TOCK
And following the tock and the tick came something long lost in Time.
IS IT OVER?
DONNNNNNG!
A minute.
An amazingly loud sound after lying silent for so long.
AHHHHH!

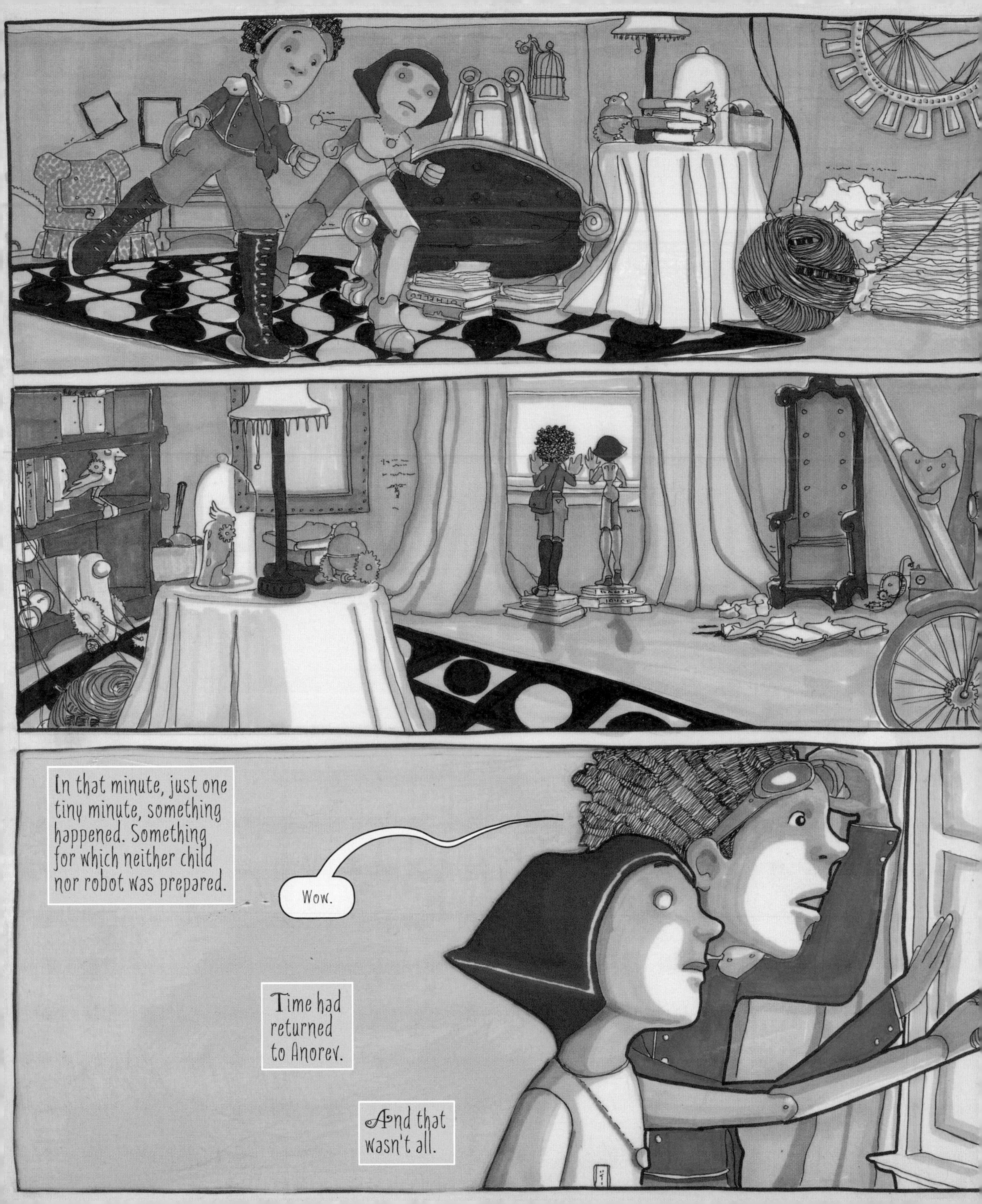
In that minute, just one tiny minute, something happened. Something for which neither child nor robot was prepared.
Wow.
Time had returned to Anorev.
And that wasn't all.

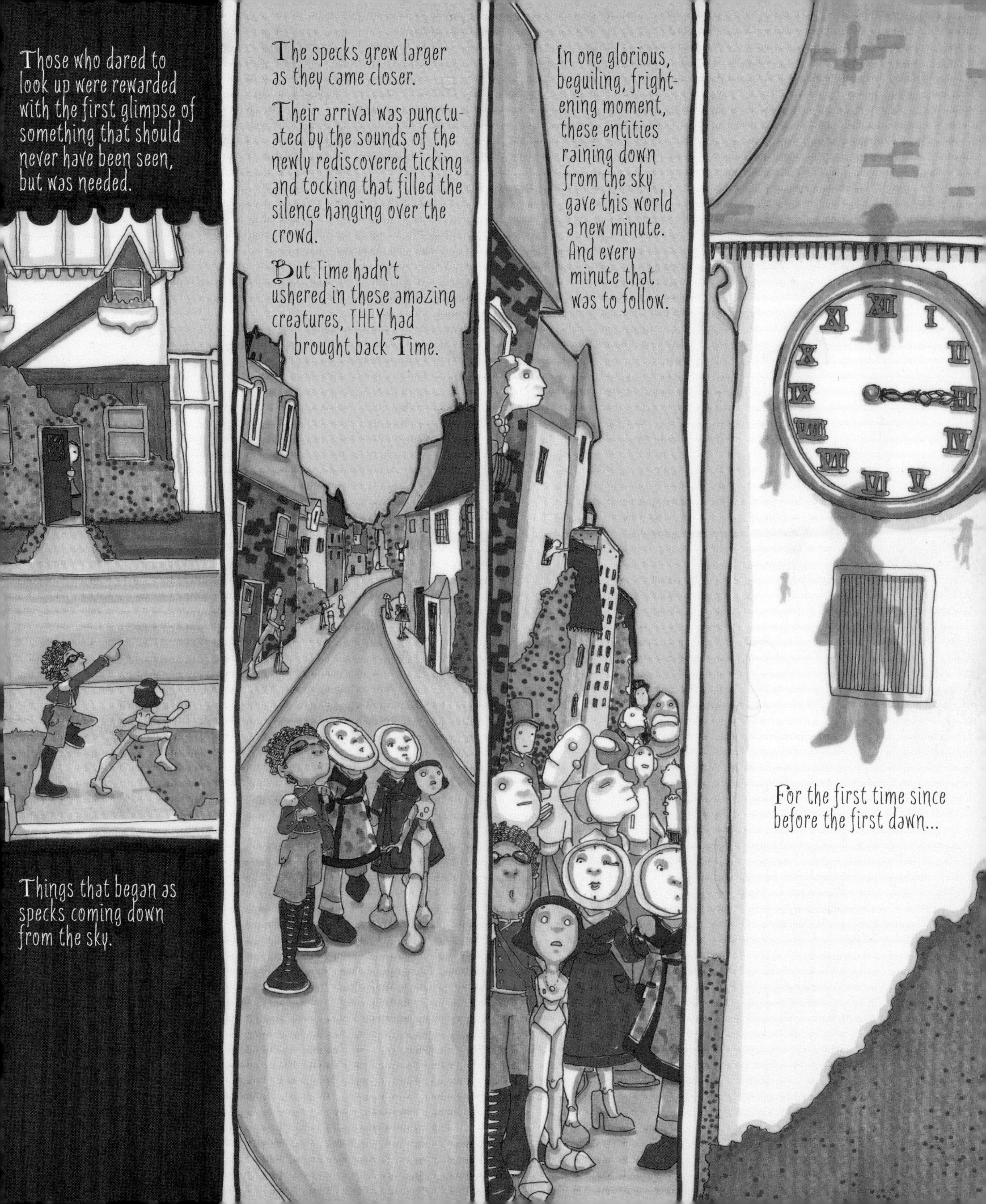
Those who dared to look up were rewarded with the first glimpse of something that should never have been seen, but was needed.
Things that began as specks coming down from the sky.
The specks grew larger as they came closer.
Their arrival was punctuated by the sounds of the newly rediscovered ticking and tocking that filled the silence hanging over the crowd.
But Time hadn't ushered in these amazing creatures, THEY had brought back Time.
In one glorious, beguiling, frightening moment, these entities raining down from the sky gave this world a new minute. And every minute that was to follow.
For the first time since before the first dawn...

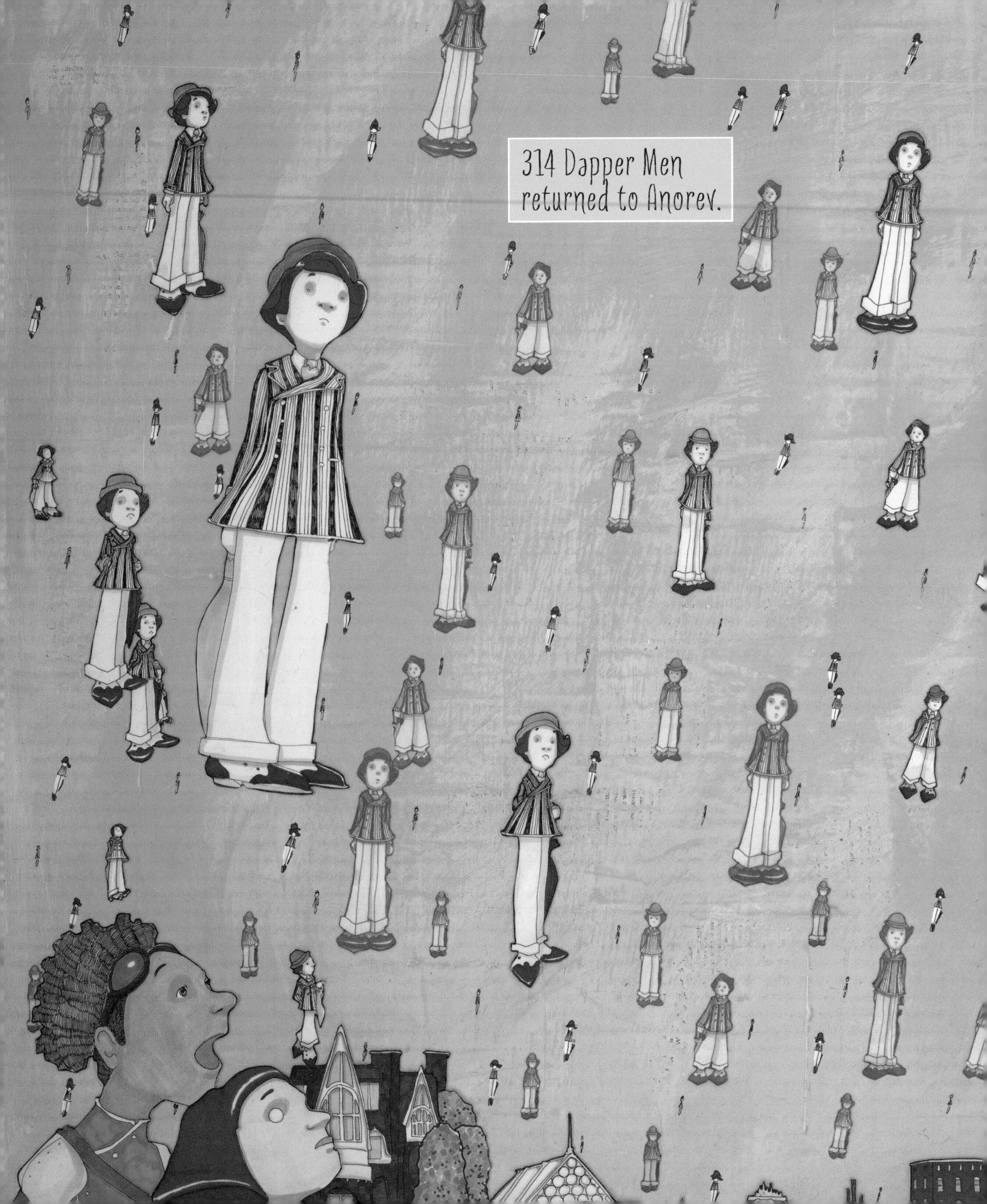
314 Dapper Men returned to Anorev.

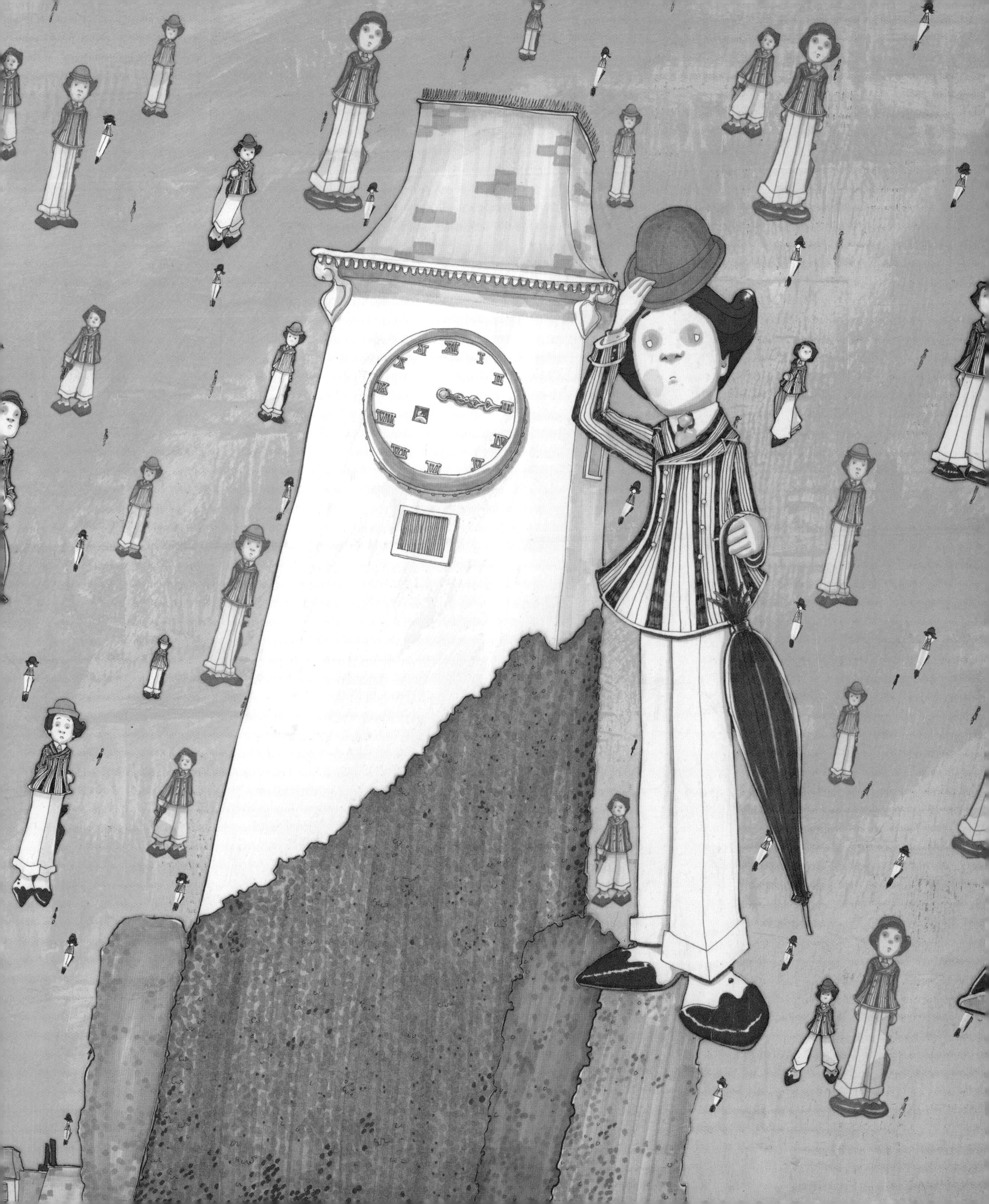

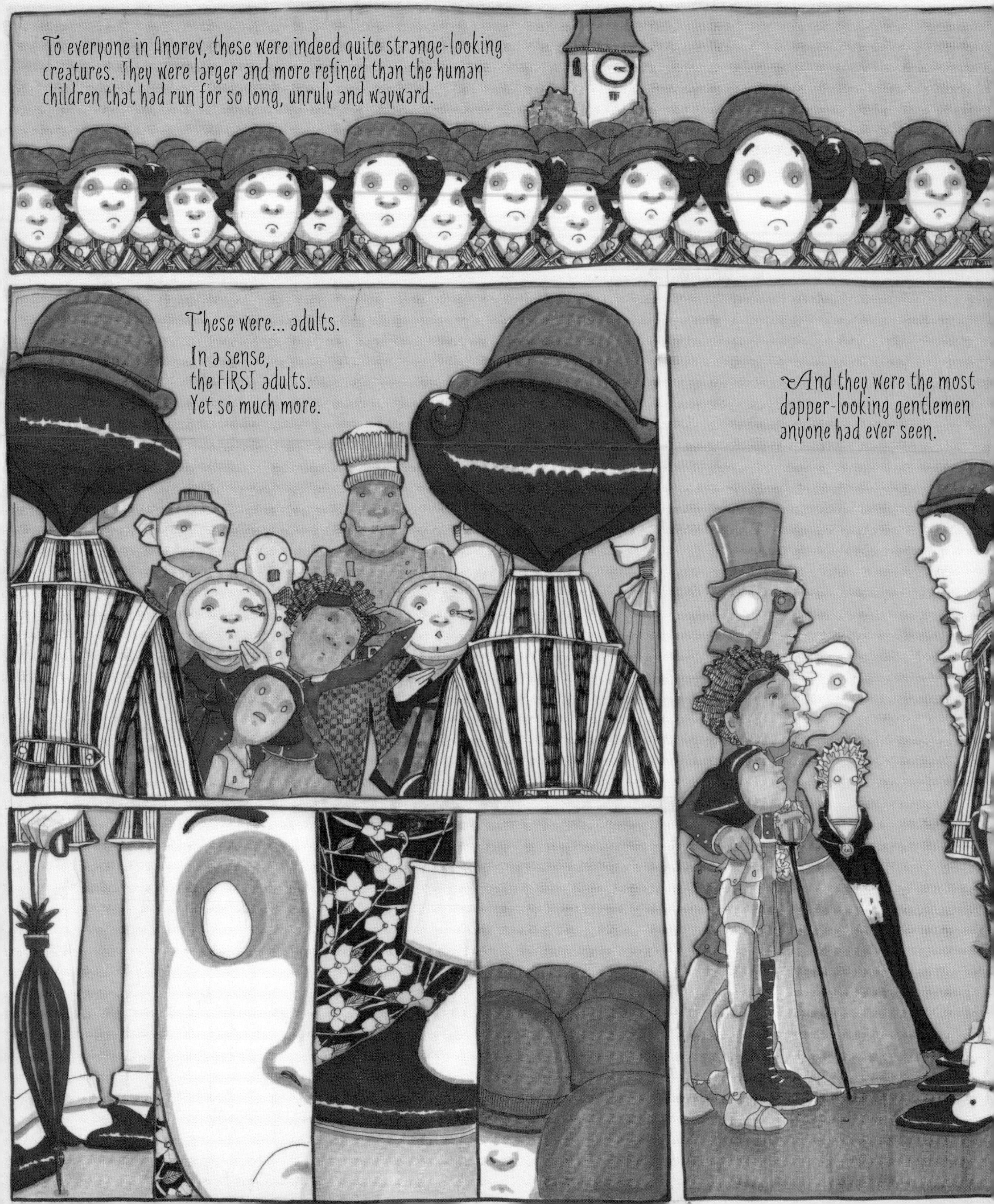

To everyone in Anorev, these were indeed quite strange-looking creatures. They were larger and more refined than the human children that had run for so long, unruly and wayward.
These were... adults.
In a sense, the FIRST adults. Yet so much more.
And they were the most dapper-looking gentlemen anyone had ever seen.

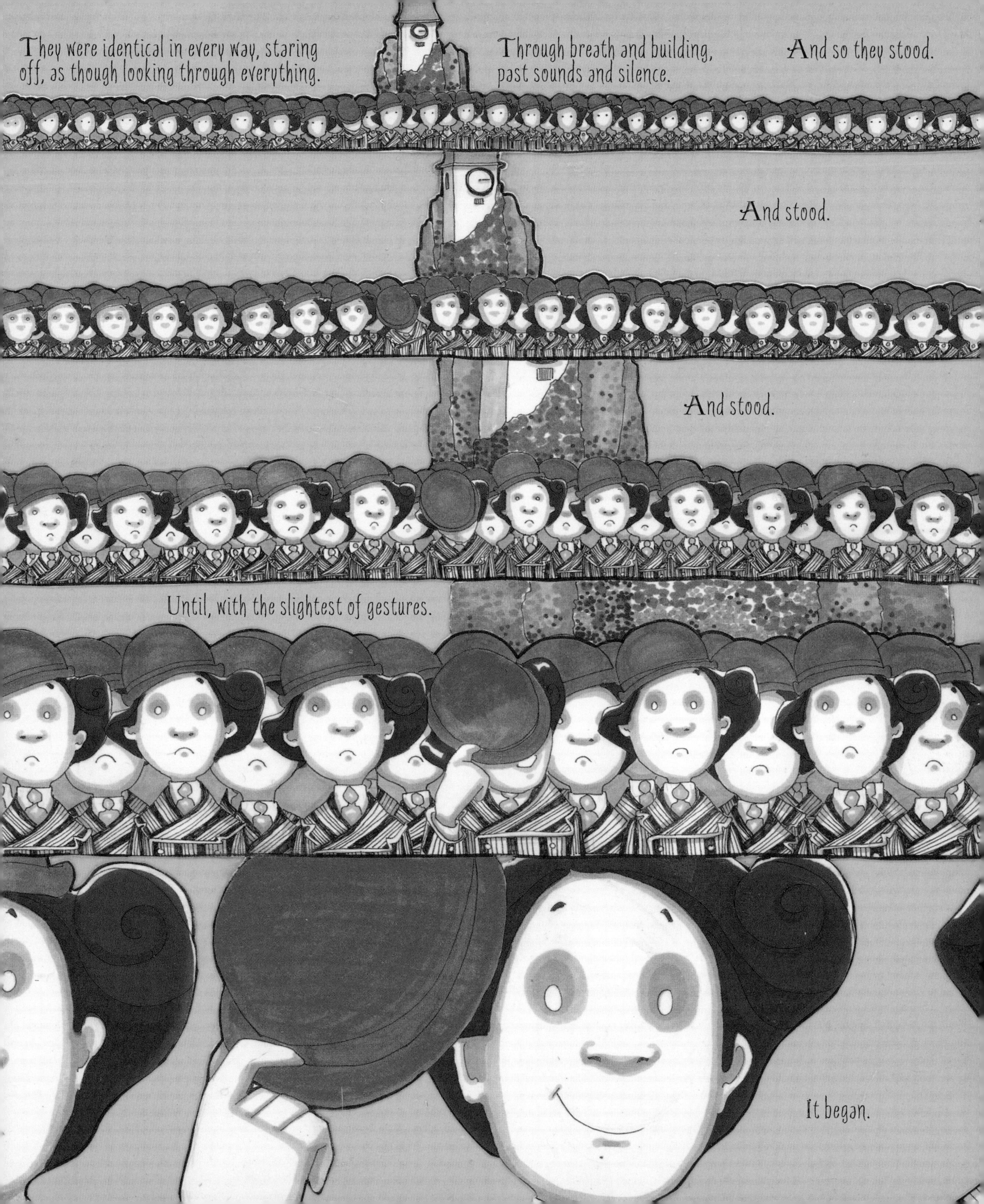
They were identical in every way, staring off, as though looking through everything.
Through breath and building, past sounds and silence.
And so they stood.
And stood.
And stood.
Until, with the slightest of gestures.
It began.

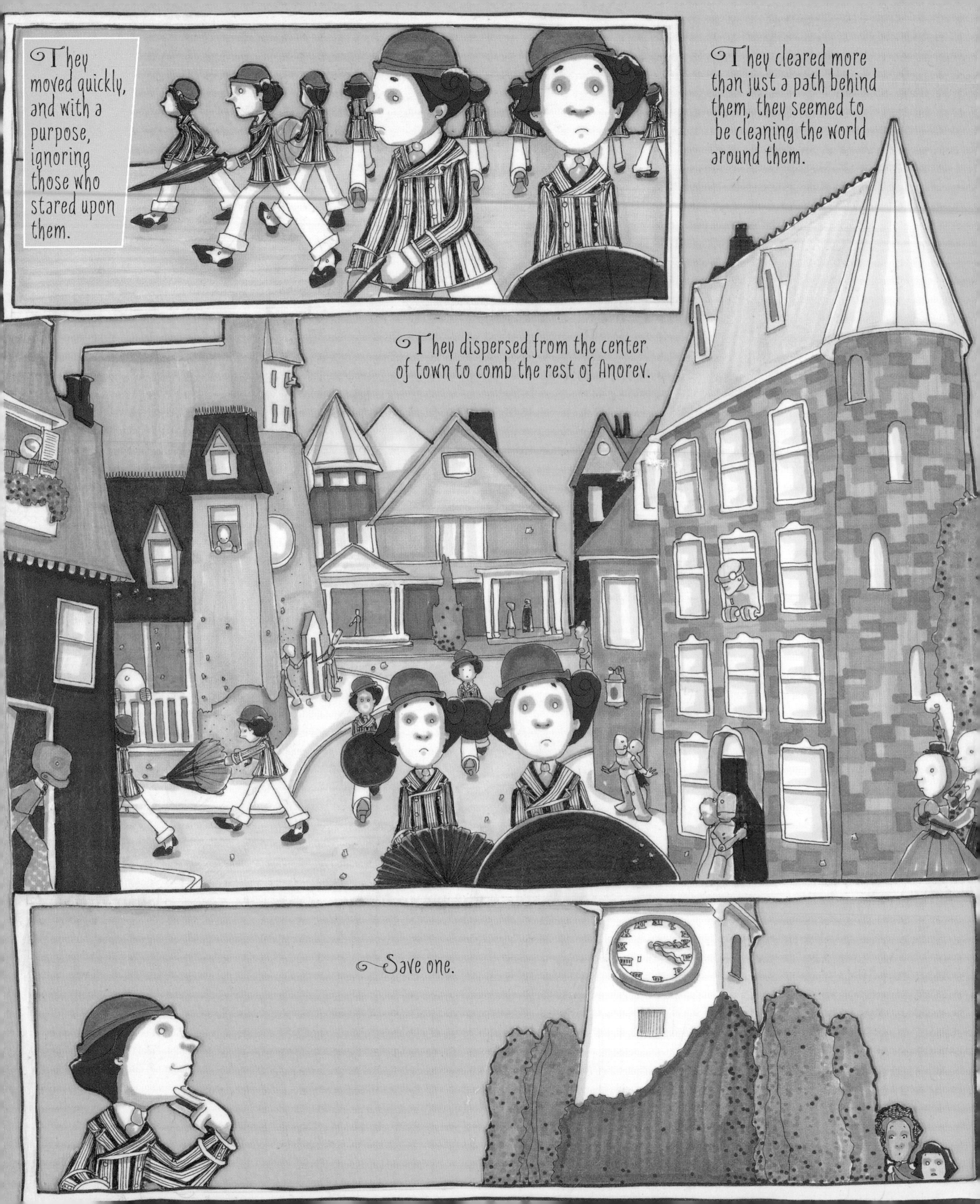
They moved quickly, and with a purpose, ignoring those who stared upon them.
They cleared more than just a path behind them, they seemed to be cleaning the world around them.
They dispersed from the center of town to comb the rest of Anorev.
Save one.

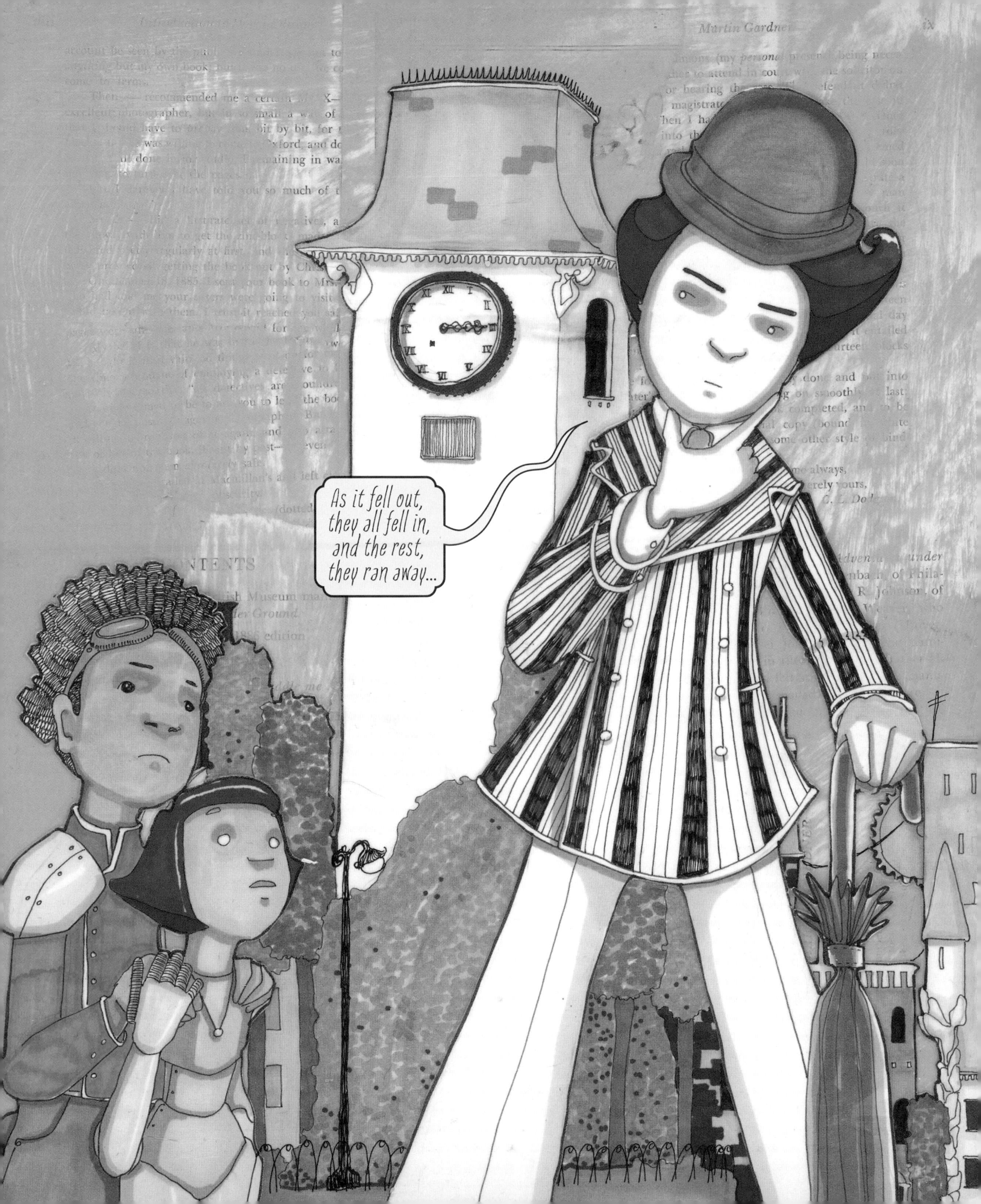
As it fell out, they all fell in, and the rest, they ran away...

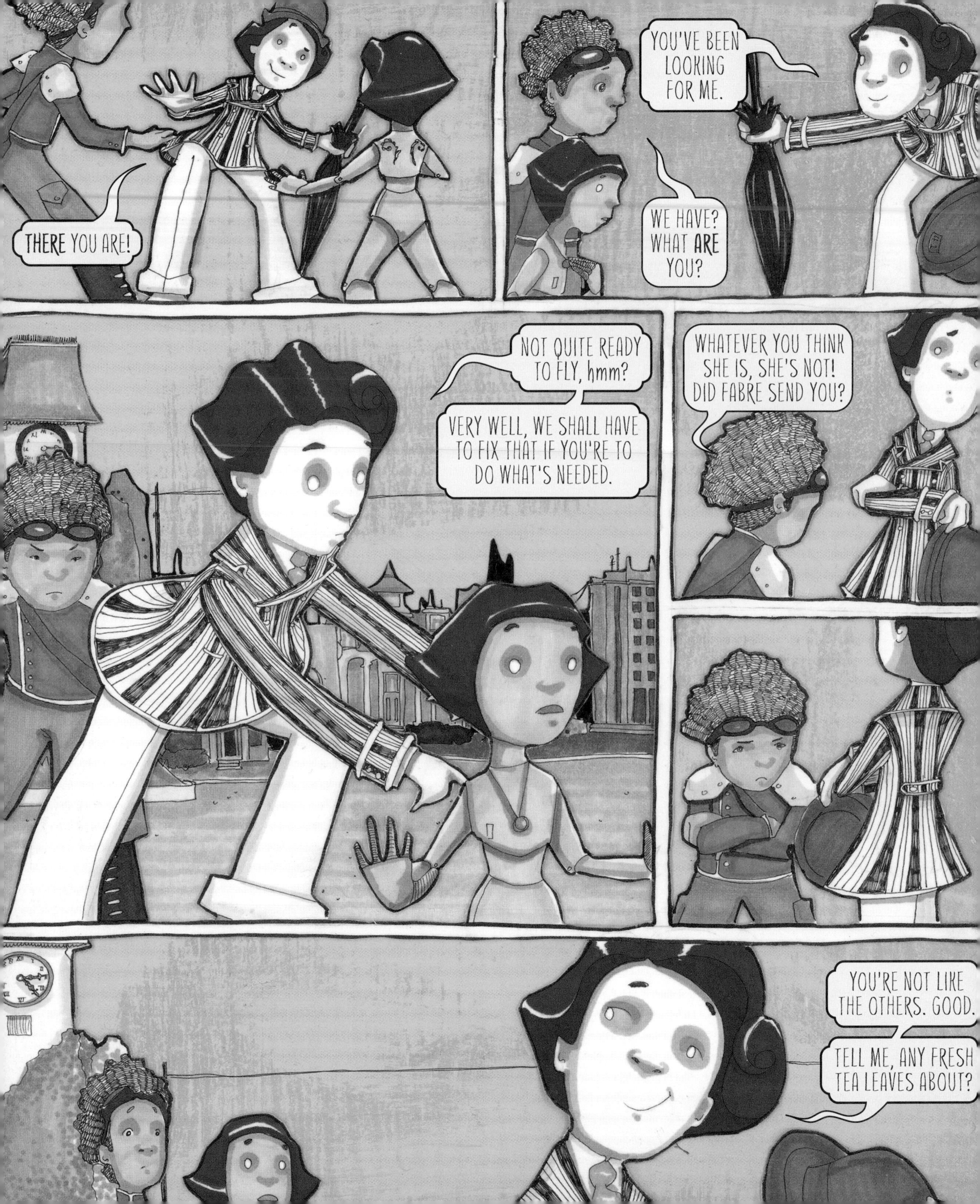
THERE YOU ARE!
YOU'VE BEEN LOOKING FOR ME.
WE HAVE? WHAT ARE YOU?
NOT QUITE READY TO FLY, hmm?
VERY WELL, WE SHALL HAVE TO FIX THAT IF YOU'RE TO DO WHAT'S NEEDED.
WHATEVER YOU THINK SHE IS, SHE'S NOT! DID FABRE SEND YOU?
YOU'RE NOT LIKE THE OTHERS. GOOD.
TELL ME, ANY FRESH TEA LEAVES ABOUT?

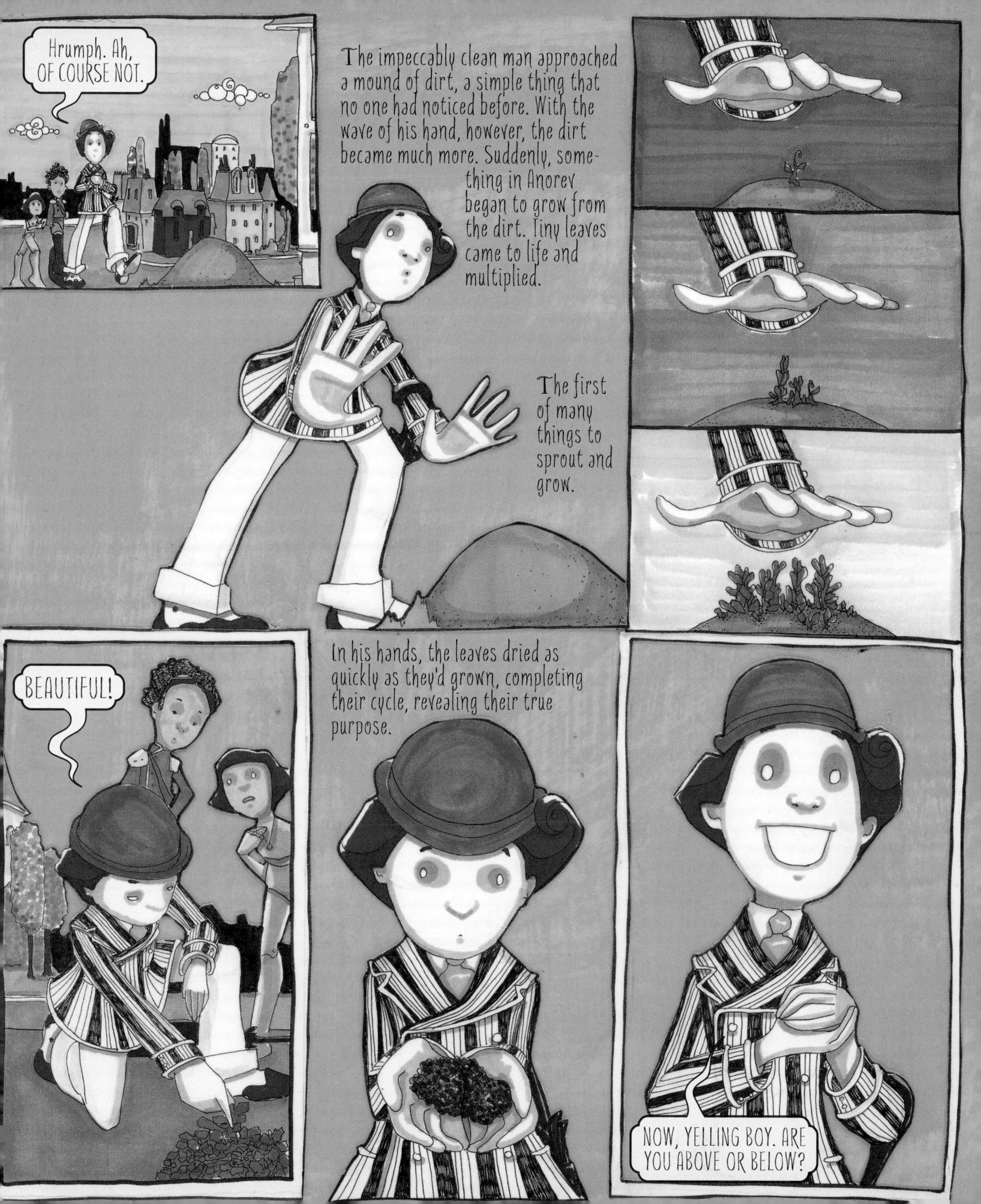
Hrumph. Ah, OF COURSE NOT.
The impeccably clean man approached a mound of dirt, a simple thing that no one had noticed before. With the wave of his hand, however, the dirt became much more. Suddenly, something in Anorev began to grow from the dirt. Tiny leaves came to life and multiplied.
The first of many things to sprout and grow.
BEAUTIFUL!
In his hands, the leaves dried as quickly as they'd grown, completing their cycle, revealing their true purpose.
NOW, YELLING BOY. ARE YOU ABOVE OR BELOW?

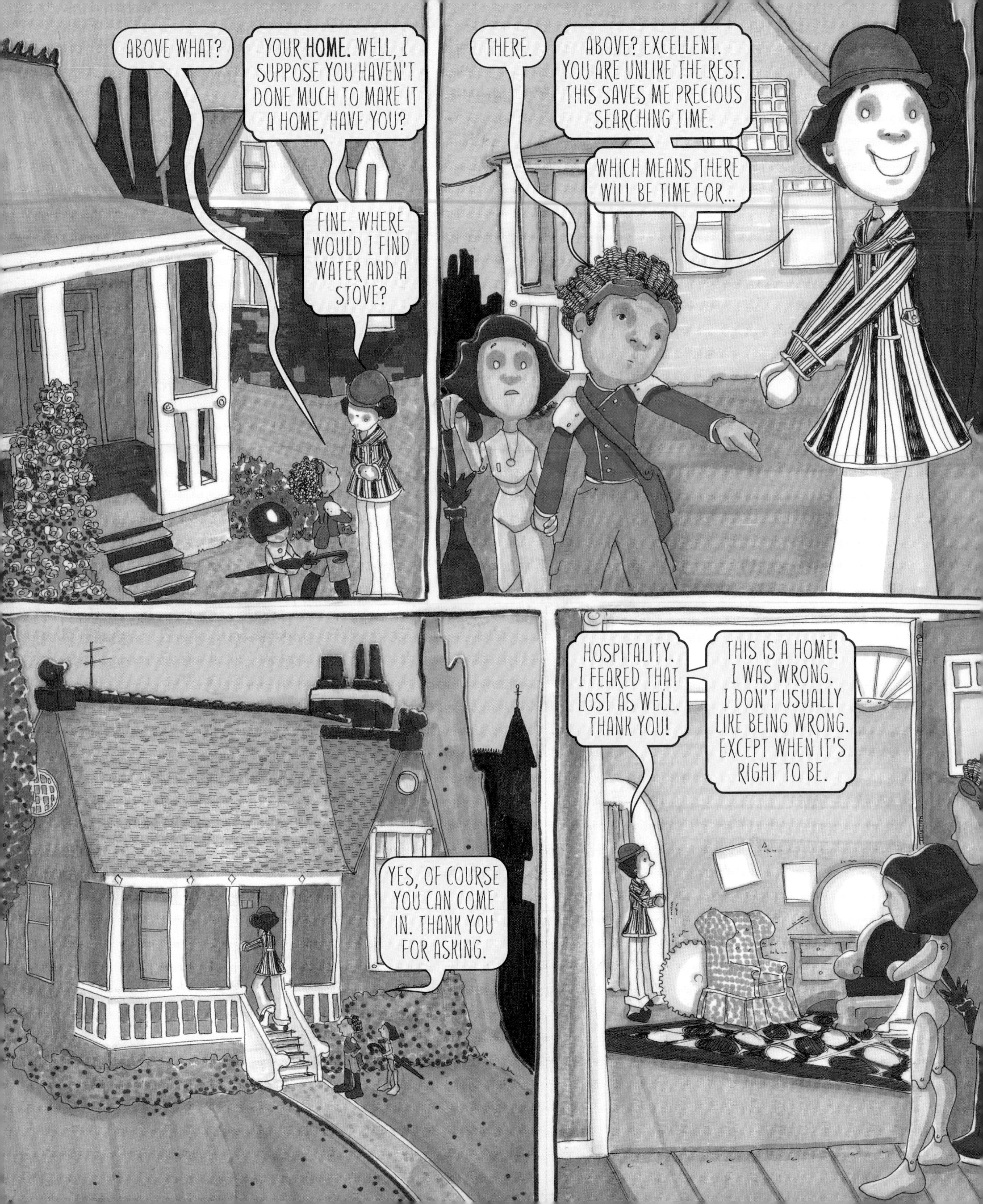
ABOVE WHAT?
YOUR **HOME.** WELL, I SUPPOSE YOU HAVEN'T DONE MUCH TO MAKE IT A HOME, HAVE YOU?
FINE. WHERE WOULD I FIND WATER AND A STOVE?
THERE.
ABOVE? EXCELLENT. YOU ARE UNLIKE THE REST. THIS SAVES ME PRECIOUS SEARCHING TIME.
WHICH MEANS THERE WILL BE TIME FOR...
YES, OF COURSE YOU CAN COME IN. THANK YOU FOR ASKING.
HOSPITALITY. I FEARED THAT LOST AS WELL. THANK YOU!
THIS IS A HOME! I WAS WRONG. I DON'T USUALLY LIKE BEING WRONG. EXCEPT WHEN IT'S RIGHT TO BE.

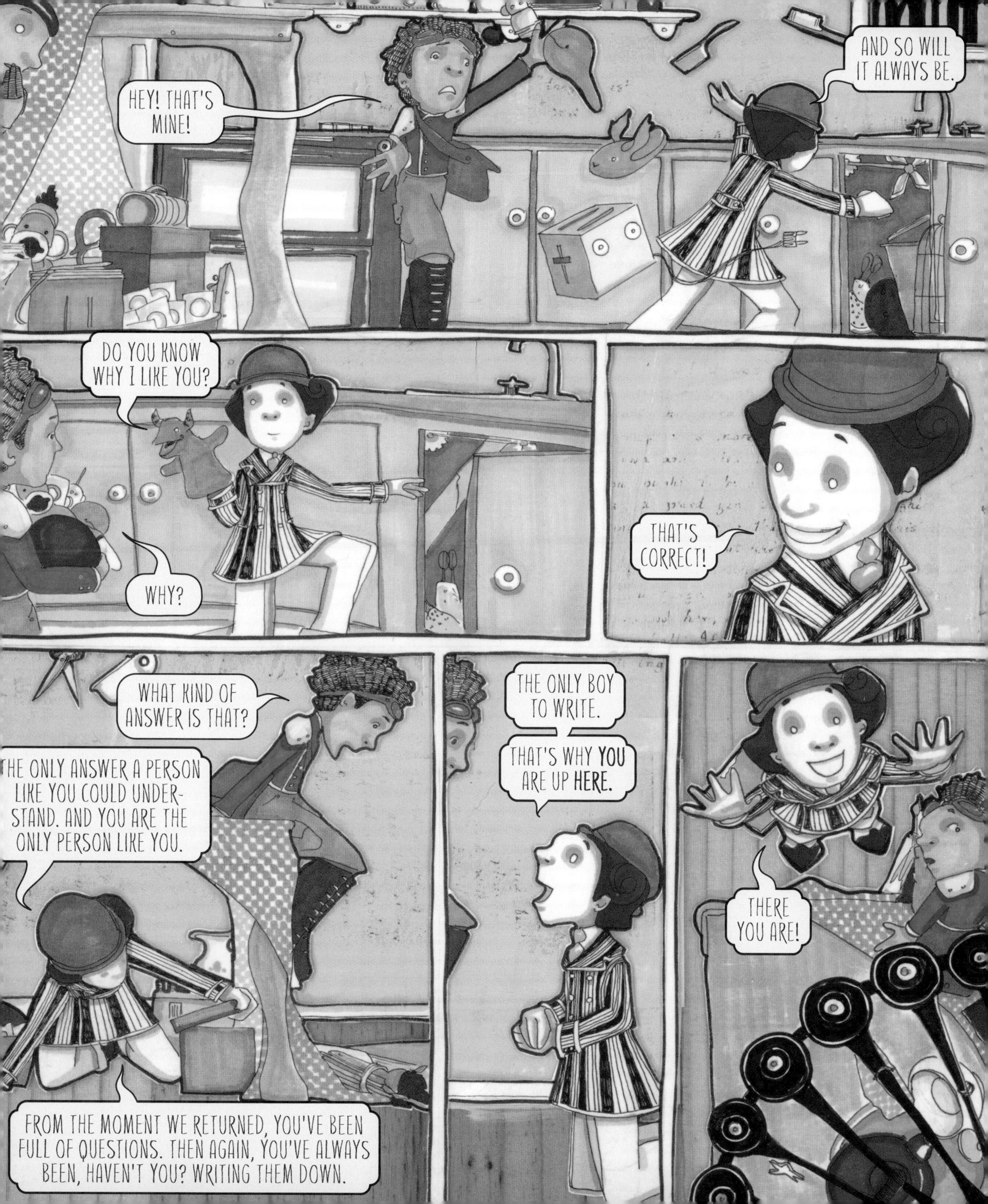
HEY! THAT'S MINE!
AND SO WILL IT ALWAYS BE.
DO YOU KNOW WHY I LIKE YOU?
WHY?
THAT'S CORRECT!
WHAT KIND OF ANSWER IS THAT?
THE ONLY ANSWER A PERSON LIKE YOU COULD UNDER-STAND. AND YOU ARE THE ONLY PERSON LIKE YOU.
FROM THE MOMENT WE RETURNED, YOU'VE BEEN FULL OF QUESTIONS. THEN AGAIN, YOU'VE ALWAYS BEEN, HAVEN'T YOU? WRITING THEM DOWN.
THE ONLY BOY TO WRITE.
THAT'S WHY YOU ARE UP HERE.
THERE YOU ARE!

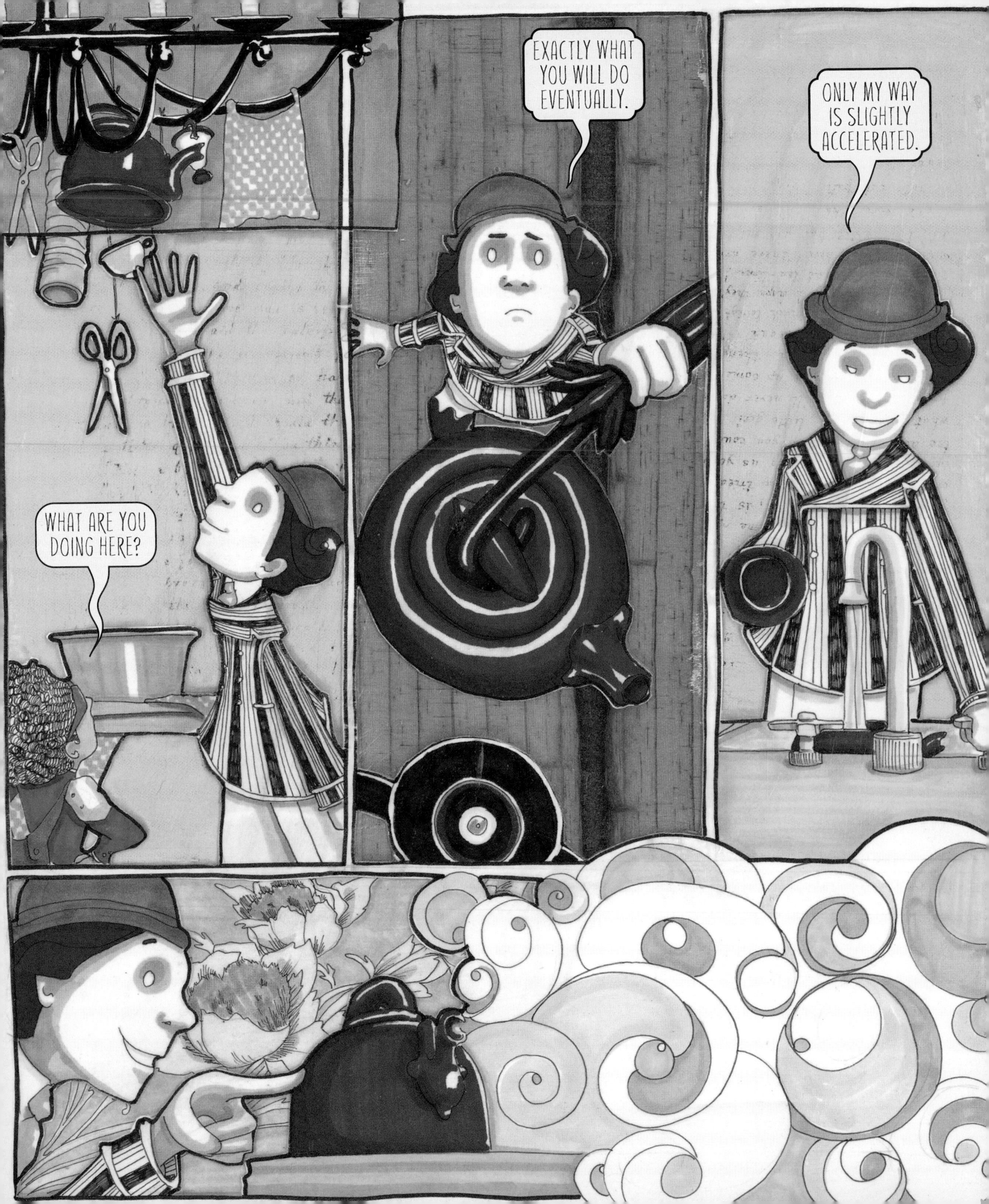
WHAT ARE YOU DOING HERE?
EXACTLY WHAT YOU WILL DO EVENTUALLY.
ONLY MY WAY IS SLIGHTLY ACCELERATED.

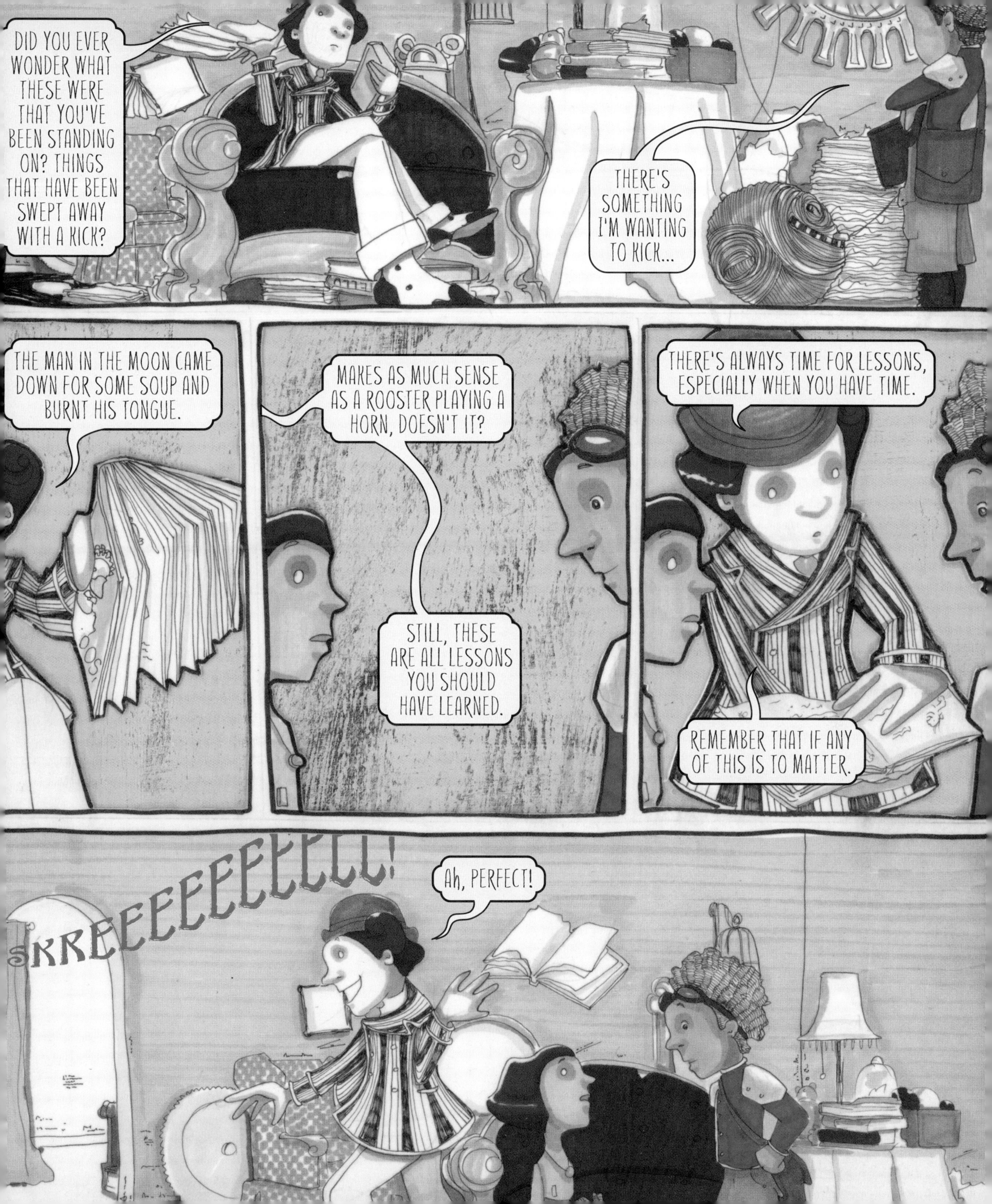
DID YOU EVER WONDER WHAT THESE WERE THAT YOU'VE BEEN STANDING ON? THINGS THAT HAVE BEEN SWEPT AWAY WITH A KICK?
THERE'S SOMETHING I'M WANTING TO KICK...
THE MAN IN THE MOON CAME DOWN FOR SOME SOUP AND BURNT HIS TONGUE.
MAKES AS MUCH SENSE AS A ROOSTER PLAYING A HORN, DOESN'T IT?
STILL, THESE ARE ALL LESSONS YOU SHOULD HAVE LEARNED.
THERE'S ALWAYS TIME FOR LESSONS, ESPECIALLY WHEN YOU HAVE TIME.
REMEMBER THAT IF ANY OF THIS IS TO MATTER.
SKREEEEEEEEEEEL!
Ah, PERFECT!

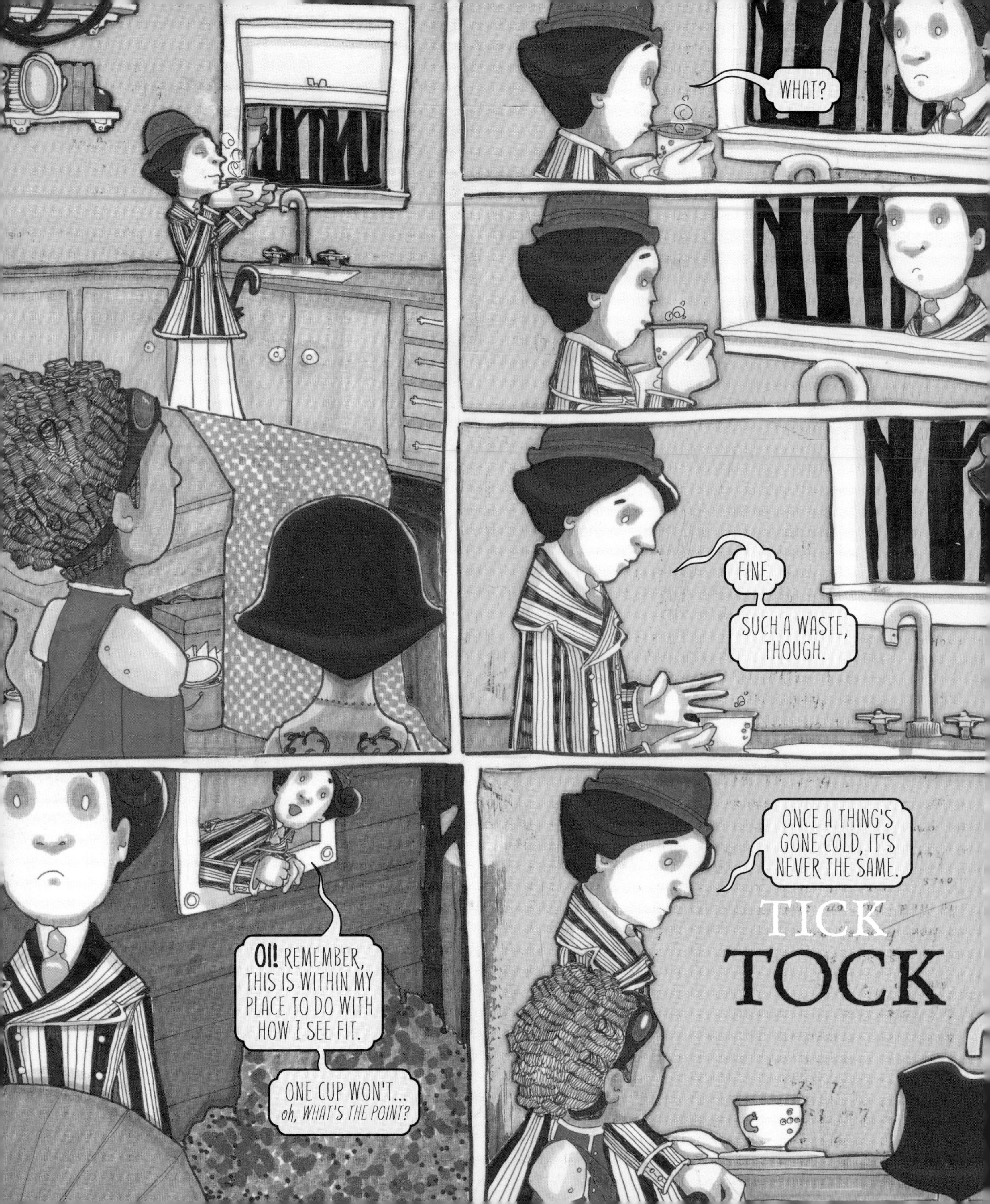

WHAT?
FINE.
SUCH A WASTE, THOUGH.
OI! REMEMBER, THIS IS WITHIN MY PLACE TO DO WITH HOW I SEE FIT.
ONE CUP WON'T... oh, WHAT'S THE POINT?
ONCE A THING'S GONE COLD, IT'S NEVER THE SAME.
TICK
TOCK

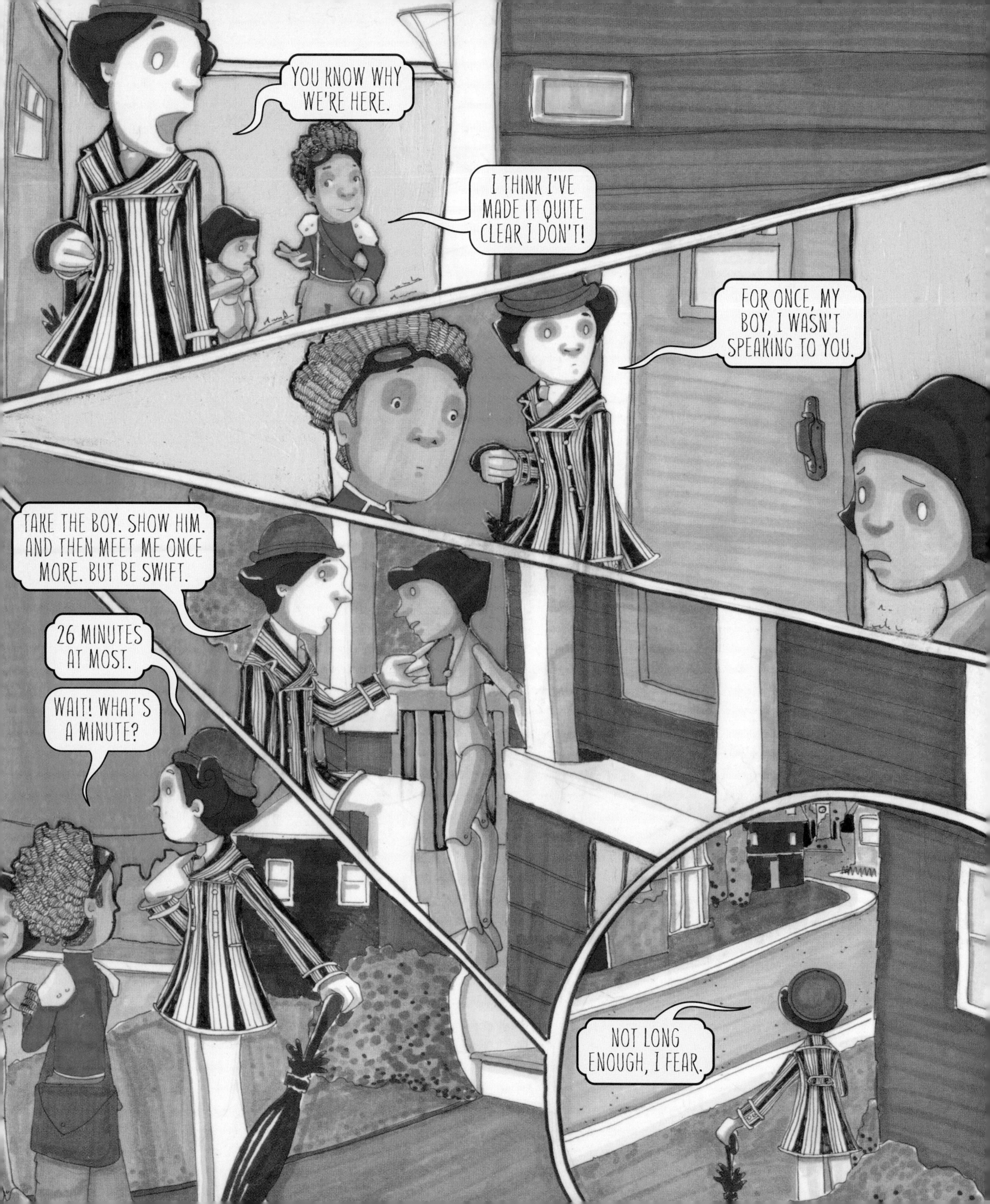
YOU KNOW WHY WE'RE HERE.
I THINK I'VE MADE IT QUITE CLEAR I DON'T!
FOR ONCE, MY BOY, I WASN'T SPEAKING TO YOU.
TAKE THE BOY. SHOW HIM. AND THEN MEET ME ONCE MORE. BUT BE SWIFT.
26 MINUTES AT MOST.
WAIT! WHAT'S A MINUTE?
NOT LONG ENOUGH, I FEAR.

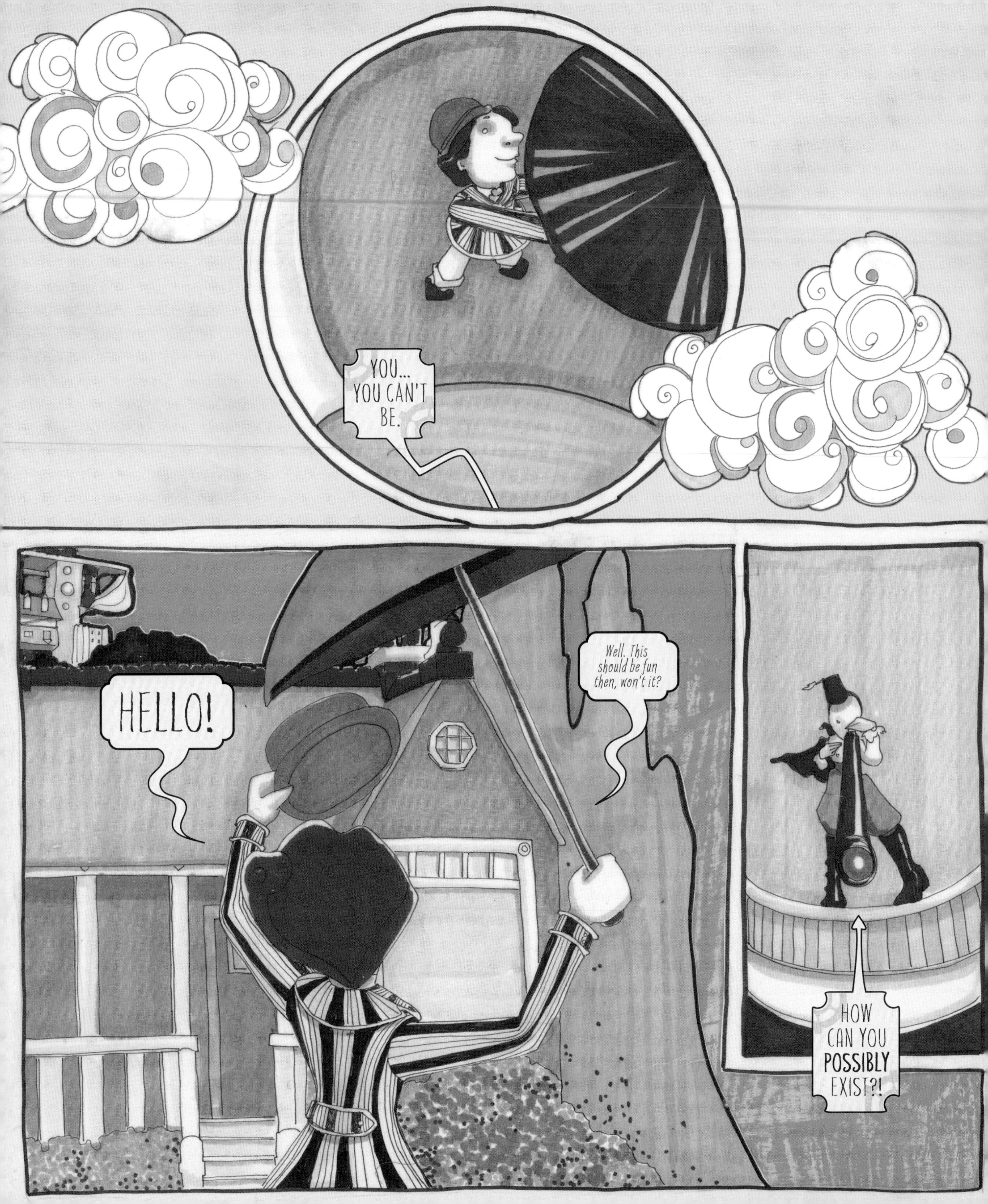
YOU... YOU CAN'T BE.
HELLO!
Well. This should be fun then, won't it?
HOW CAN YOU **POSSIBLY** EXIST?!

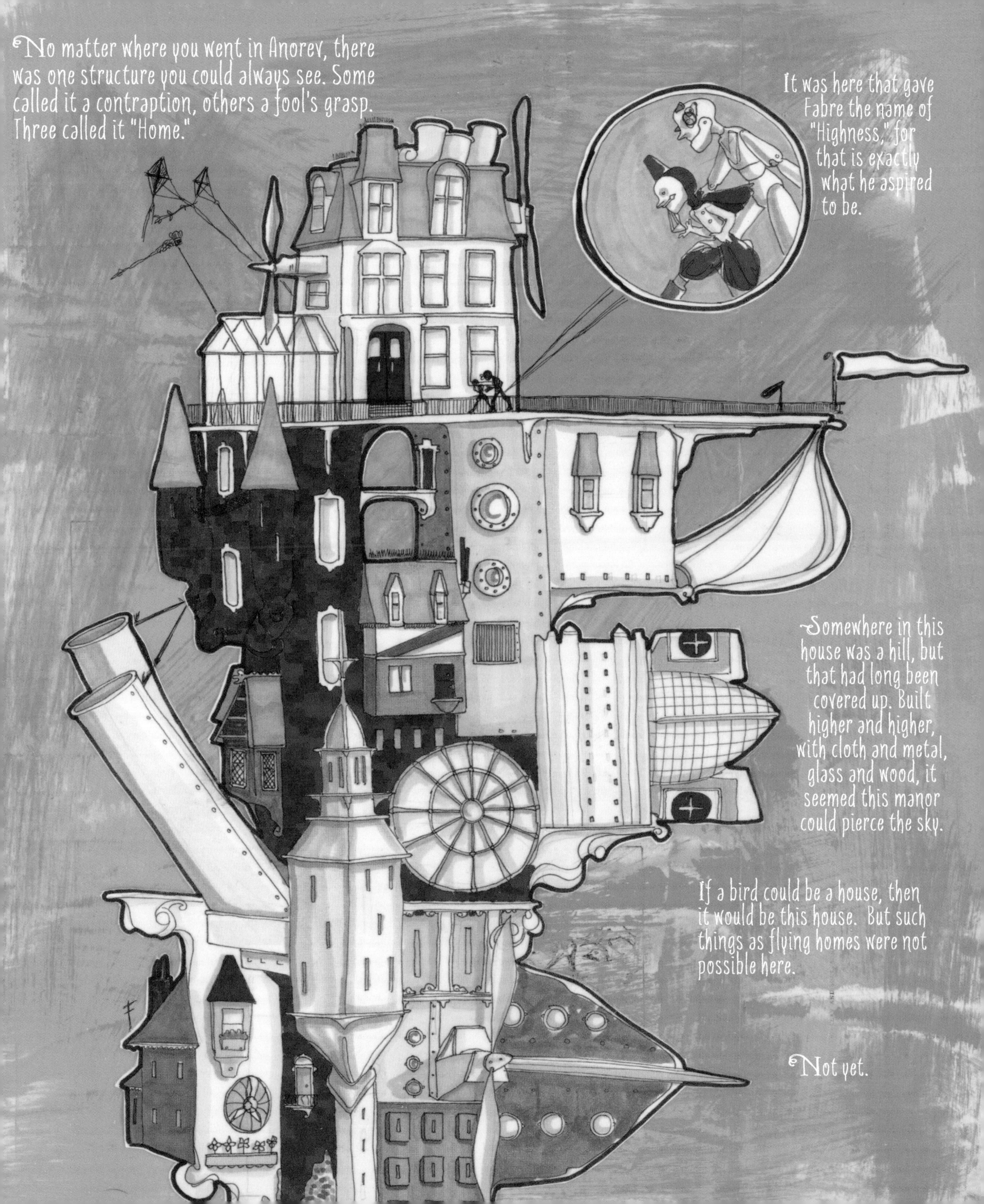
No matter where you went in Anorev, there was one structure you could always see. Some called it a contraption, others a fool's grasp. Three called it "Home."
It was here that gave Fabre the name of "Highness," for that is exactly what he aspired to be.
Somewhere in this house was a hill, but that had long been covered up. Built higher and higher, with cloth and metal, glass and wood, it seemed this manor could pierce the sky.
If a bird could be a house, then it would be this house. But such things as flying homes were not possible here.
Not yet.

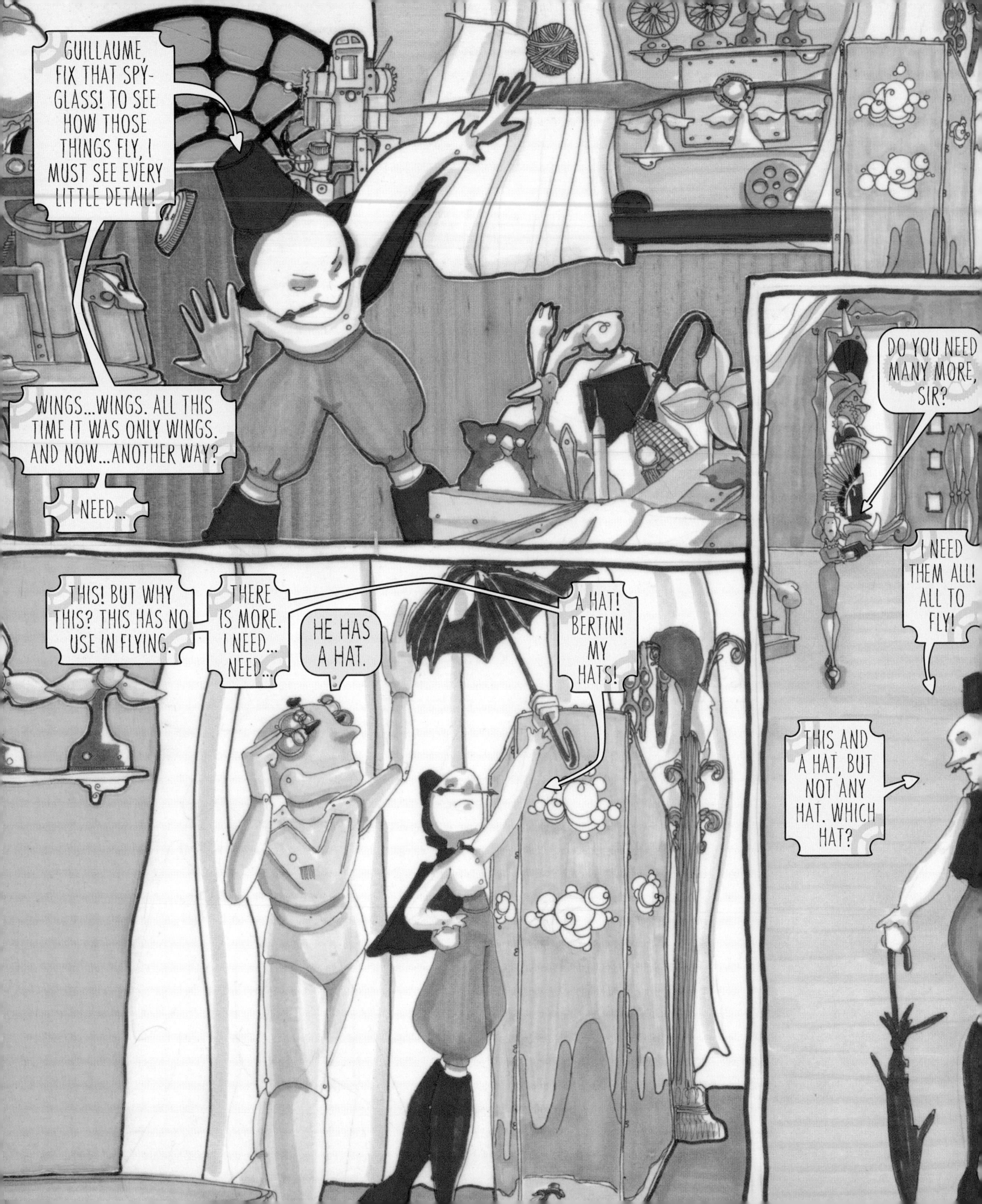
GUILLAUME, FIX THAT SPY-GLASS! TO SEE HOW THOSE THINGS FLY, I MUST SEE EVERY LITTLE DETAIL!
WINGS...WINGS. ALL THIS TIME IT WAS ONLY WINGS. AND NOW...ANOTHER WAY?
I NEED...
DO YOU NEED MANY MORE, SIR?
I NEED THEM ALL! ALL TO FLY!
THIS! BUT WHY THIS? THIS HAS NO USE IN FLYING.
THERE IS MORE. I NEED... NEED...
HE HAS A HAT.
A HAT! BERTIN! MY HATS!
THIS AND A HAT, BUT NOT ANY HAT. WHICH HAT?

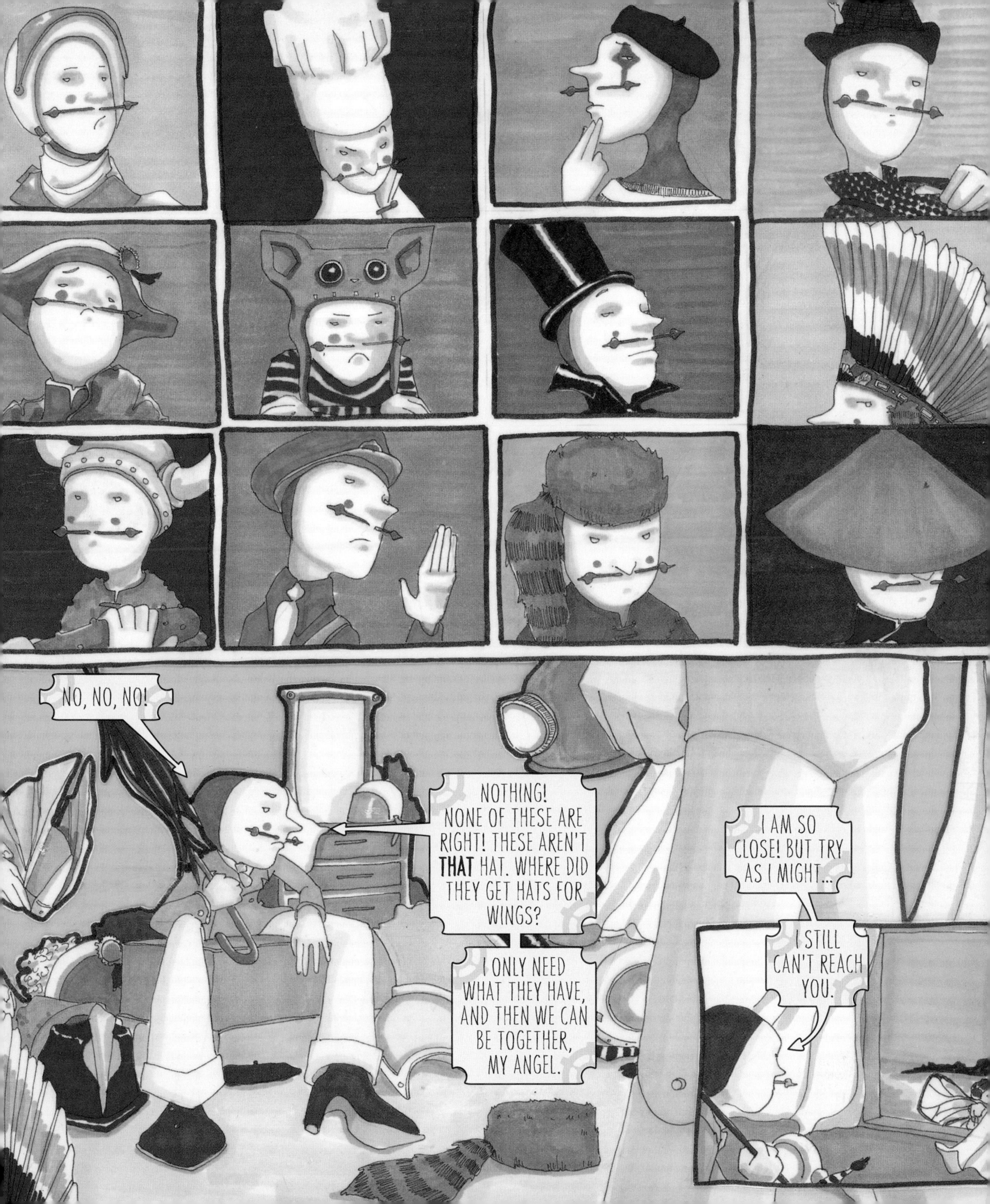
NO, NO, NO!
NOTHING! NONE OF THESE ARE RIGHT! THESE AREN'T **THAT** HAT. WHERE DID THEY GET HATS FOR WINGS?
I ONLY NEED WHAT THEY HAVE, AND THEN WE CAN BE TOGETHER, MY ANGEL.
I AM SO CLOSE! BUT TRY AS I MIGHT...
I STILL CAN'T REACH YOU.

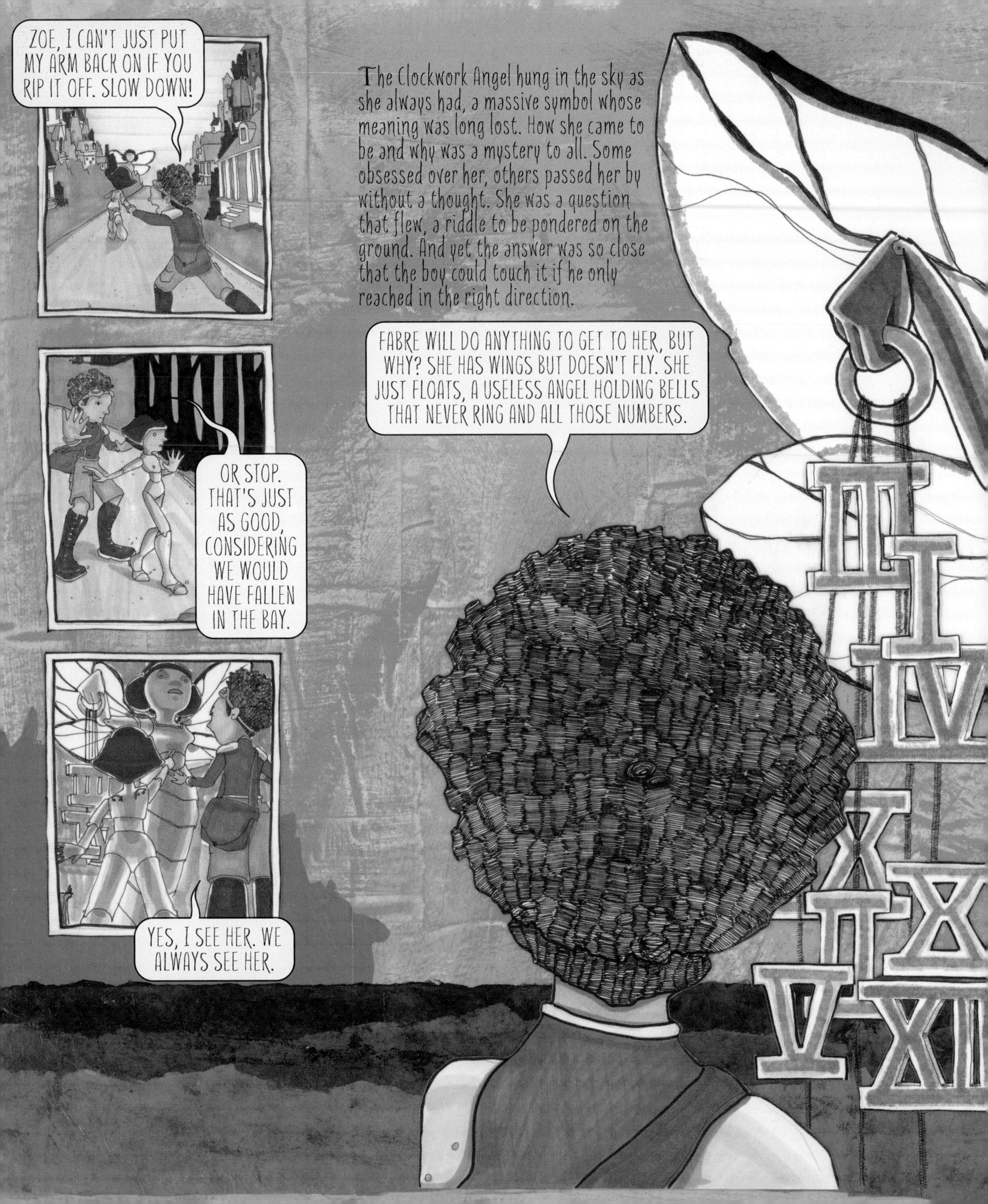
The Clockwork Angel hung in the sky as she always had, a massive symbol whose meaning was long lost. How she came to be and why was a mystery to all. Some obsessed over her, others passed her by without a thought. She was a question that flew, a riddle to be pondered on the ground. And yet the answer was so close that the boy could touch it if he only reached in the right direction.
ZOE, I CAN'T JUST PUT MY ARM BACK ON IF YOU RIP IT OFF. SLOW DOWN!
OR STOP. THAT'S JUST AS GOOD, CONSIDERING WE WOULD HAVE FALLEN IN THE BAY.
YES, I SEE HER. WE ALWAYS SEE HER.
FABRE WILL DO ANYTHING TO GET TO HER, BUT WHY? SHE HAS WINGS BUT DOESN'T FLY. SHE JUST FLOATS, A USELESS ANGEL HOLDING BELLS THAT NEVER RING AND ALL THOSE NUMBERS.

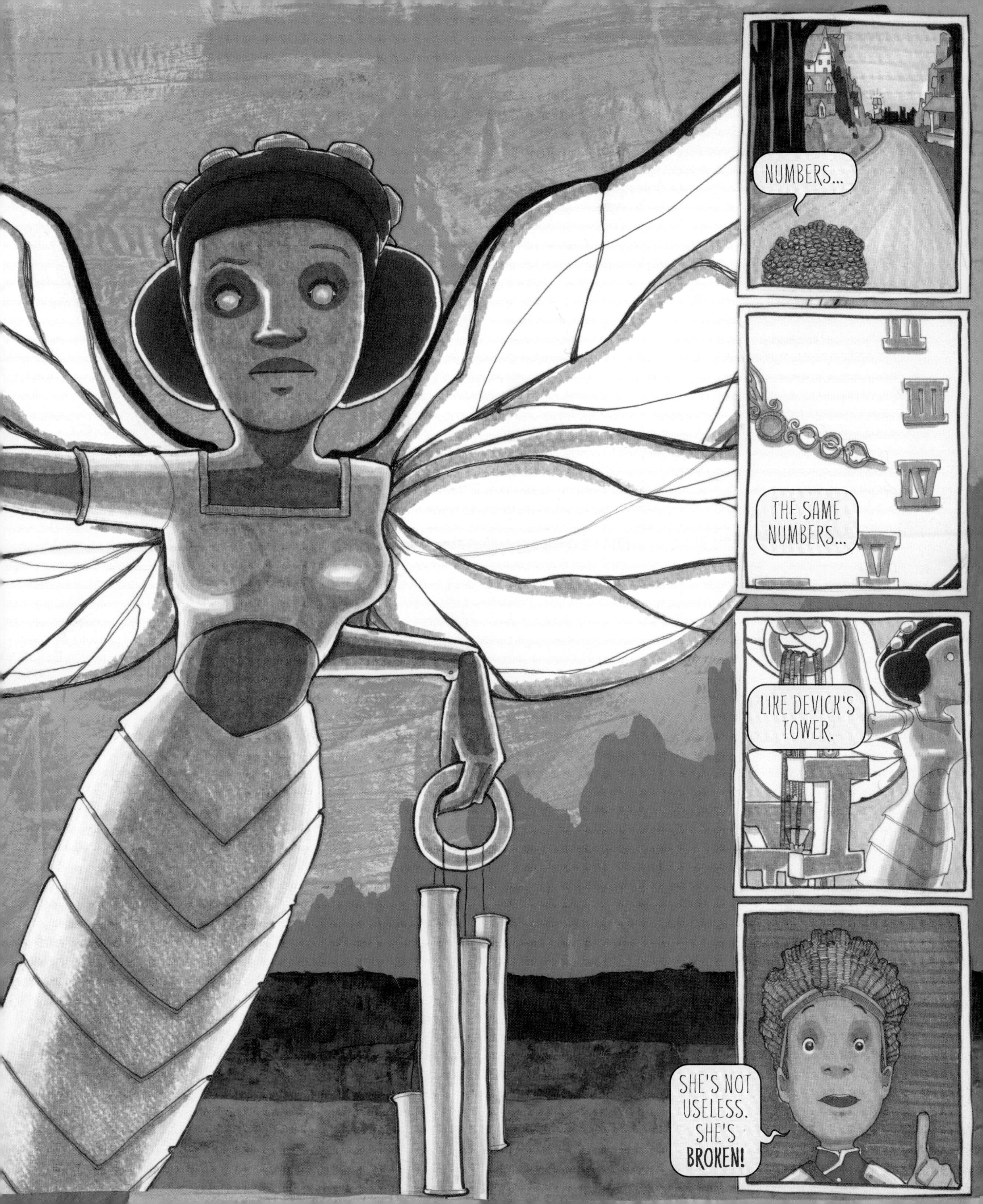
NUMBERS...
THE SAME NUMBERS...
LIKE DEVICK'S TOWER.
SHE'S NOT USELESS. SHE'S **BROKEN!**

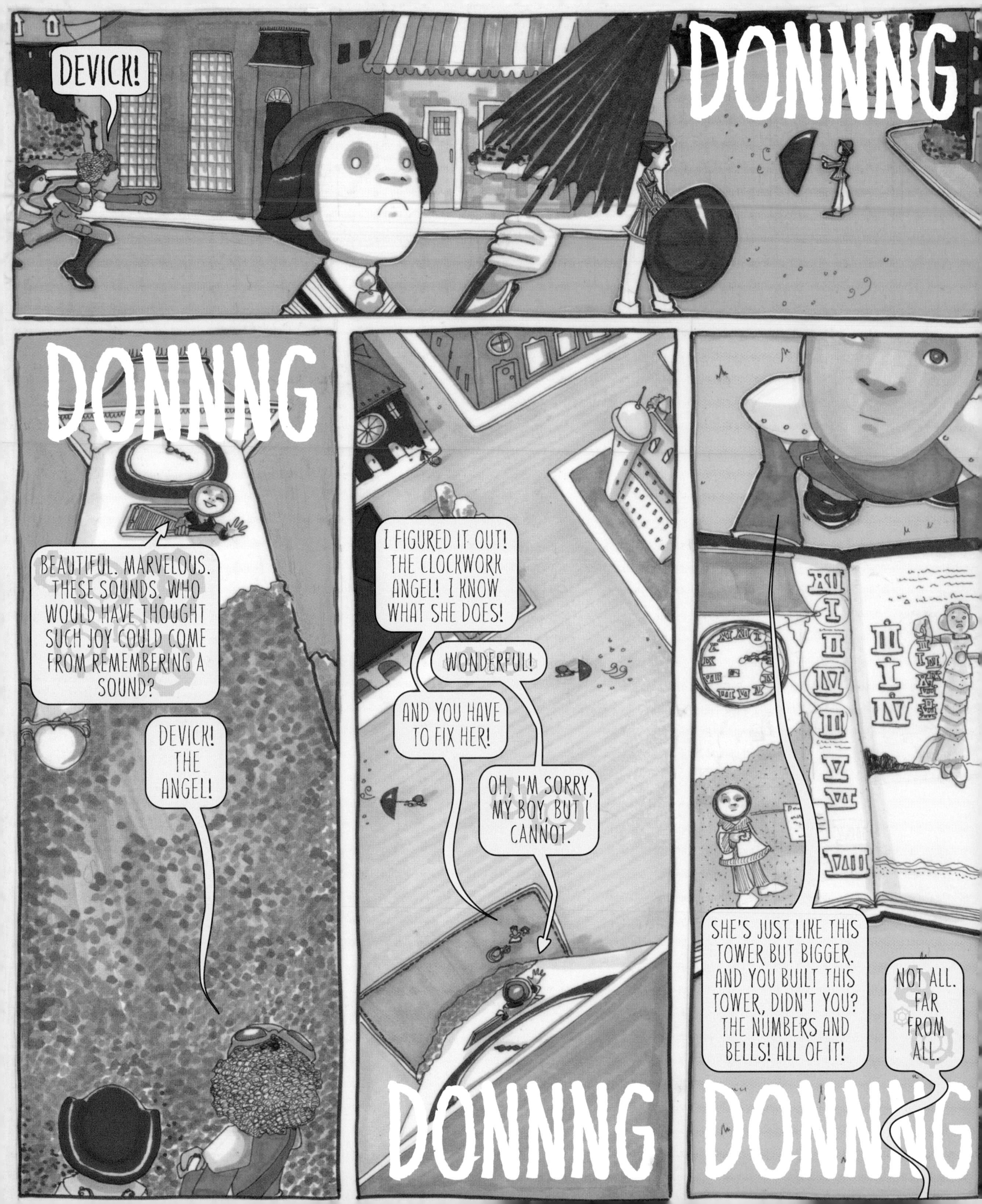
DEVICK!
DONNNG
DONNNG
BEAUTIFUL. MARVELOUS. THESE SOUNDS. WHO WOULD HAVE THOUGHT SUCH JOY COULD COME FROM REMEMBERING A SOUND?
DEVICK! THE ANGEL!
I FIGURED IT OUT! THE CLOCKWORK ANGEL! I KNOW WHAT SHE DOES!
WONDERFUL!
AND YOU HAVE TO FIX HER!
OH, I'M SORRY, MY BOY, BUT I CANNOT.
DONNNG
SHE'S JUST LIKE THIS TOWER BUT BIGGER. AND YOU BUILT THIS TOWER, DIDN'T YOU? THE NUMBERS AND BELLS! ALL OF IT!
NOT ALL. FAR FROM ALL.
DONNNG

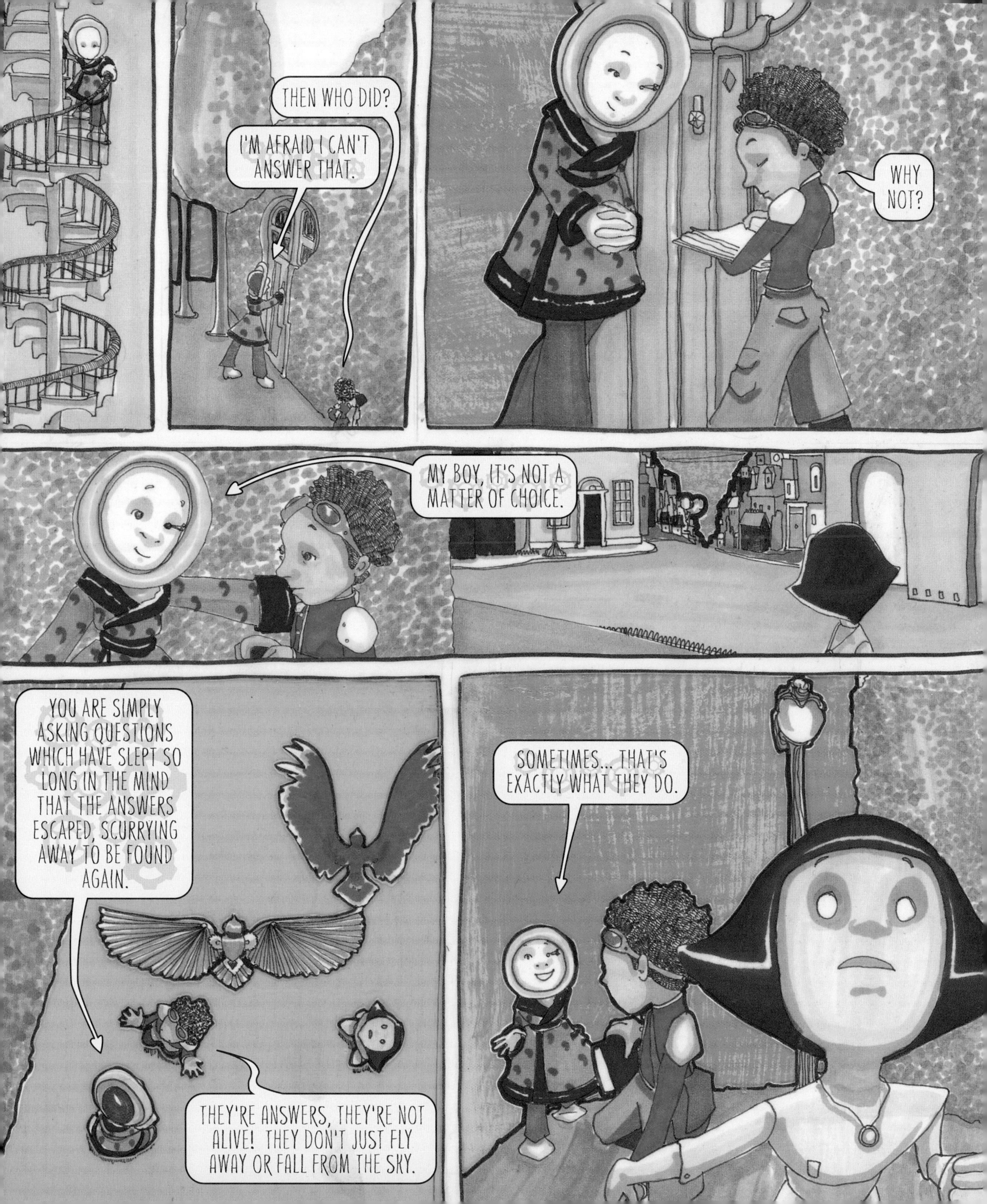
THEN WHO DID?
I'M AFRAID I CAN'T ANSWER THAT.
WHY NOT?
MY BOY, IT'S NOT A MATTER OF CHOICE.
YOU ARE SIMPLY ASKING QUESTIONS WHICH HAVE SLEPT SO LONG IN THE MIND THAT THE ANSWERS ESCAPED, SCURRYING AWAY TO BE FOUND AGAIN.
THEY'RE ANSWERS, THEY'RE NOT ALIVE! THEY DON'T JUST FLY AWAY OR FALL FROM THE SKY.
SOMETIMES... THAT'S EXACTLY WHAT THEY DO.

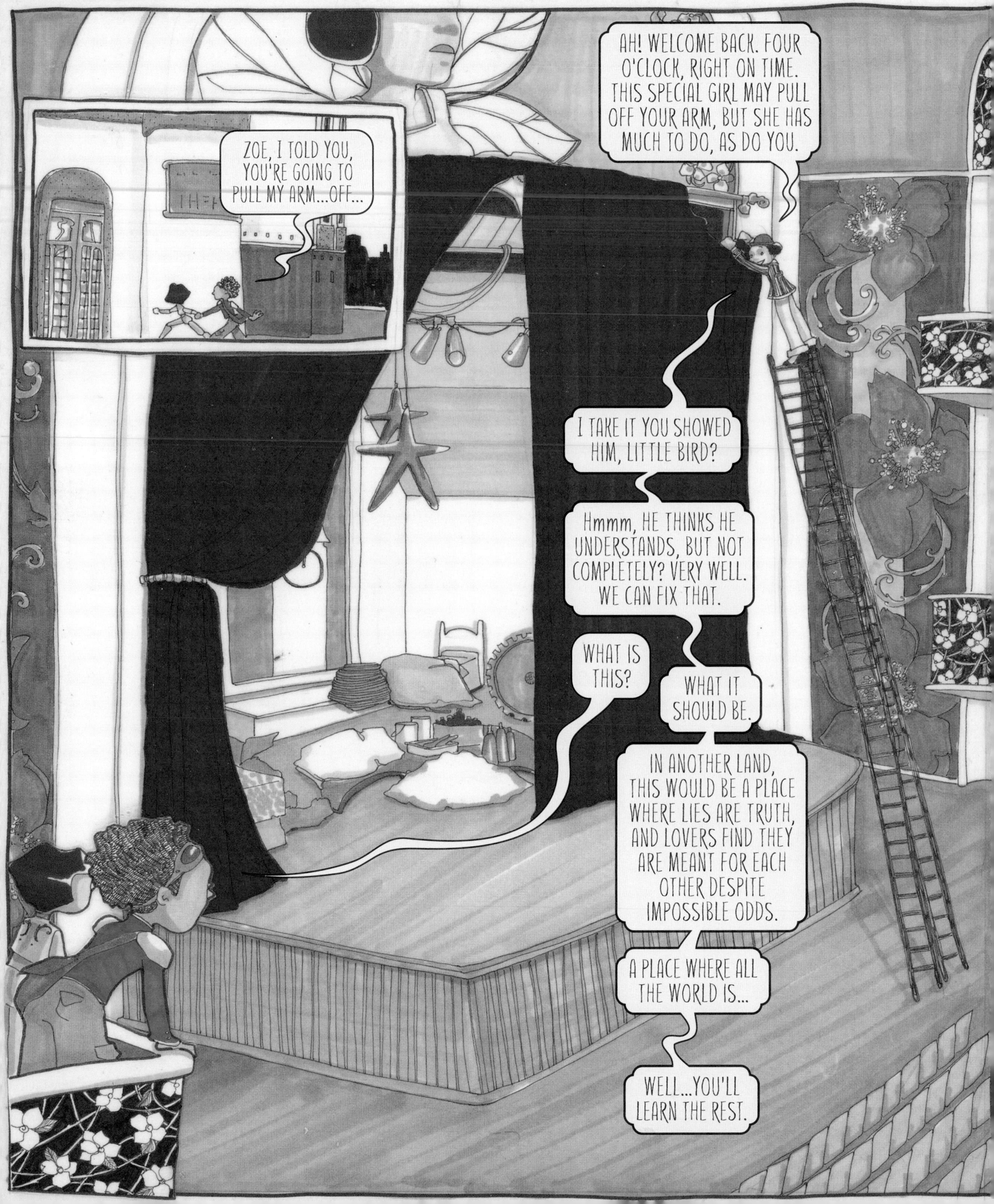
ZOE, I TOLD YOU, YOU'RE GOING TO PULL MY ARM...OFF...
AH! WELCOME BACK. FOUR O'CLOCK, RIGHT ON TIME. THIS SPECIAL GIRL MAY PULL OFF YOUR ARM, BUT SHE HAS MUCH TO DO, AS DO YOU.
I TAKE IT YOU SHOWED HIM, LITTLE BIRD?
Hmmm, HE THINKS HE UNDERSTANDS, BUT NOT COMPLETELY? VERY WELL. WE CAN FIX THAT.
WHAT IS THIS?
WHAT IT SHOULD BE.
IN ANOTHER LAND, THIS WOULD BE A PLACE WHERE LIES ARE TRUTH, AND LOVERS FIND THEY ARE MEANT FOR EACH OTHER DESPITE IMPOSSIBLE ODDS.
A PLACE WHERE ALL THE WORLD IS...
WELL...YOU'LL LEARN THE REST.

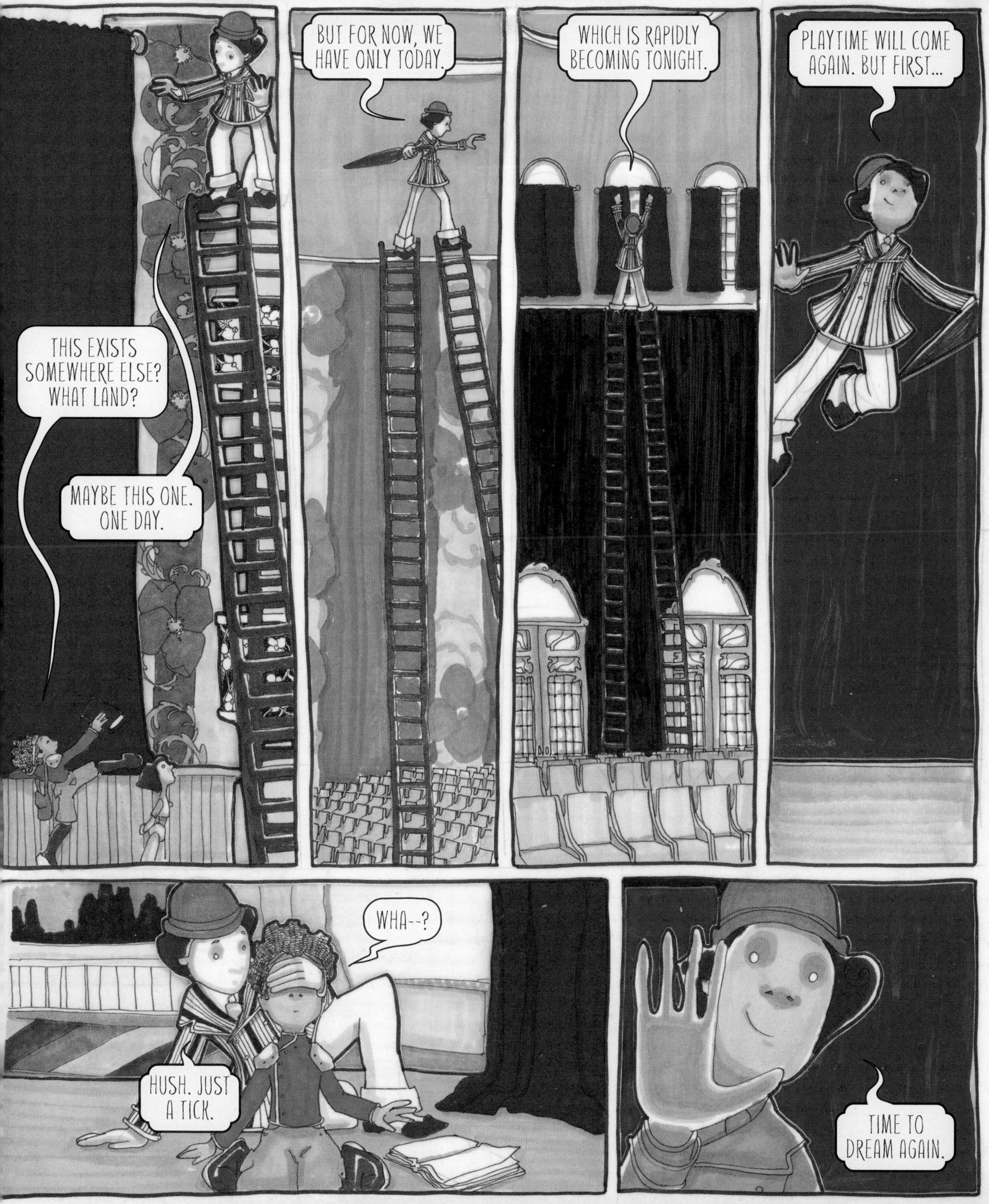
THIS EXISTS SOMEWHERE ELSE? WHAT LAND?
MAYBE THIS ONE. ONE DAY.
BUT FOR NOW, WE HAVE ONLY TODAY.
WHICH IS RAPIDLY BECOMING TONIGHT.
PLAYTIME WILL COME AGAIN. BUT FIRST...
WHA--?
HUSH. JUST A TICK.
TIME TO DREAM AGAIN.

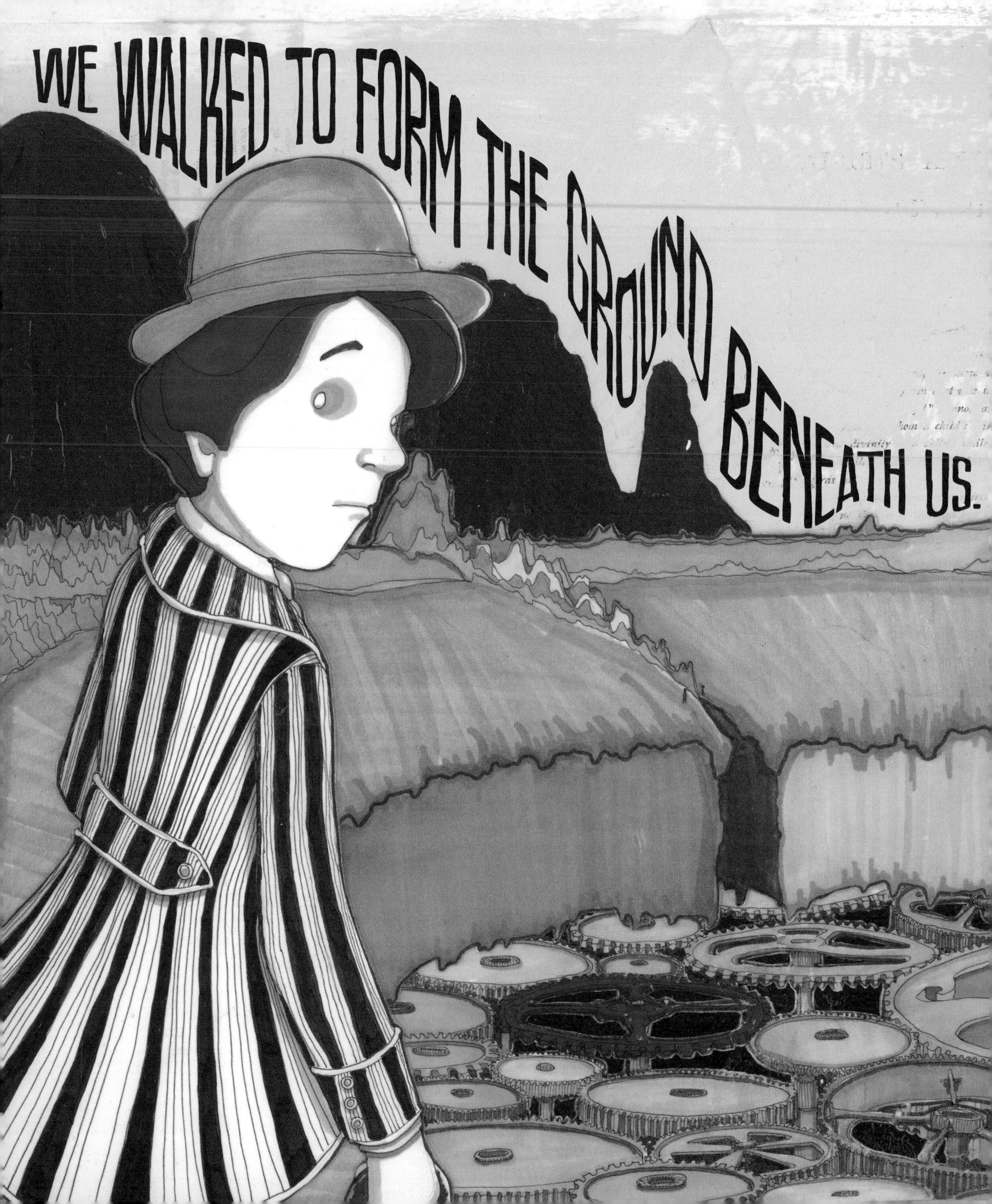
WE WALKED TO FORM THE GROUND BENEATH US.

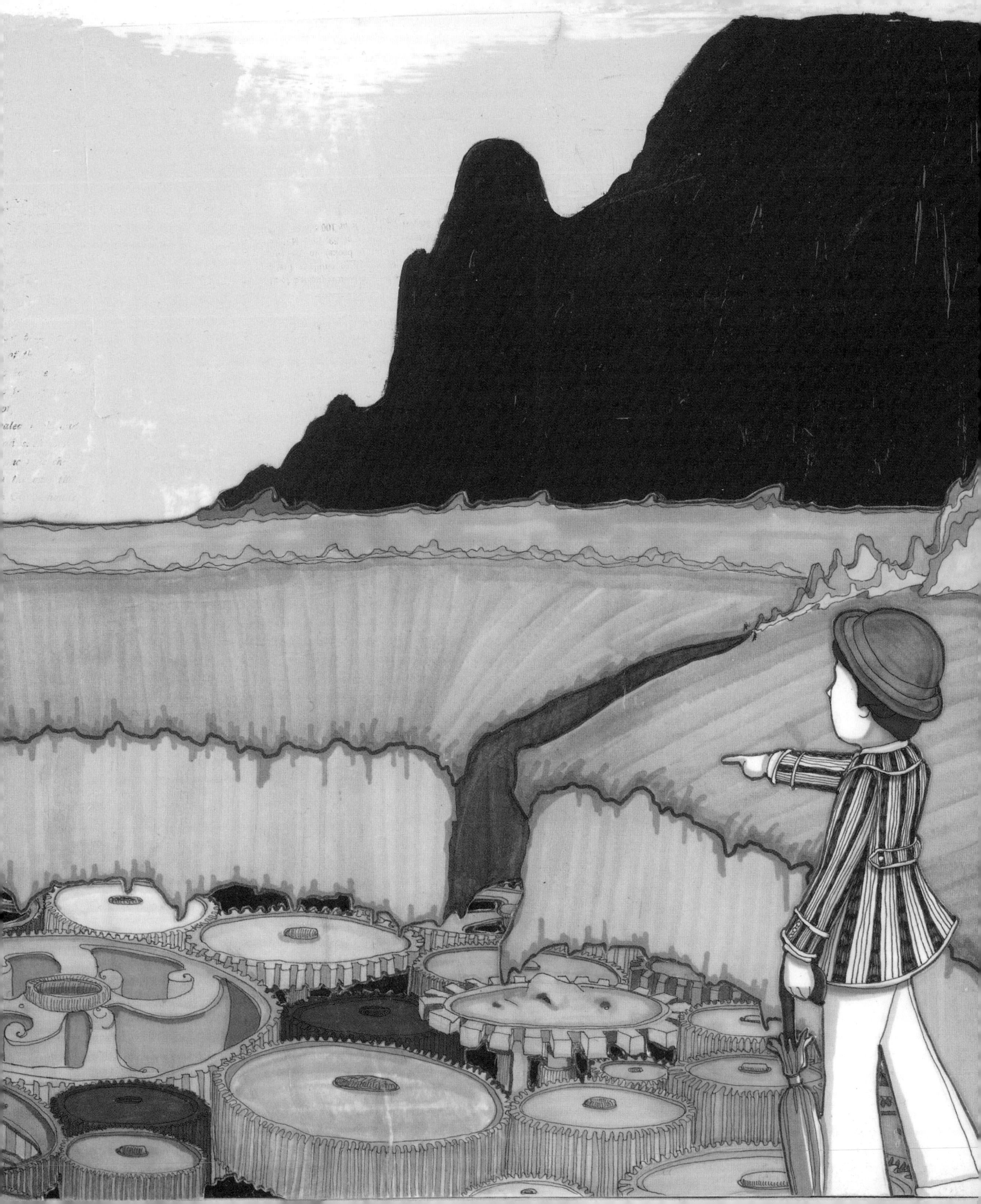

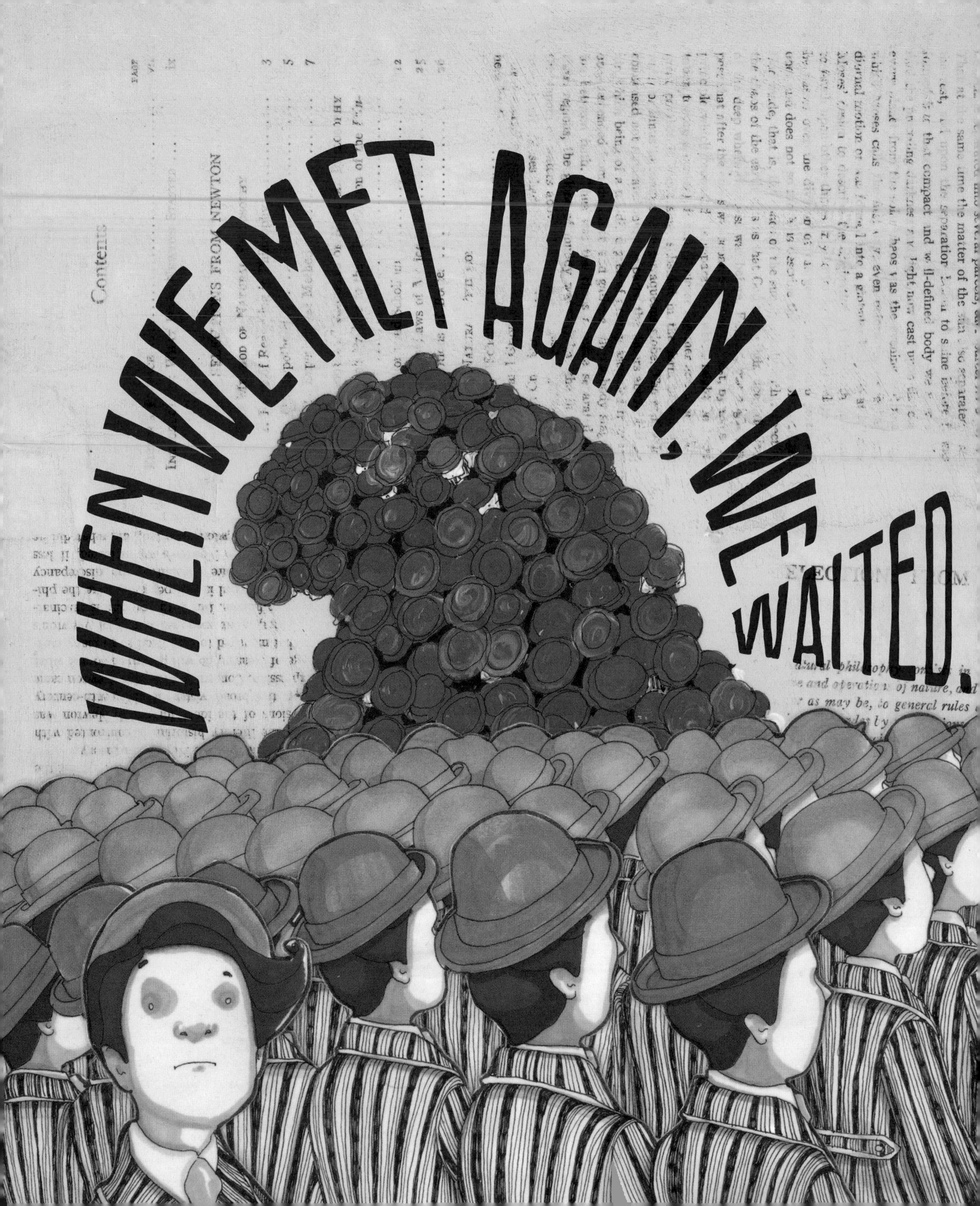
WHEN WE MET AGAIN, WE WAITED.

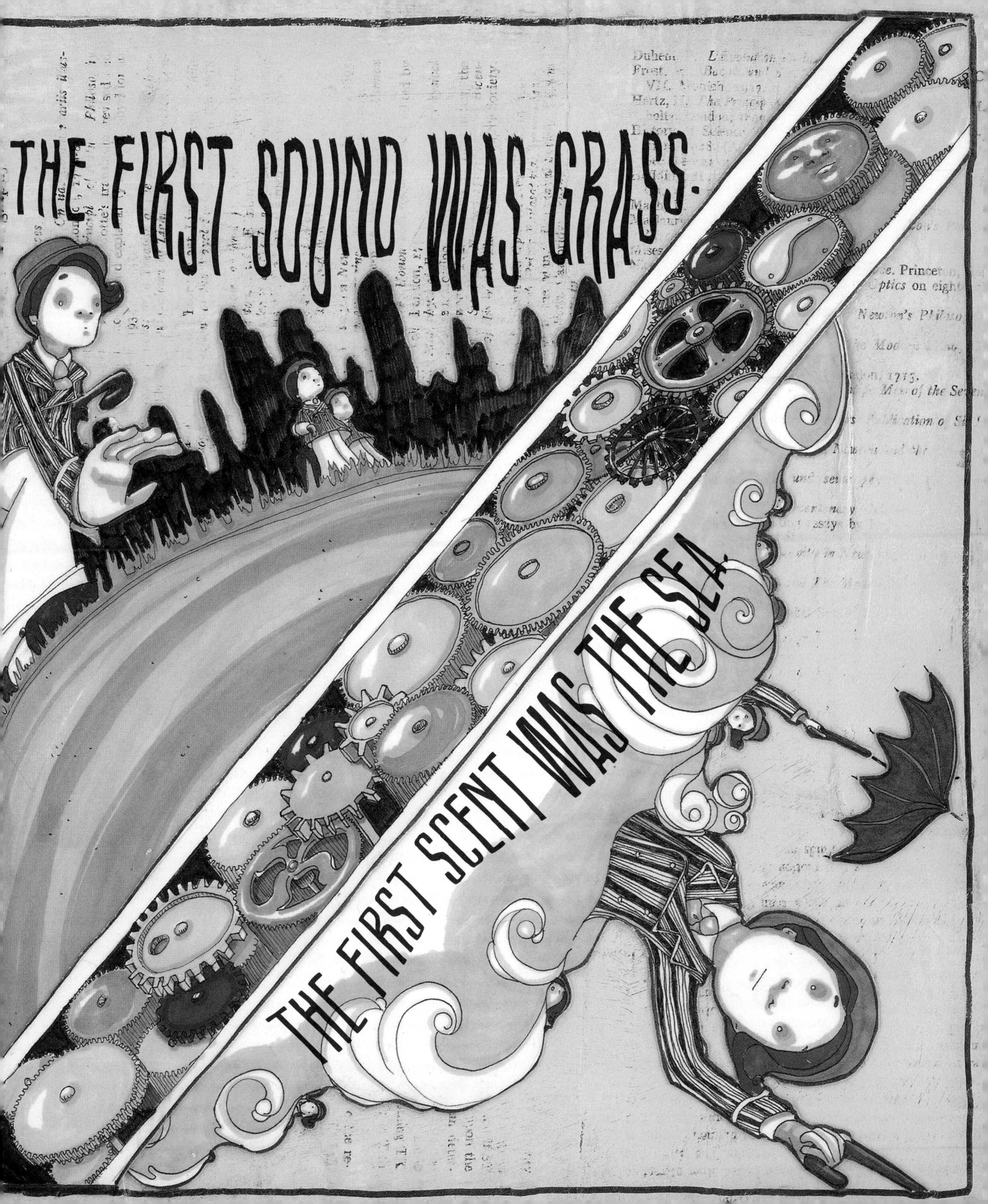
THE FIRST SOUND WAS GRASS.
THE FIRST SCENT WAS THE SEA

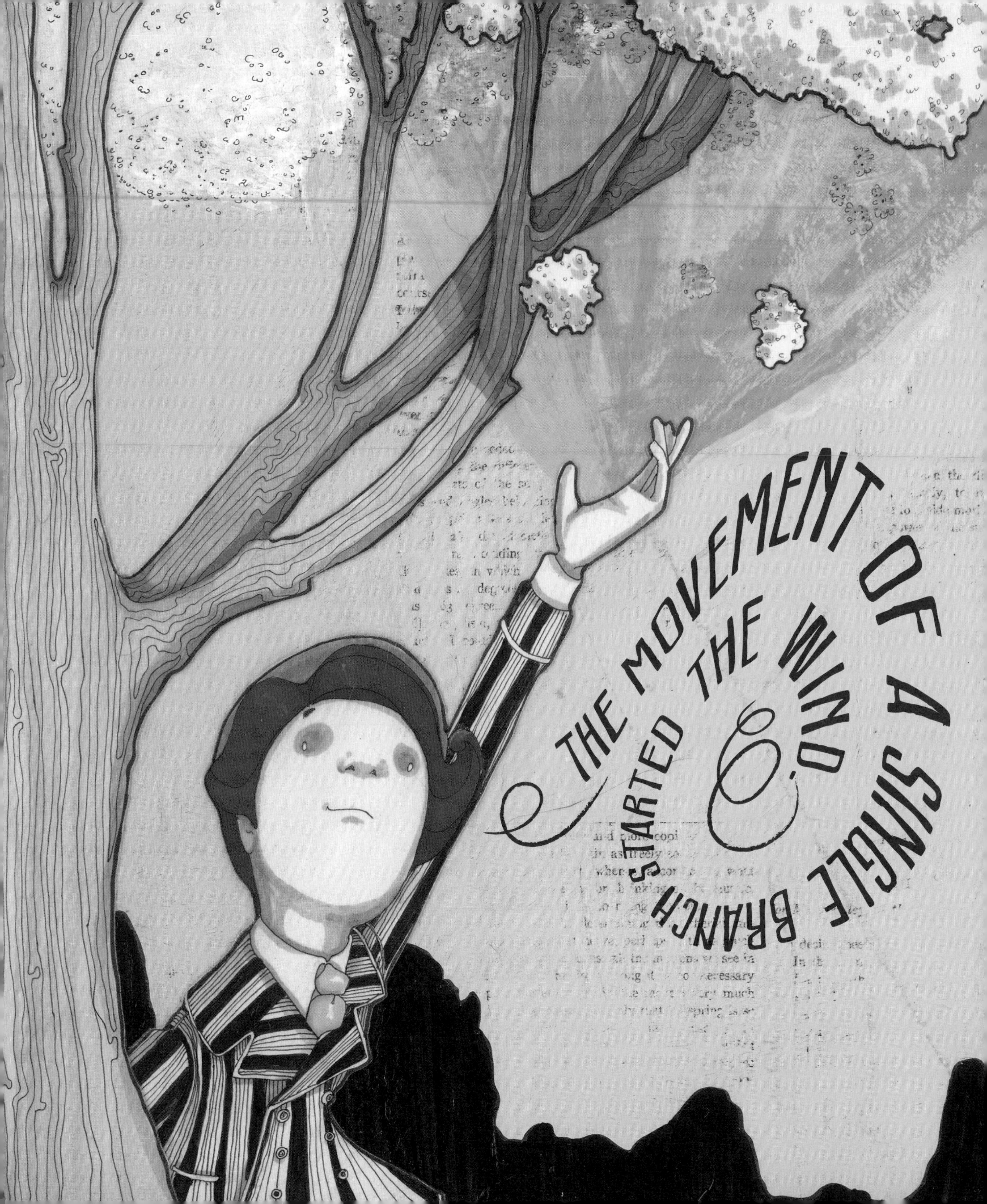
THE MOVEMENT OF A SINGLE BRANCH
STARTED THE WIND.

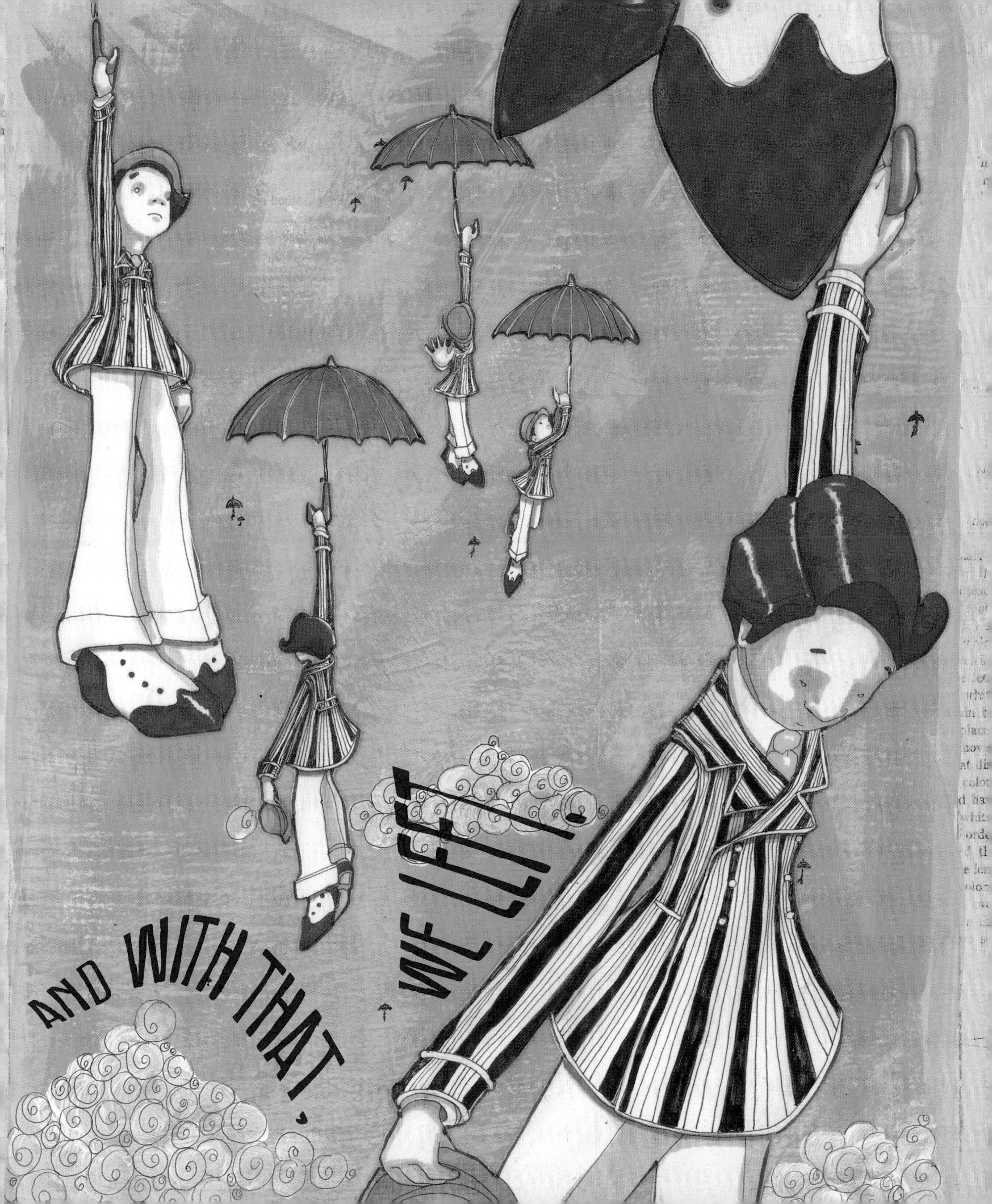
AND WITH THAT,
WE LEFT.

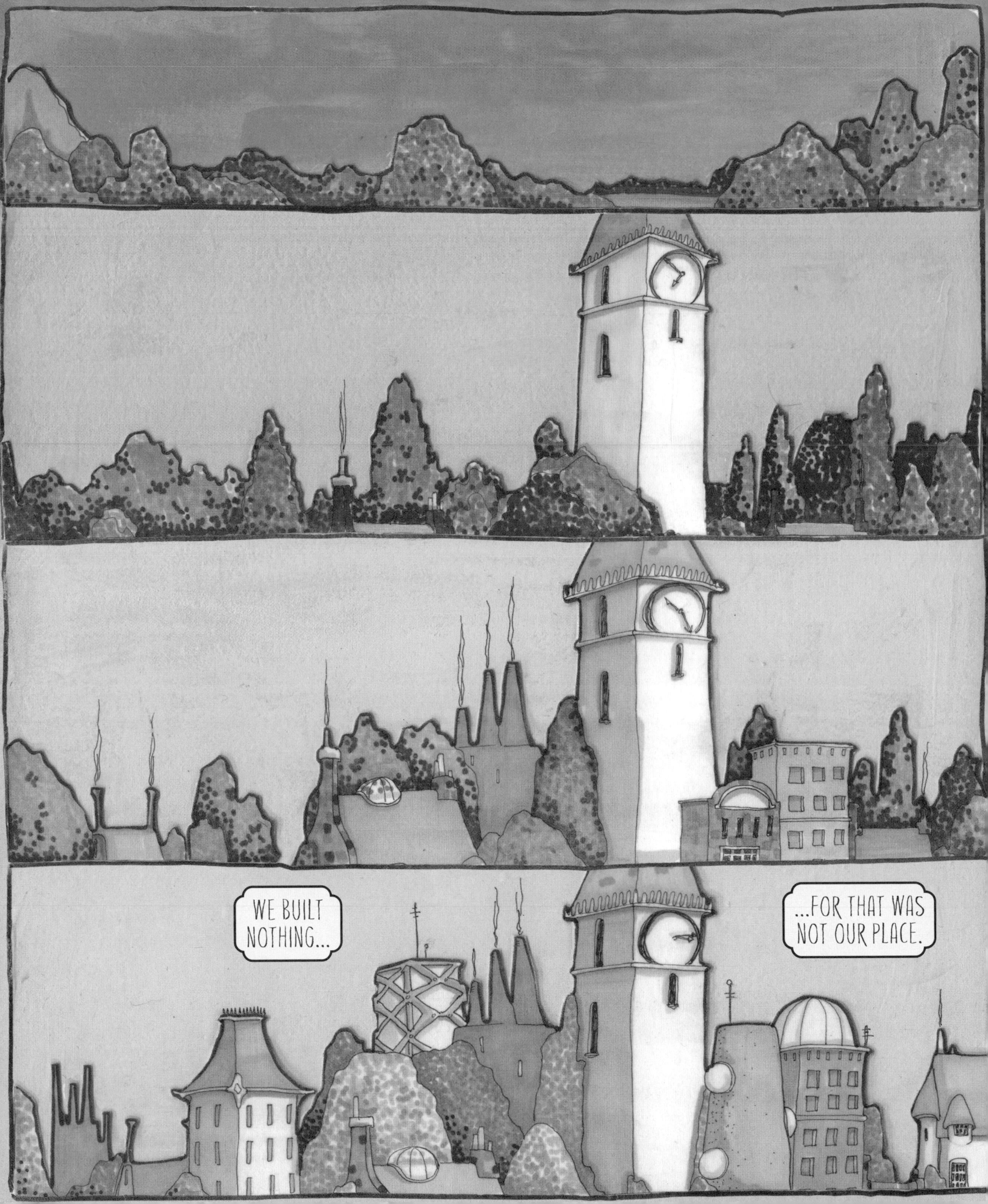
WE BUILT NOTHING...
...FOR THAT WAS NOT OUR PLACE.

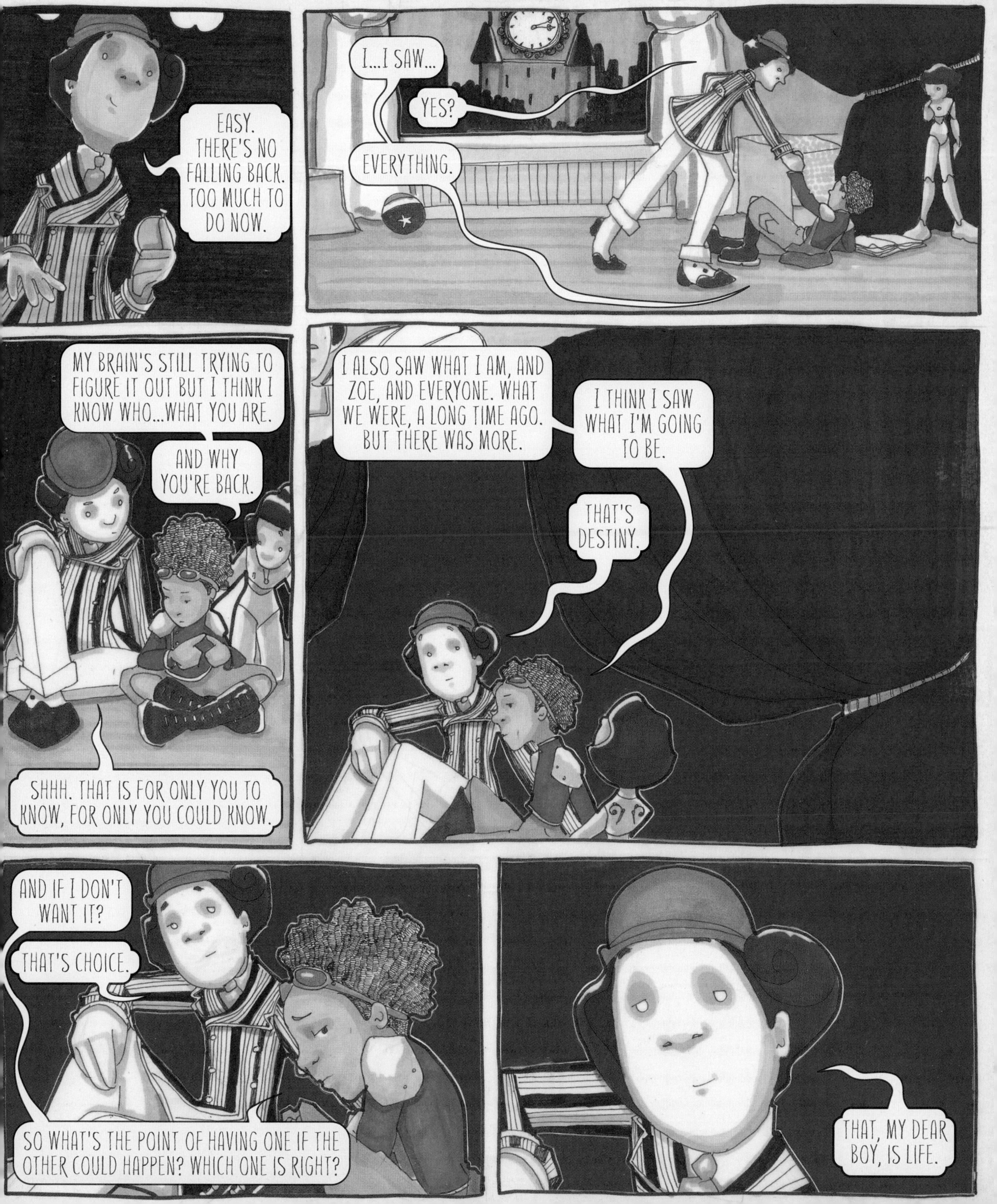
EASY. THERE'S NO FALLING BACK. TOO MUCH TO DO NOW.
I...I SAW...
YES?
EVERYTHING.
MY BRAIN'S STILL TRYING TO FIGURE IT OUT BUT I THINK I KNOW WHO...WHAT YOU ARE.
AND WHY YOU'RE BACK.
SHHH. THAT IS FOR ONLY YOU TO KNOW, FOR ONLY YOU COULD KNOW.
I ALSO SAW WHAT I AM, AND ZOE, AND EVERYONE. WHAT WE WERE, A LONG TIME AGO. BUT THERE WAS MORE.
I THINK I SAW WHAT I'M GOING TO BE.
THAT'S DESTINY.
AND IF I DON'T WANT IT?
THAT'S CHOICE.
SO WHAT'S THE POINT OF HAVING ONE IF THE OTHER COULD HAPPEN? WHICH ONE IS RIGHT?
THAT, MY DEAR BOY, IS LIFE.

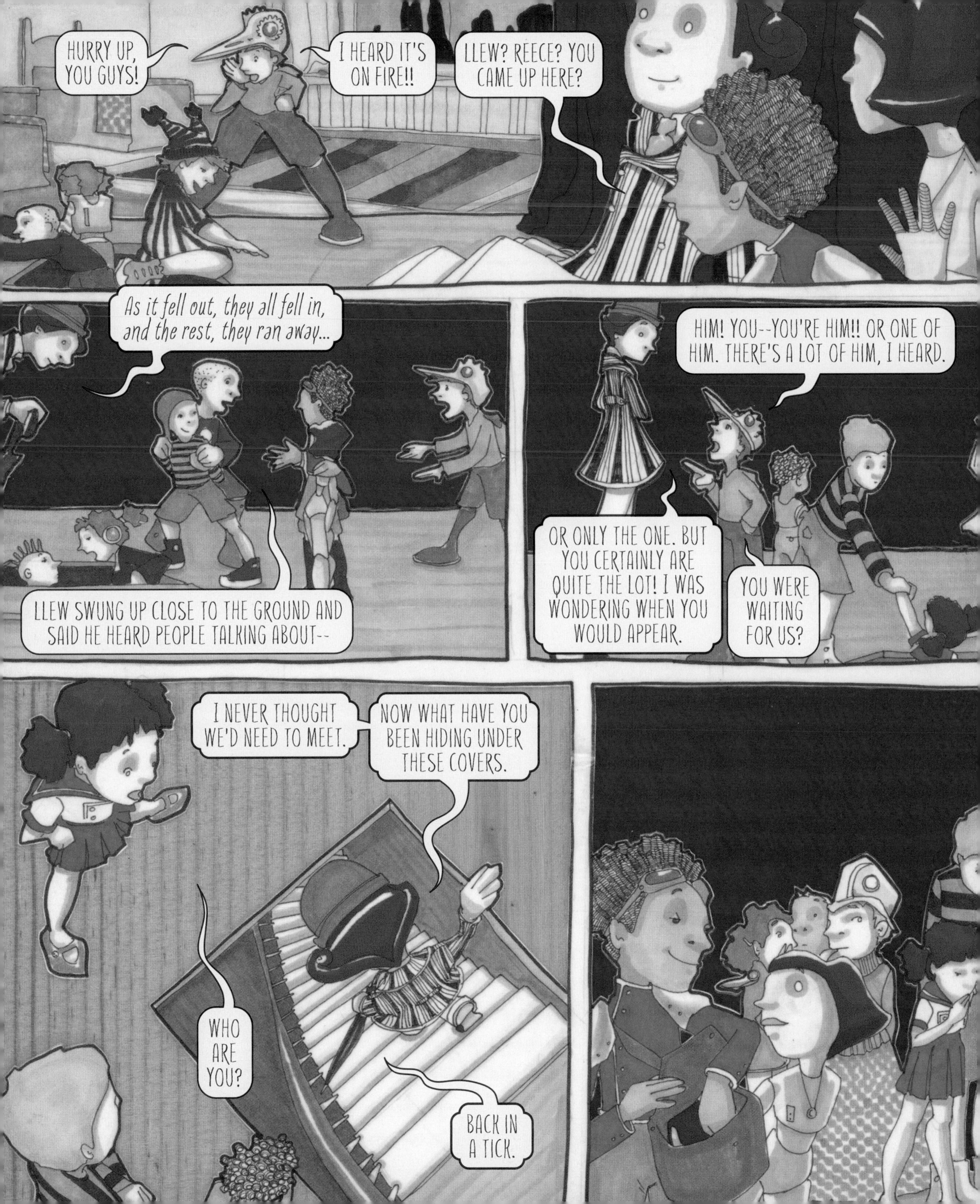
HURRY UP, YOU GUYS!
I HEARD IT'S ON FIRE!!
LLEW? REECE? YOU CAME UP HERE?
As it fell out, they all fell in, and the rest, they ran away...
LLEW SWUNG UP CLOSE TO THE GROUND AND SAID HE HEARD PEOPLE TALKING ABOUT--
HIM! YOU--YOU'RE HIM!! OR ONE OF HIM. THERE'S A LOT OF HIM, I HEARD.
OR ONLY THE ONE. BUT YOU CERTAINLY ARE QUITE THE LOT! I WAS WONDERING WHEN YOU WOULD APPEAR.
YOU WERE WAITING FOR US?
I NEVER THOUGHT WE'D NEED TO MEET.
NOW WHAT HAVE YOU BEEN HIDING UNDER THESE COVERS.
WHO ARE YOU?
BACK IN A TICK.

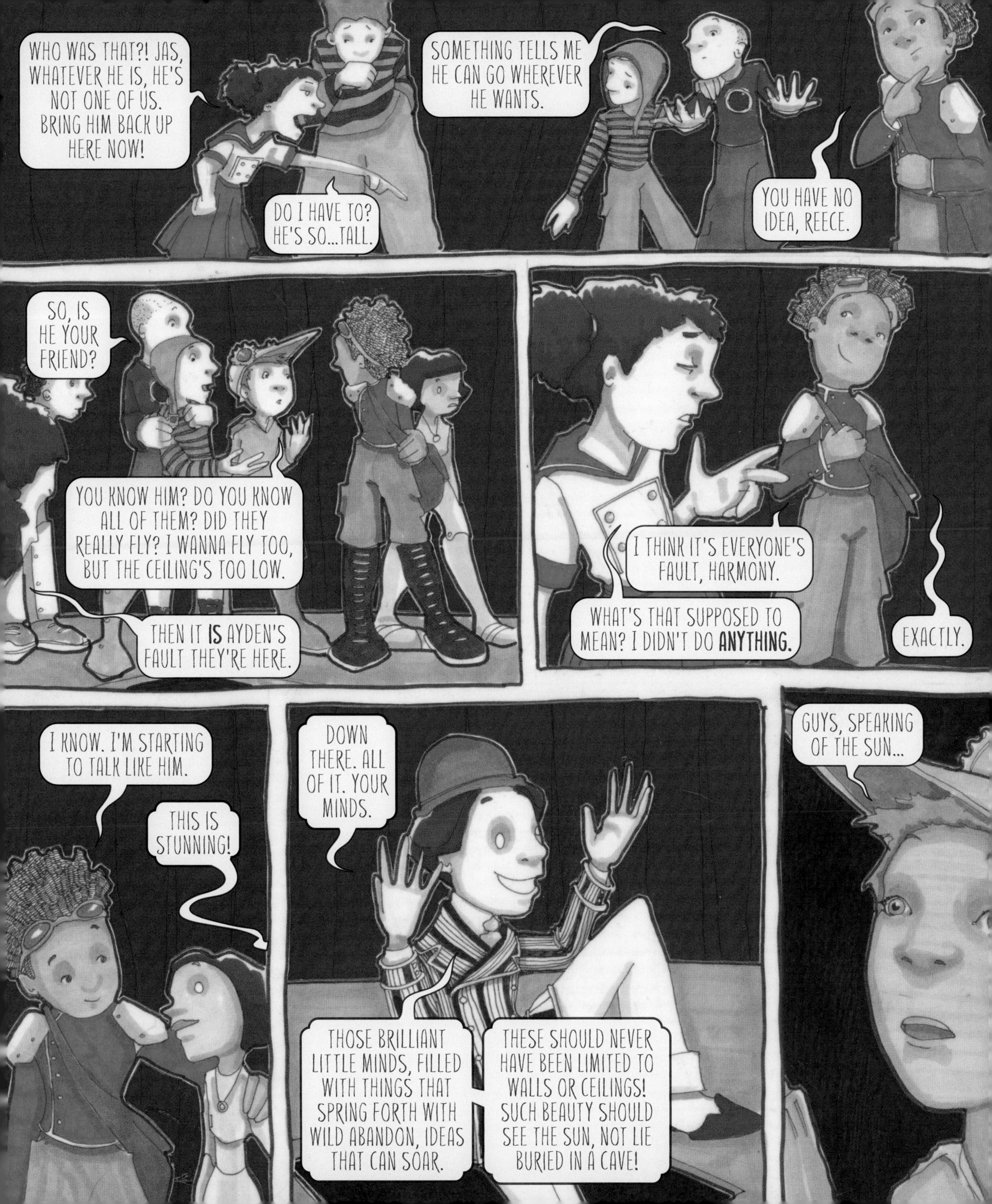
WHO WAS THAT?! JAS, WHATEVER HE IS, HE'S NOT ONE OF US. BRING HIM BACK UP HERE NOW!
DO I HAVE TO? HE'S SO...TALL.
SOMETHING TELLS ME HE CAN GO WHEREVER HE WANTS.
YOU HAVE NO IDEA, REECE.
SO, IS HE YOUR FRIEND?
YOU KNOW HIM? DO YOU KNOW ALL OF THEM? DID THEY REALLY FLY? I WANNA FLY TOO, BUT THE CEILING'S TOO LOW.
THEN IT **IS** AYDEN'S FAULT THEY'RE HERE.
I THINK IT'S EVERYONE'S FAULT, HARMONY.
WHAT'S THAT SUPPOSED TO MEAN? I DIDN'T DO **ANYTHING.**
EXACTLY.
I KNOW. I'M STARTING TO TALK LIKE HIM.
THIS IS STUNNING!
DOWN THERE. ALL OF IT. YOUR MINDS.
THOSE BRILLIANT LITTLE MINDS, FILLED WITH THINGS THAT SPRING FORTH WITH WILD ABANDON, IDEAS THAT CAN SOAR.
THESE SHOULD NEVER HAVE BEEN LIMITED TO WALLS OR CEILINGS! SUCH BEAUTY SHOULD SEE THE SUN, NOT LIE BURIED IN A CAVE!
GUYS, SPEAKING OF THE SUN...

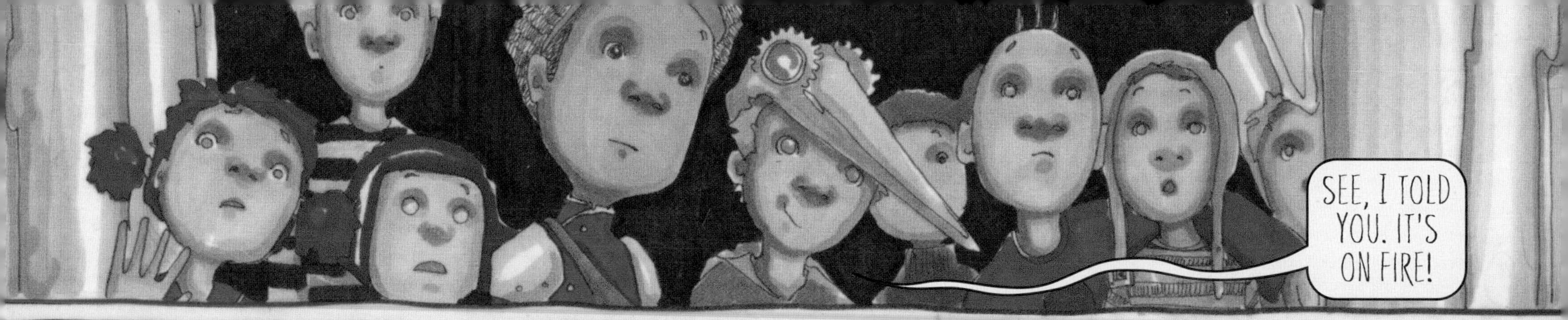
SEE, I TOLD YOU. IT'S ON FIRE!

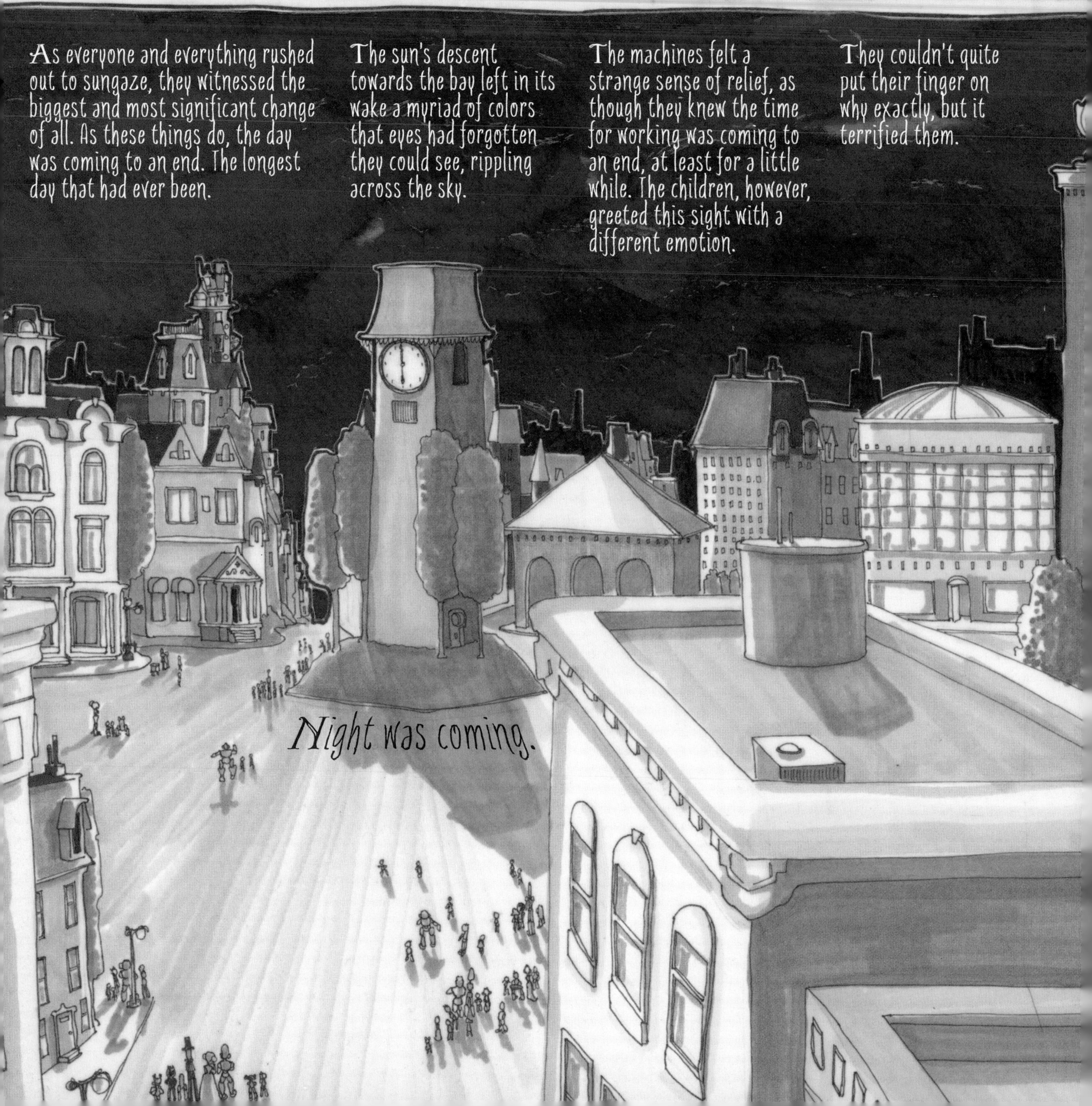
As everyone and everything rushed out to sungaze, they witnessed the biggest and most significant change of all. As these things do, the day was coming to an end. The longest day that had ever been.
The sun's descent towards the bay left in its wake a myriad of colors that eyes had forgotten they could see, rippling across the sky.
The machines felt a strange sense of relief, as though they knew the time for working was coming to an end, at least for a little while. The children, however, greeted this sight with a different emotion.
They couldn't quite put their finger on why exactly, but it terrified them.
Night was coming.

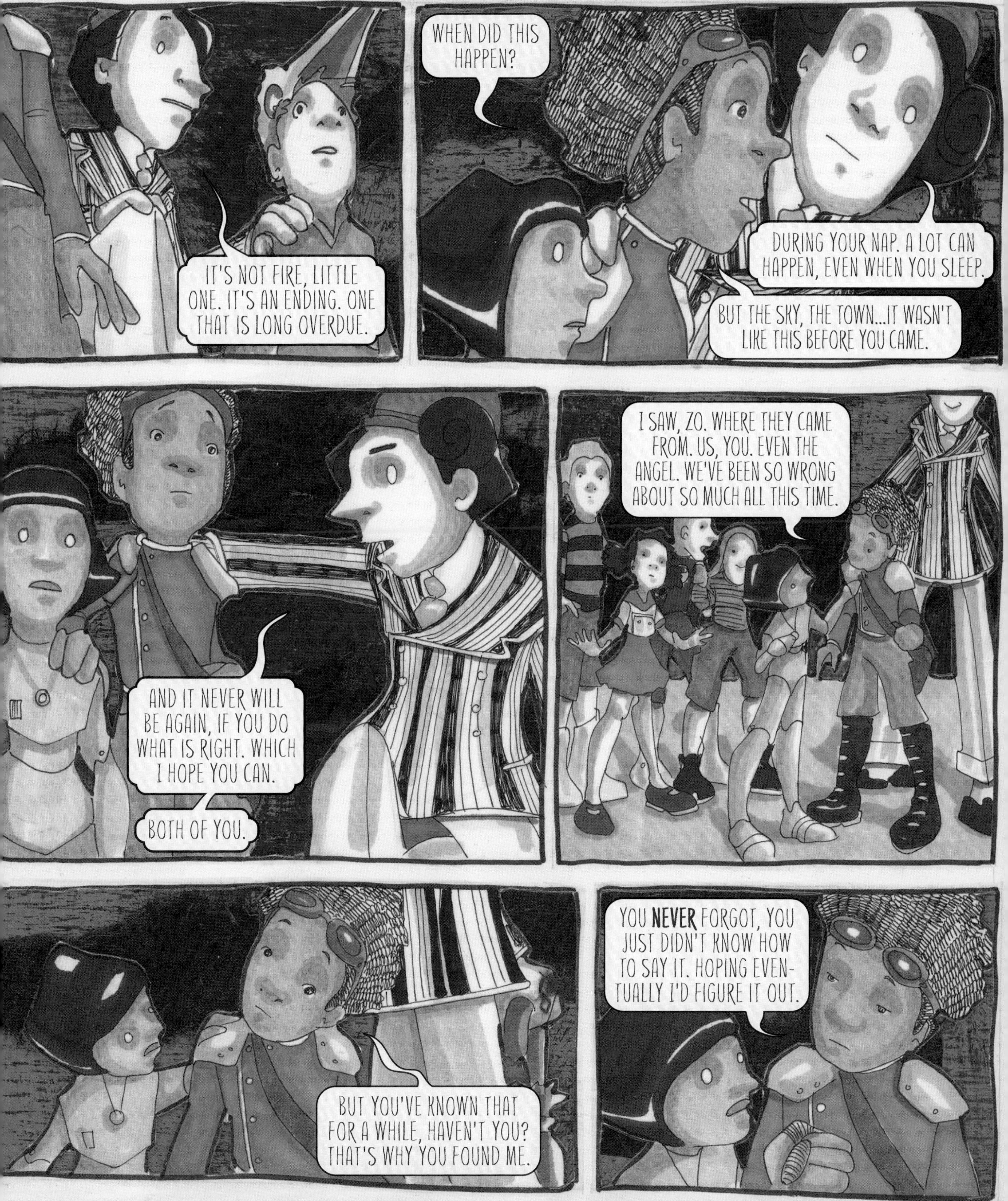
IT'S NOT FIRE, LITTLE ONE. IT'S AN ENDING. ONE THAT IS LONG OVERDUE.
WHEN DID THIS HAPPEN?
DURING YOUR NAP. A LOT CAN HAPPEN, EVEN WHEN YOU SLEEP.
BUT THE SKY, THE TOWN...IT WASN'T LIKE THIS BEFORE YOU CAME.
AND IT NEVER WILL BE AGAIN, IF YOU DO WHAT IS RIGHT. WHICH I HOPE YOU CAN.
BOTH OF YOU.
I SAW, ZO. WHERE THEY CAME FROM. US, YOU. EVEN THE ANGEL. WE'VE BEEN SO WRONG ABOUT SO MUCH ALL THIS TIME.
BUT YOU'VE KNOWN THAT FOR A WHILE, HAVEN'T YOU? THAT'S WHY YOU FOUND ME.
YOU **NEVER** FORGOT, YOU JUST DIDN'T KNOW HOW TO SAY IT. HOPING EVENTUALLY I'D FIGURE IT OUT.

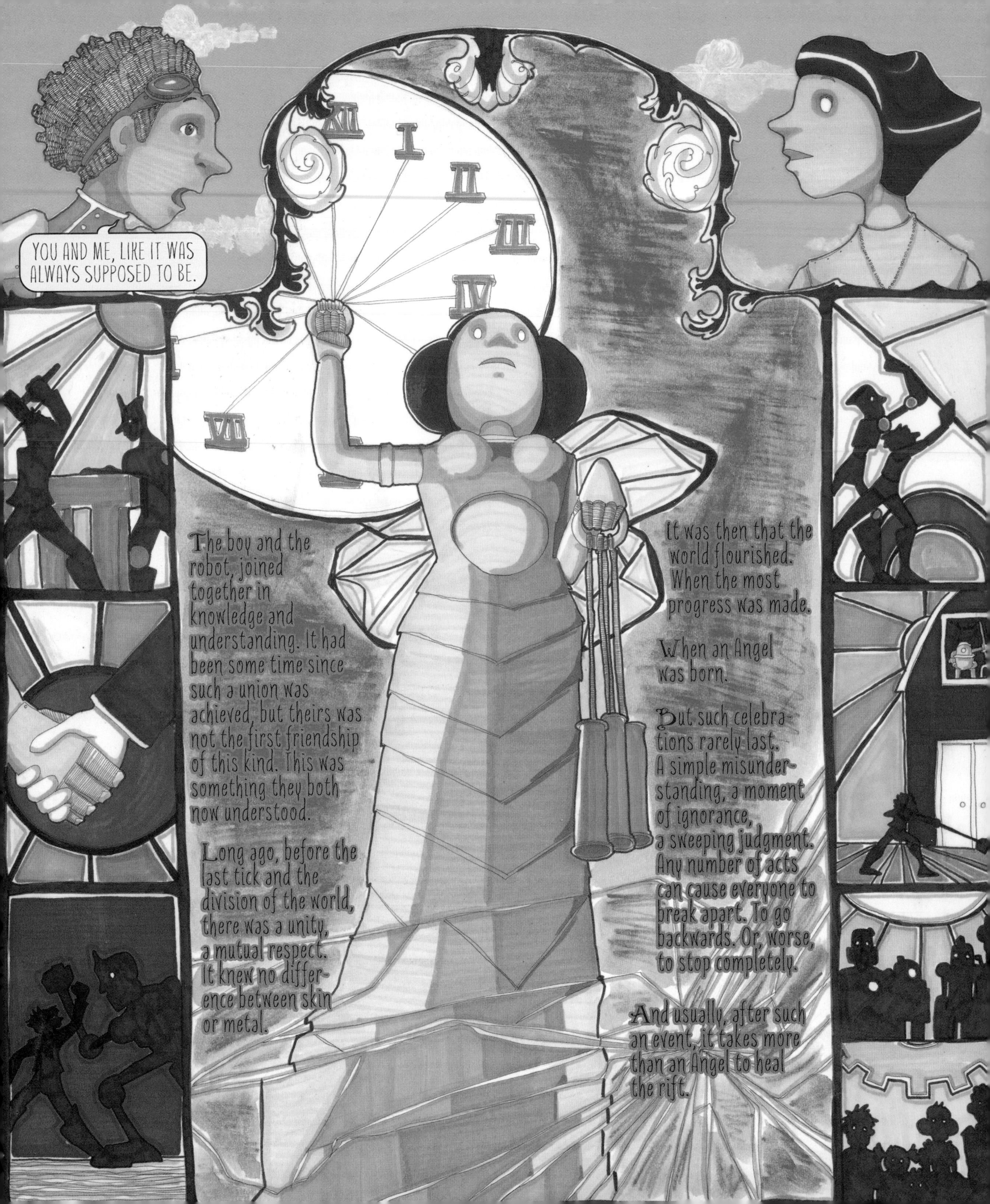
YOU AND ME, LIKE IT WAS ALWAYS SUPPOSED TO BE.
The boy and the robot, joined together in knowledge and understanding. It had been some time since such a union was achieved, but theirs was not the first friendship of this kind. This was something they both now understood.
Long ago, before the last tick and the division of the world, there was a unity, a mutual respect. It knew no difference between skin or metal.
It was then that the world flourished. When the most progress was made.
When an Angel was born.
But such celebrations rarely last. A simple misunderstanding, a moment of ignorance, a sweeping judgment. Any number of acts can cause everyone to break apart. To go backwards. Or, worse, to stop completely.
And usually, after such an event, it takes more than an Angel to heal the rift.

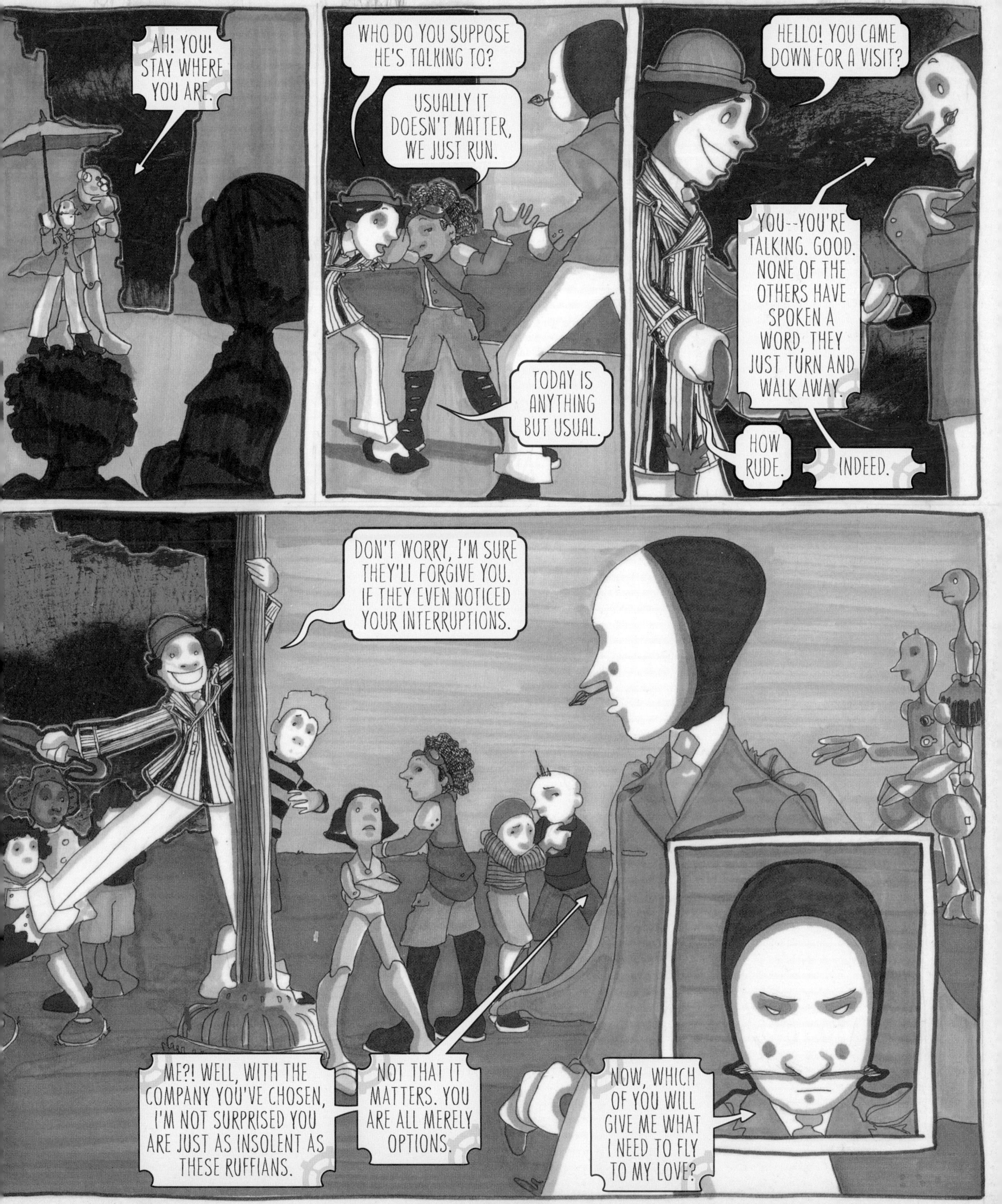
AH! YOU! STAY WHERE YOU ARE.
WHO DO YOU SUPPOSE HE'S TALKING TO?
USUALLY IT DOESN'T MATTER, WE JUST RUN.
TODAY IS ANYTHING BUT USUAL.
HELLO! YOU CAME DOWN FOR A VISIT?
YOU--YOU'RE TALKING. GOOD. NONE OF THE OTHERS HAVE SPOKEN A WORD, THEY JUST TURN AND WALK AWAY.
HOW RUDE.
INDEED.
DON'T WORRY, I'M SURE THEY'LL FORGIVE YOU. IF THEY EVEN NOTICED YOUR INTERRUPTIONS.
ME?! WELL, WITH THE COMPANY YOU'VE CHOSEN, I'M NOT SURPRISED YOU ARE JUST AS INSOLENT AS THESE RUFFIANS.
NOT THAT IT MATTERS. YOU ARE ALL MERELY OPTIONS.
NOW, WHICH OF YOU WILL GIVE ME WHAT I NEED TO FLY TO MY LOVE?

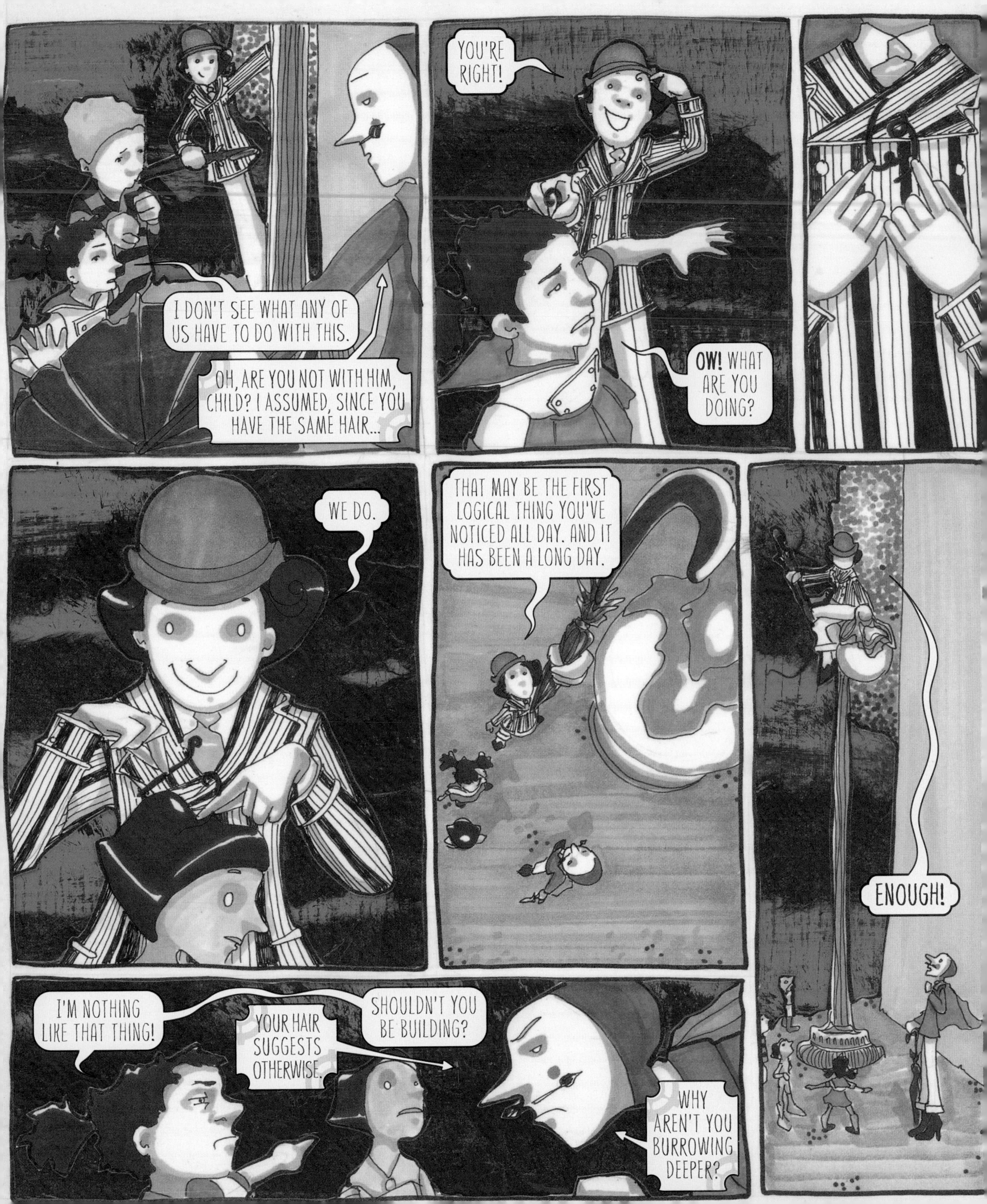

I DON'T SEE WHAT ANY OF US HAVE TO DO WITH THIS.
OH, ARE YOU NOT WITH HIM, CHILD? I ASSUMED, SINCE YOU HAVE THE SAME HAIR...
YOU'RE RIGHT!
OW! WHAT ARE YOU DOING?
WE DO.
THAT MAY BE THE FIRST LOGICAL THING YOU'VE NOTICED ALL DAY. AND IT HAS BEEN A LONG DAY.
ENOUGH!
I'M NOTHING LIKE THAT THING!
YOUR HAIR SUGGESTS OTHERWISE.
SHOULDN'T YOU BE BUILDING?
WHY AREN'T YOU BURROWING DEEPER?

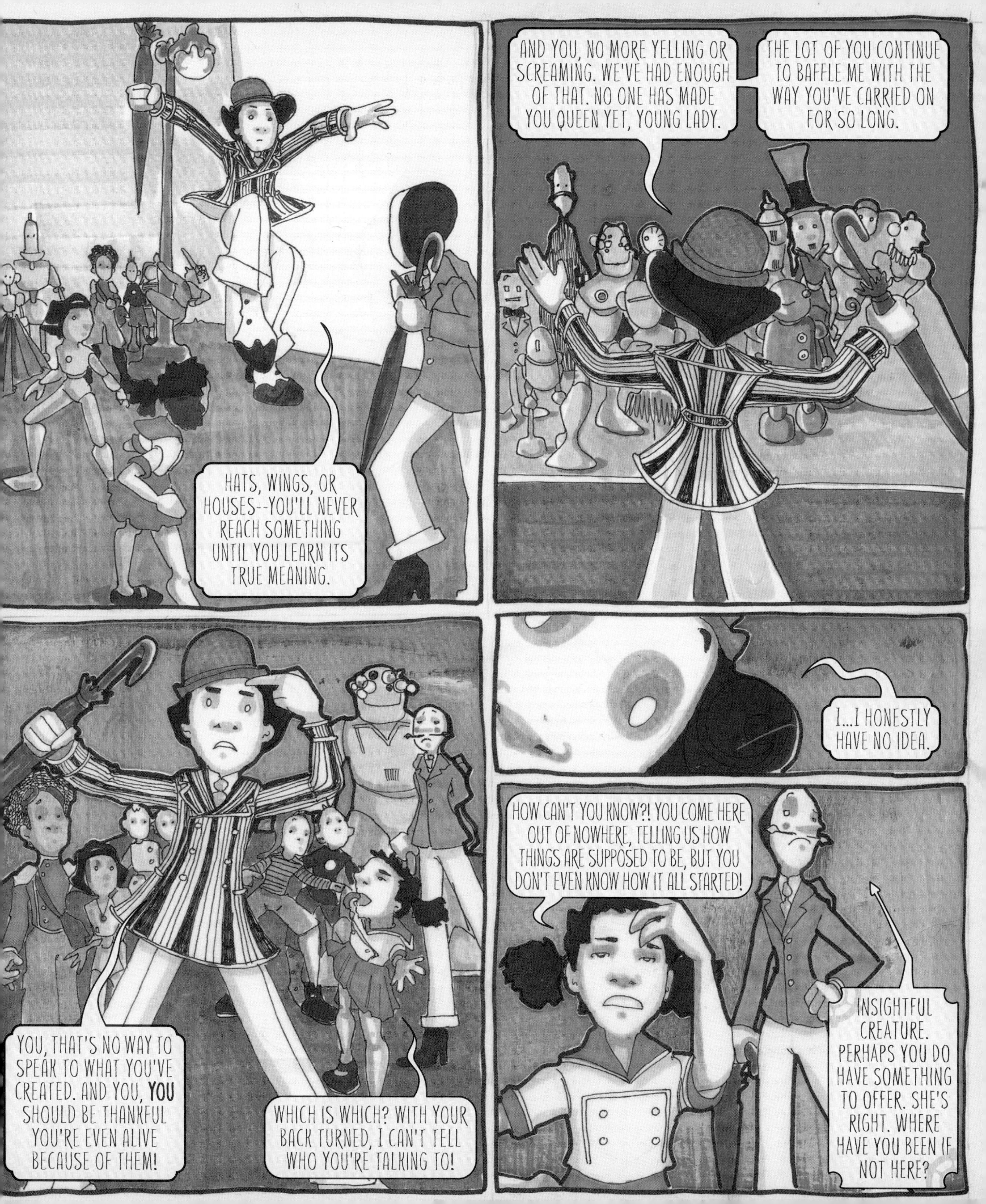
HATS, WINGS, OR HOUSES--YOU'LL NEVER REACH SOMETHING UNTIL YOU LEARN ITS TRUE MEANING.
AND YOU, NO MORE YELLING OR SCREAMING. WE'VE HAD ENOUGH OF THAT. NO ONE HAS MADE YOU QUEEN YET, YOUNG LADY.
THE LOT OF YOU CONTINUE TO BAFFLE ME WITH THE WAY YOU'VE CARRIED ON FOR SO LONG.
YOU, THAT'S NO WAY TO SPEAK TO WHAT YOU'VE CREATED. AND YOU, **YOU** SHOULD BE THANKFUL YOU'RE EVEN ALIVE BECAUSE OF THEM!
WHICH IS WHICH? WITH YOUR BACK TURNED, I CAN'T TELL WHO YOU'RE TALKING TO!
I...I HONESTLY HAVE NO IDEA.
HOW CAN'T YOU KNOW?! YOU COME HERE OUT OF NOWHERE, TELLING US HOW THINGS ARE SUPPOSED TO BE, BUT YOU DON'T EVEN KNOW HOW IT ALL STARTED!
INSIGHTFUL CREATURE. PERHAPS YOU DO HAVE SOMETHING TO OFFER. SHE'S RIGHT. WHERE HAVE YOU BEEN IF NOT HERE?

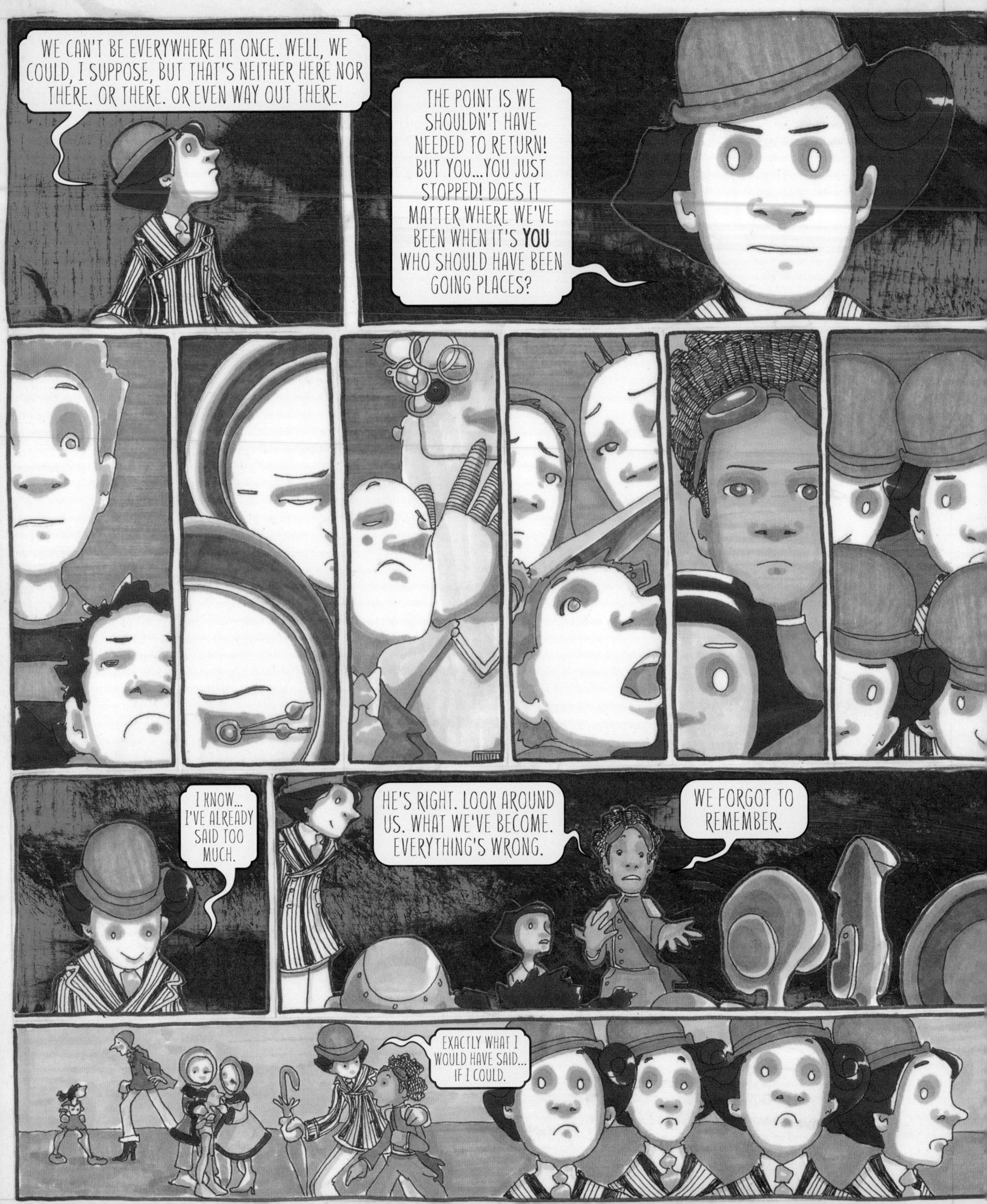
WE CAN'T BE EVERYWHERE AT ONCE. WELL, WE COULD, I SUPPOSE, BUT THAT'S NEITHER HERE NOR THERE. OR THERE. OR EVEN WAY OUT THERE.
THE POINT IS WE SHOULDN'T HAVE NEEDED TO RETURN! BUT YOU...YOU JUST STOPPED! DOES IT MATTER WHERE WE'VE BEEN WHEN IT'S **YOU** WHO SHOULD HAVE BEEN GOING PLACES?
I KNOW... I'VE ALREADY SAID TOO MUCH.
HE'S RIGHT. LOOK AROUND US. WHAT WE'VE BECOME. EVERYTHING'S WRONG.
WE FORGOT TO REMEMBER.
EXACTLY WHAT I WOULD HAVE SAID... IF I COULD.

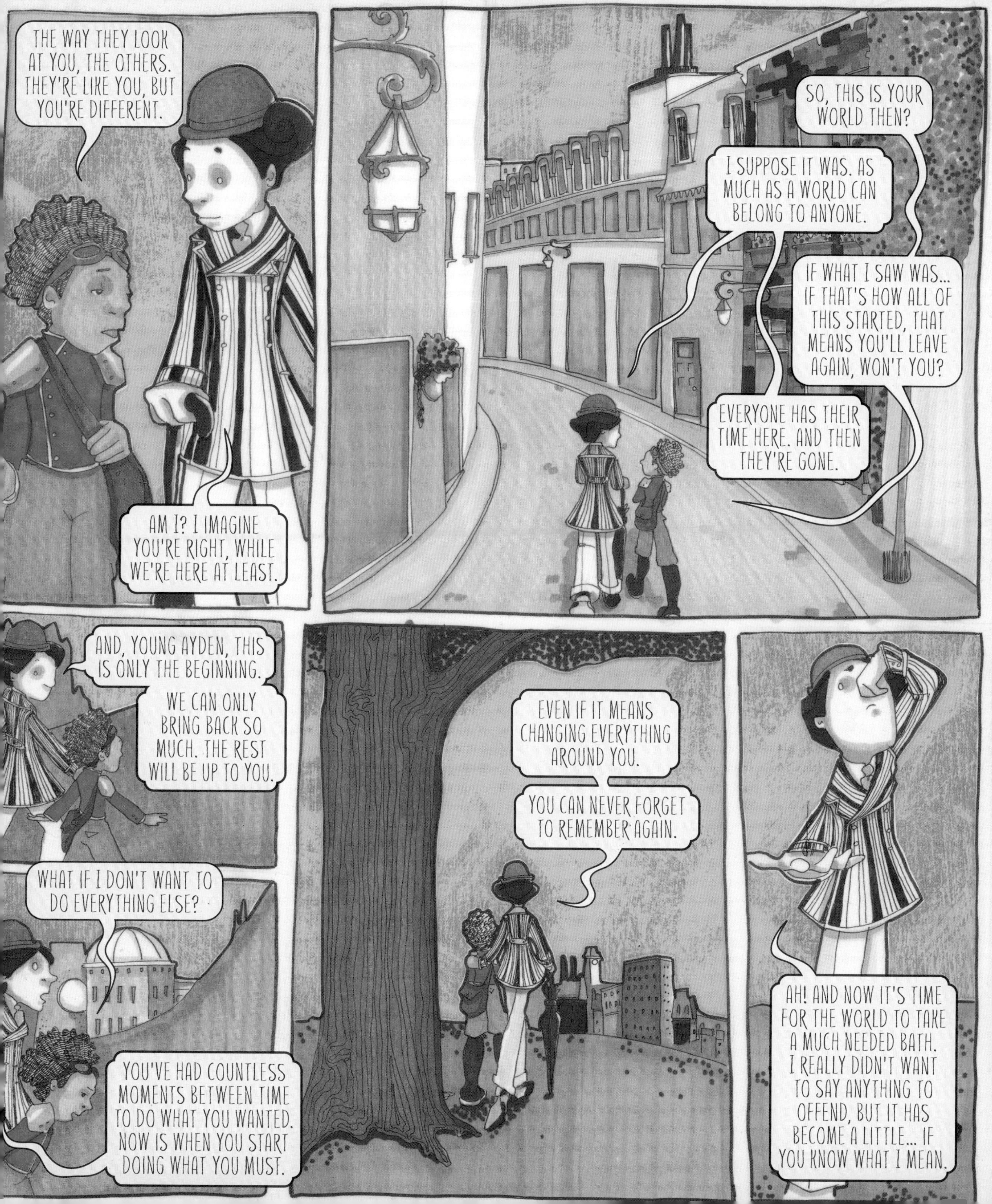
THE WAY THEY LOOK AT YOU, THE OTHERS. THEY'RE LIKE YOU, BUT YOU'RE DIFFERENT.
AM I? I IMAGINE YOU'RE RIGHT, WHILE WE'RE HERE AT LEAST.
SO, THIS IS YOUR WORLD THEN?
I SUPPOSE IT WAS. AS MUCH AS A WORLD CAN BELONG TO ANYONE.
IF WHAT I SAW WAS... IF THAT'S HOW ALL OF THIS STARTED, THAT MEANS YOU'LL LEAVE AGAIN, WON'T YOU?
EVERYONE HAS THEIR TIME HERE. AND THEN THEY'RE GONE.
AND, YOUNG AYDEN, THIS IS ONLY THE BEGINNING.
WE CAN ONLY BRING BACK SO MUCH. THE REST WILL BE UP TO YOU.
WHAT IF I DON'T WANT TO DO EVERYTHING ELSE?
YOU'VE HAD COUNTLESS MOMENTS BETWEEN TIME TO DO WHAT YOU WANTED. NOW IS WHEN YOU START DOING WHAT YOU MUST.
EVEN IF IT MEANS CHANGING EVERYTHING AROUND YOU.
YOU CAN NEVER FORGET TO REMEMBER AGAIN.
AH! AND NOW IT'S TIME FOR THE WORLD TO TAKE A MUCH NEEDED BATH. I REALLY DIDN'T WANT TO SAY ANYTHING TO OFFEND, BUT IT HAS BECOME A LITTLE... IF YOU KNOW WHAT I MEAN.

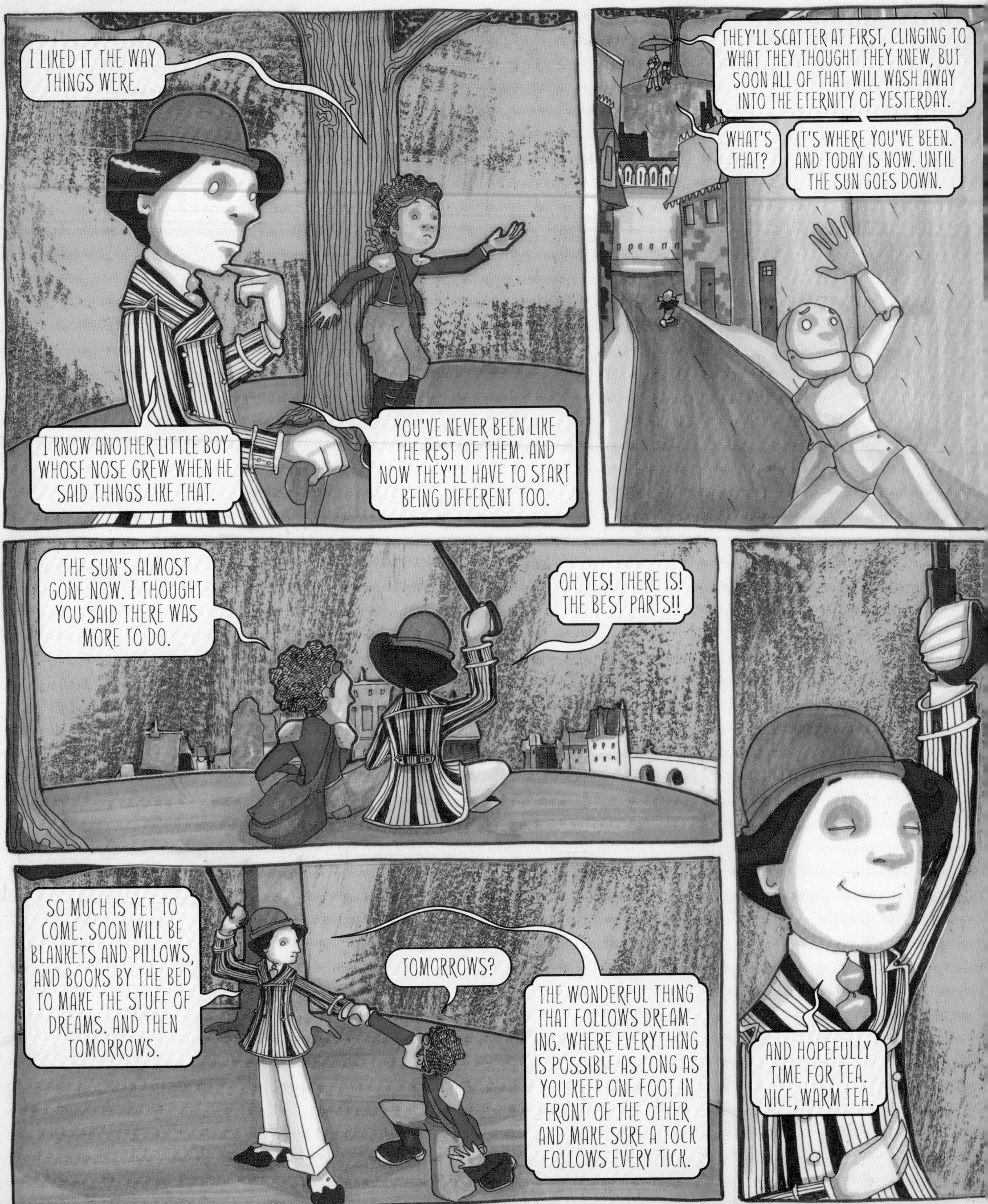
I LIKED IT THE WAY THINGS WERE.
YOU'VE NEVER BEEN LIKE THE REST OF THEM. AND NOW THEY'LL HAVE TO START BEING DIFFERENT TOO.
I KNOW ANOTHER LITTLE BOY WHOSE NOSE GREW WHEN HE SAID THINGS LIKE THAT.
THEY'LL SCATTER AT FIRST, CLINGING TO WHAT THEY THOUGHT THEY KNEW, BUT SOON ALL OF THAT WILL WASH AWAY INTO THE ETERNITY OF YESTERDAY.
WHAT'S THAT?
IT'S WHERE YOU'VE BEEN. AND TODAY IS NOW. UNTIL THE SUN GOES DOWN.
THE SUN'S ALMOST GONE NOW. I THOUGHT YOU SAID THERE WAS MORE TO DO.
OH YES! THERE IS! THE BEST PARTS!!
SO MUCH IS YET TO COME. SOON WILL BE BLANKETS AND PILLOWS, AND BOOKS BY THE BED TO MAKE THE STUFF OF DREAMS. AND THEN TOMORROWS.
TOMORROWS?
THE WONDERFUL THING THAT FOLLOWS DREAM-ING. WHERE EVERYTHING IS POSSIBLE AS LONG AS YOU KEEP ONE FOOT IN FRONT OF THE OTHER AND MAKE SURE A TOCK FOLLOWS EVERY TICK.
AND HOPEFULLY TIME FOR TEA. NICE, WARM TEA.

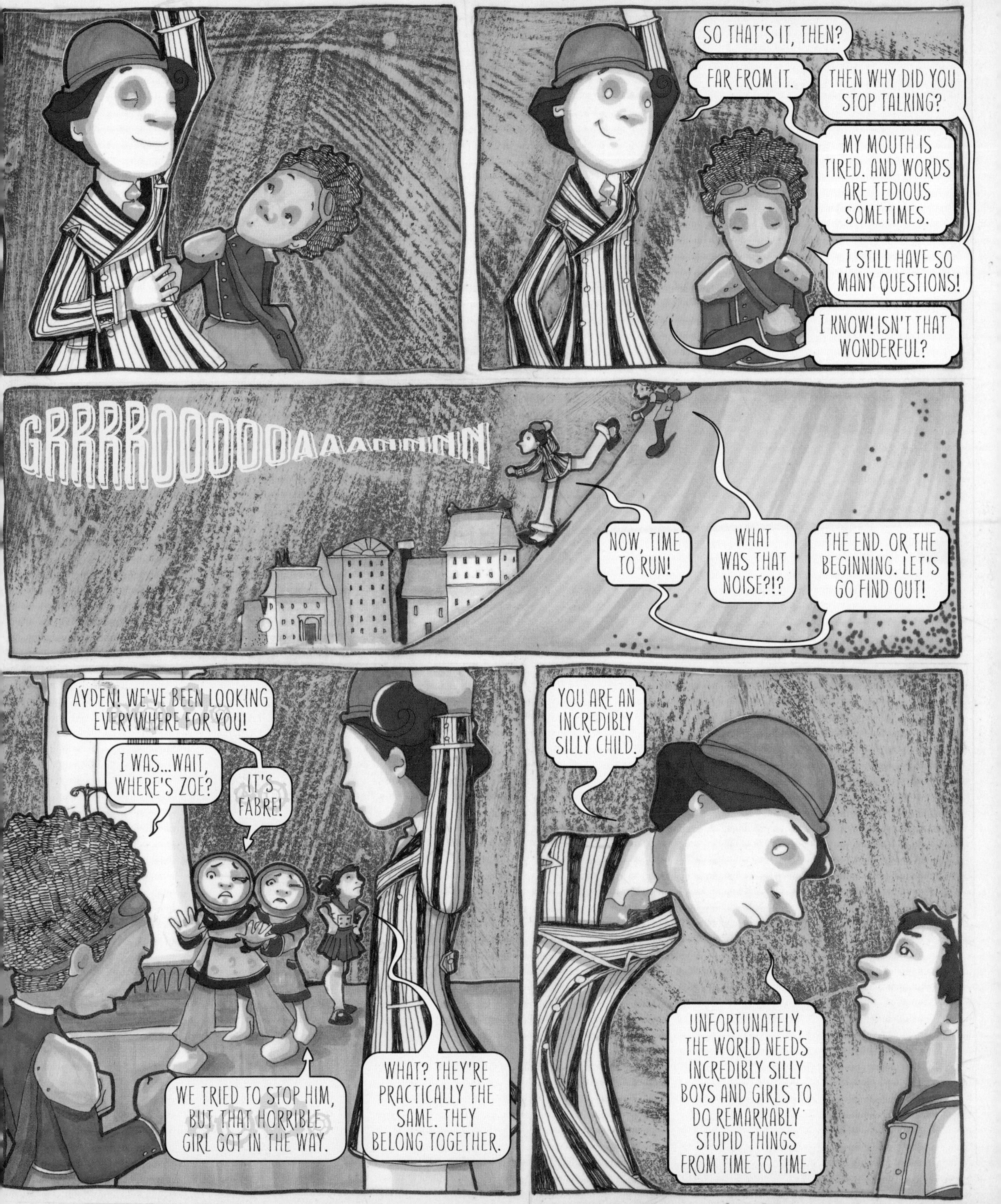
SO THAT'S IT, THEN?
FAR FROM IT.
THEN WHY DID YOU STOP TALKING?
MY MOUTH IS TIRED. AND WORDS ARE TEDIOUS SOMETIMES.
I STILL HAVE SO MANY QUESTIONS!
I KNOW! ISN'T THAT WONDERFUL?
GRRRROOOOOOAAAANNNN
NOW, TIME TO RUN!
WHAT WAS THAT NOISE?!?
THE END. OR THE BEGINNING. LET'S GO FIND OUT!
AYDEN! WE'VE BEEN LOOKING EVERYWHERE FOR YOU!
I WAS...WAIT, WHERE'S ZOE?
IT'S FABRE!
WE TRIED TO STOP HIM, BUT THAT HORRIBLE GIRL GOT IN THE WAY.
WHAT? THEY'RE PRACTICALLY THE SAME. THEY BELONG TOGETHER.
YOU ARE AN INCREDIBLY SILLY CHILD.
UNFORTUNATELY, THE WORLD NEEDS INCREDIBLY SILLY BOYS AND GIRLS TO DO REMARKABLY STUPID THINGS FROM TIME TO TIME.

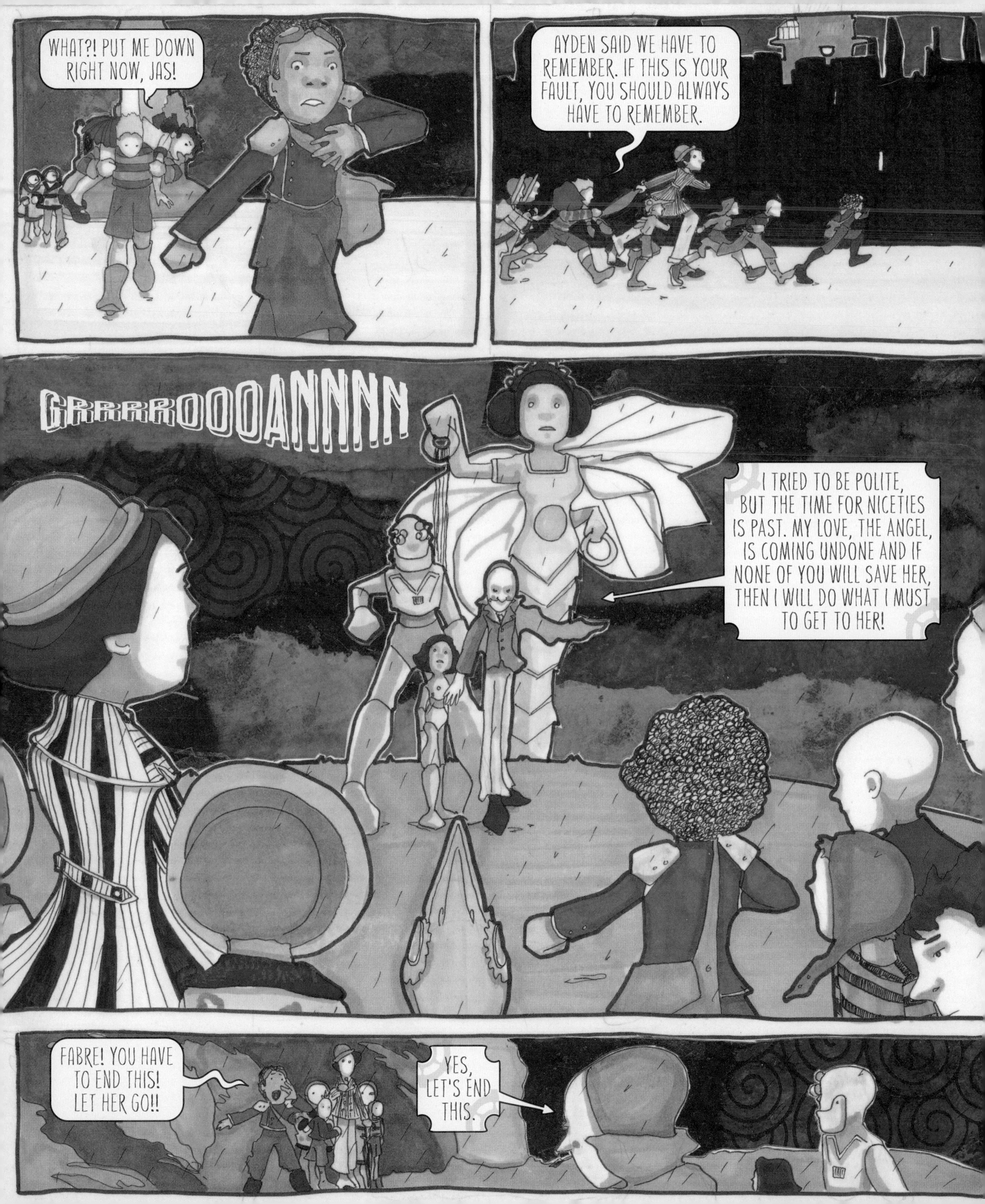
WHAT?! PUT ME DOWN RIGHT NOW, JAS!
AYDEN SAID WE HAVE TO REMEMBER. IF THIS IS YOUR FAULT, YOU SHOULD ALWAYS HAVE TO REMEMBER.
GRRRRROOOOANNNNN
I TRIED TO BE POLITE, BUT THE TIME FOR NICETIES IS PAST. MY LOVE, THE ANGEL, IS COMING UNDONE AND IF NONE OF YOU WILL SAVE HER, THEN I WILL DO WHAT I MUST TO GET TO HER!
FABRE! YOU HAVE TO END THIS! LET HER GO!!
YES, LET'S END THIS.

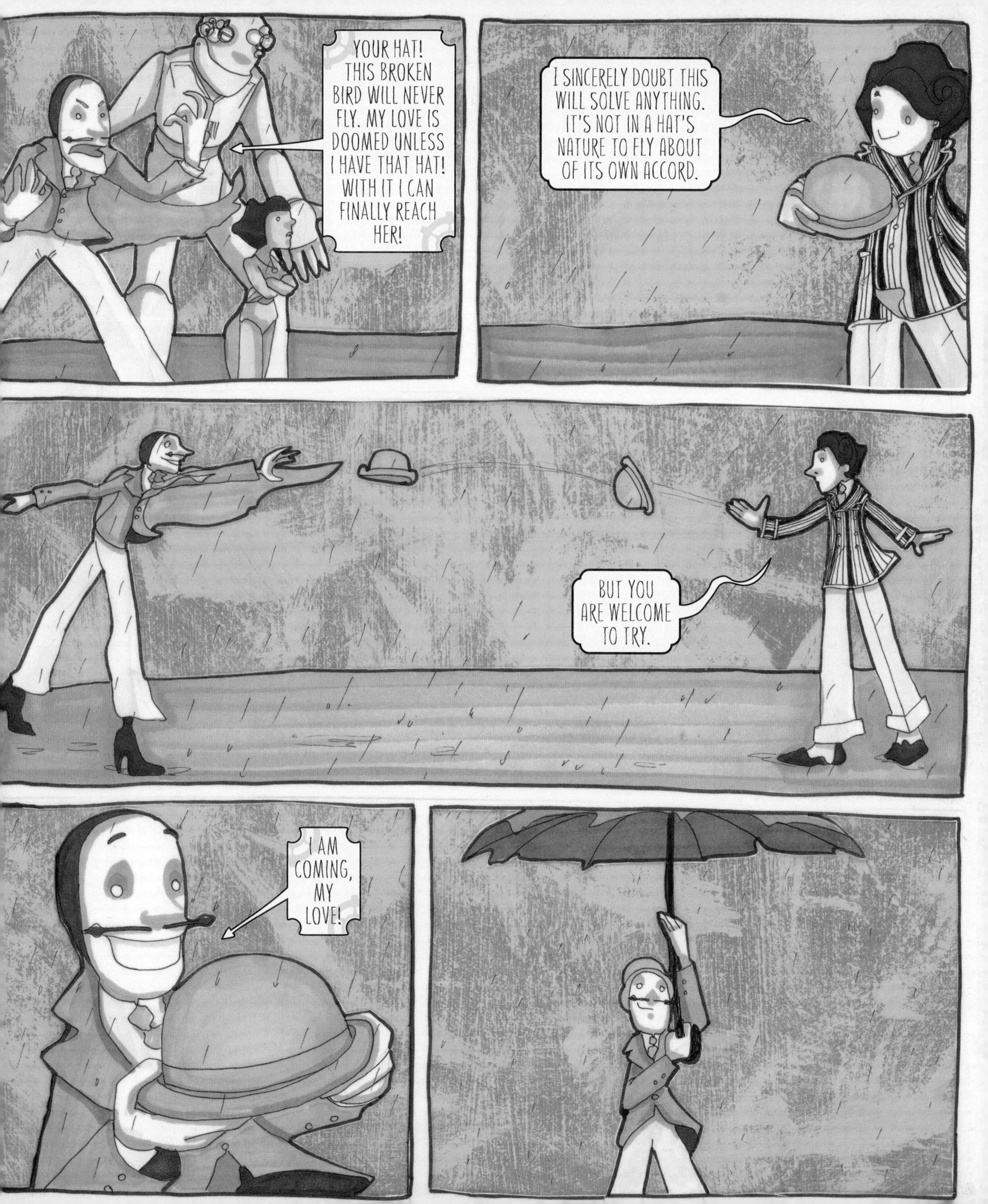
YOUR HAT! THIS BROKEN BIRD WILL NEVER FLY. MY LOVE IS DOOMED UNLESS I HAVE THAT HAT! WITH IT I CAN FINALLY REACH HER!
I SINCERELY DOUBT THIS WILL SOLVE ANYTHING. IT'S NOT IN A HAT'S NATURE TO FLY ABOUT OF ITS OWN ACCORD.
BUT YOU ARE WELCOME TO TRY.
I AM COMING, MY LOVE!

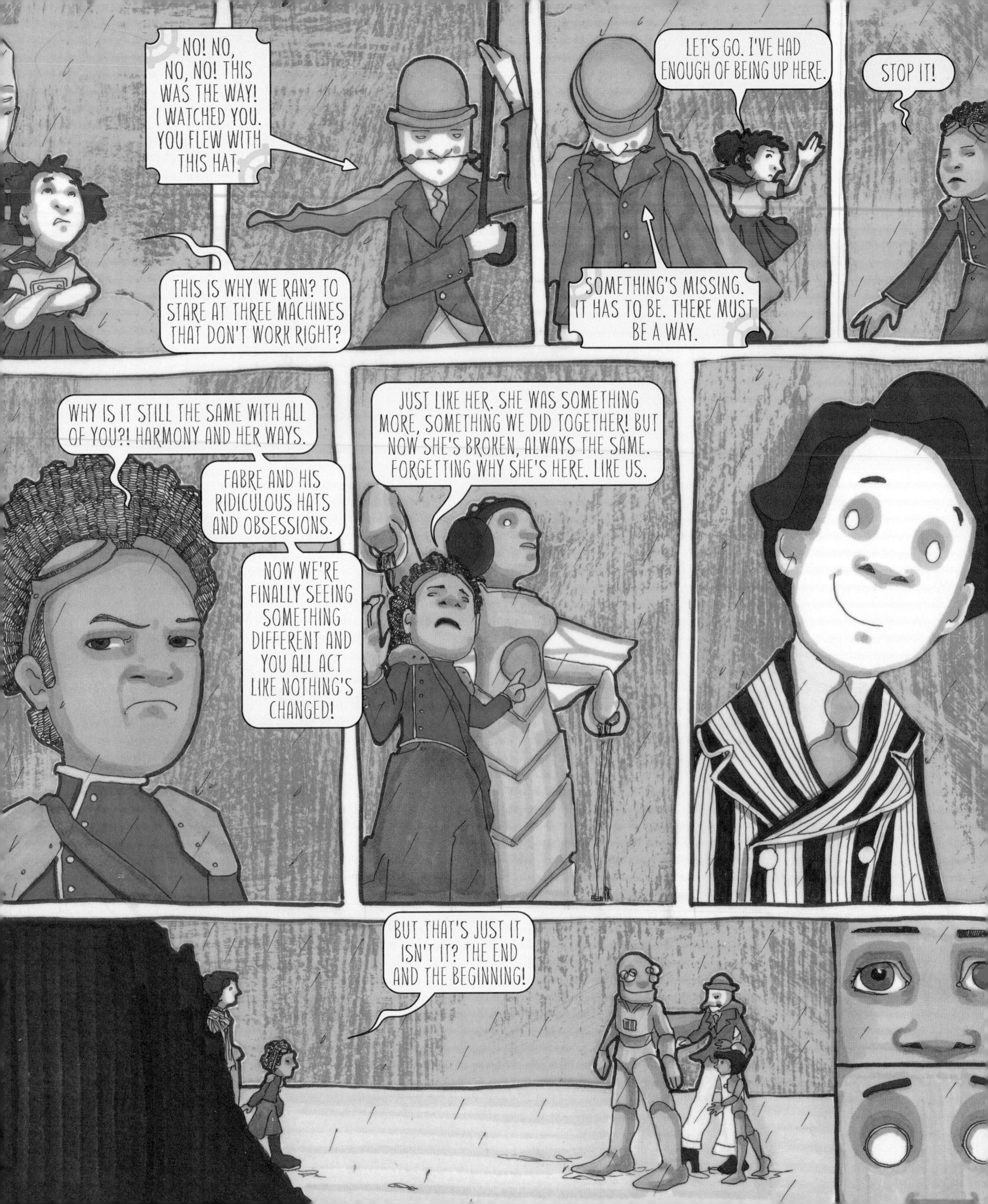
NO! NO, NO, NO! THIS WAS THE WAY! I WATCHED YOU. YOU FLEW WITH THIS HAT.
THIS IS WHY WE RAN? TO STARE AT THREE MACHINES THAT DON'T WORK RIGHT?
LET'S GO. I'VE HAD ENOUGH OF BEING UP HERE.
SOMETHING'S MISSING. IT HAS TO BE. THERE MUST BE A WAY.
STOP IT!
WHY IS IT STILL THE SAME WITH ALL OF YOU?! HARMONY AND HER WAYS.
FABRE AND HIS RIDICULOUS HATS AND OBSESSIONS.
NOW WE'RE FINALLY SEEING SOMETHING DIFFERENT AND YOU ALL ACT LIKE NOTHING'S CHANGED!
JUST LIKE HER. SHE WAS SOMETHING MORE, SOMETHING WE DID TOGETHER! BUT NOW SHE'S BROKEN, ALWAYS THE SAME. FORGETTING WHY SHE'S HERE. LIKE US.
BUT THAT'S JUST IT, ISN'T IT? THE END AND THE BEGINNING!

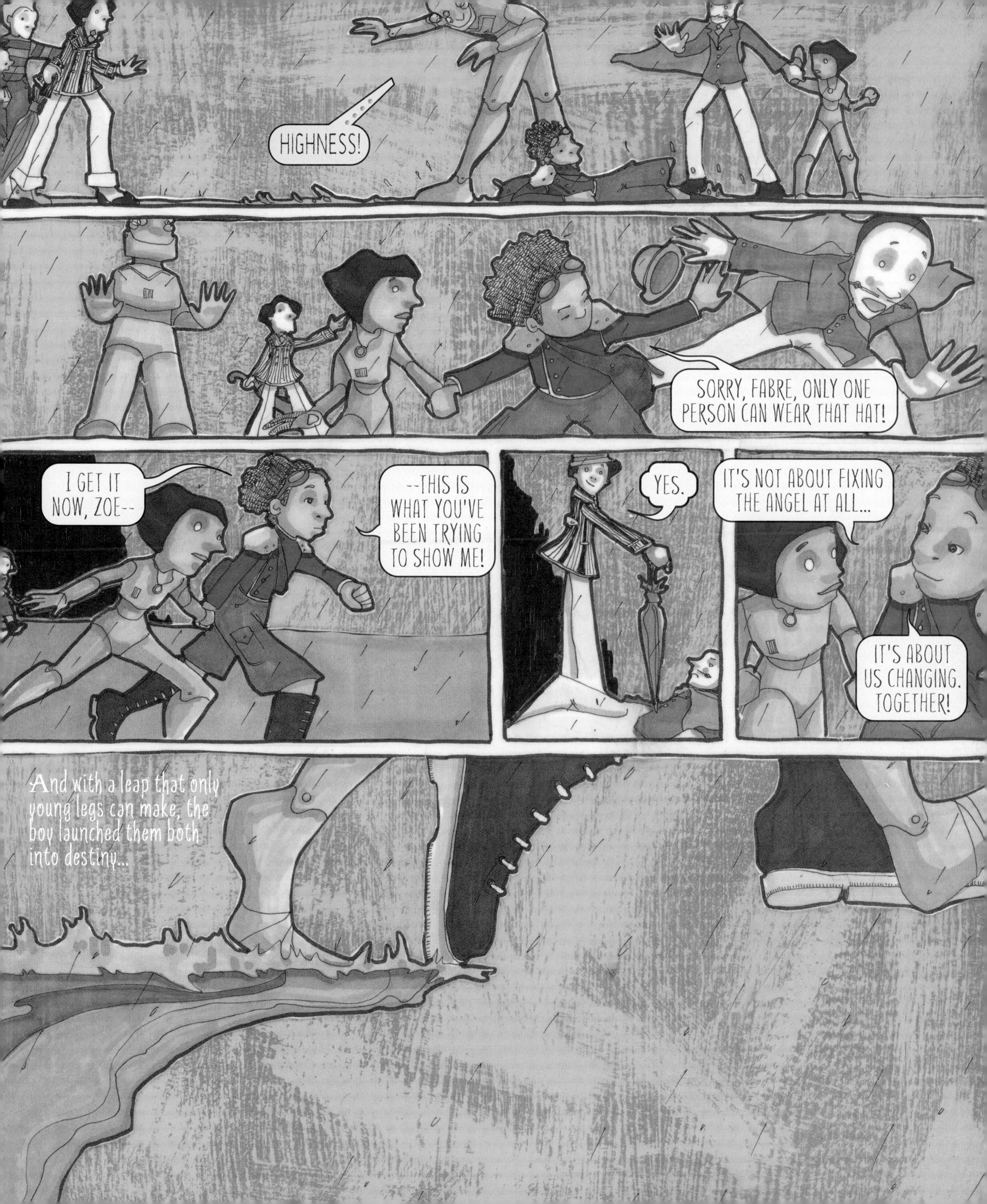
HIGHNESS!
SORRY, FABRE, ONLY ONE PERSON CAN WEAR THAT HAT!
I GET IT NOW, ZOE--
--THIS IS WHAT YOU'VE BEEN TRYING TO SHOW ME!
YES.
IT'S NOT ABOUT FIXING THE ANGEL AT ALL...
IT'S ABOUT US CHANGING. TOGETHER!
And with a leap that only young legs can make, the boy launched them both into destiny...

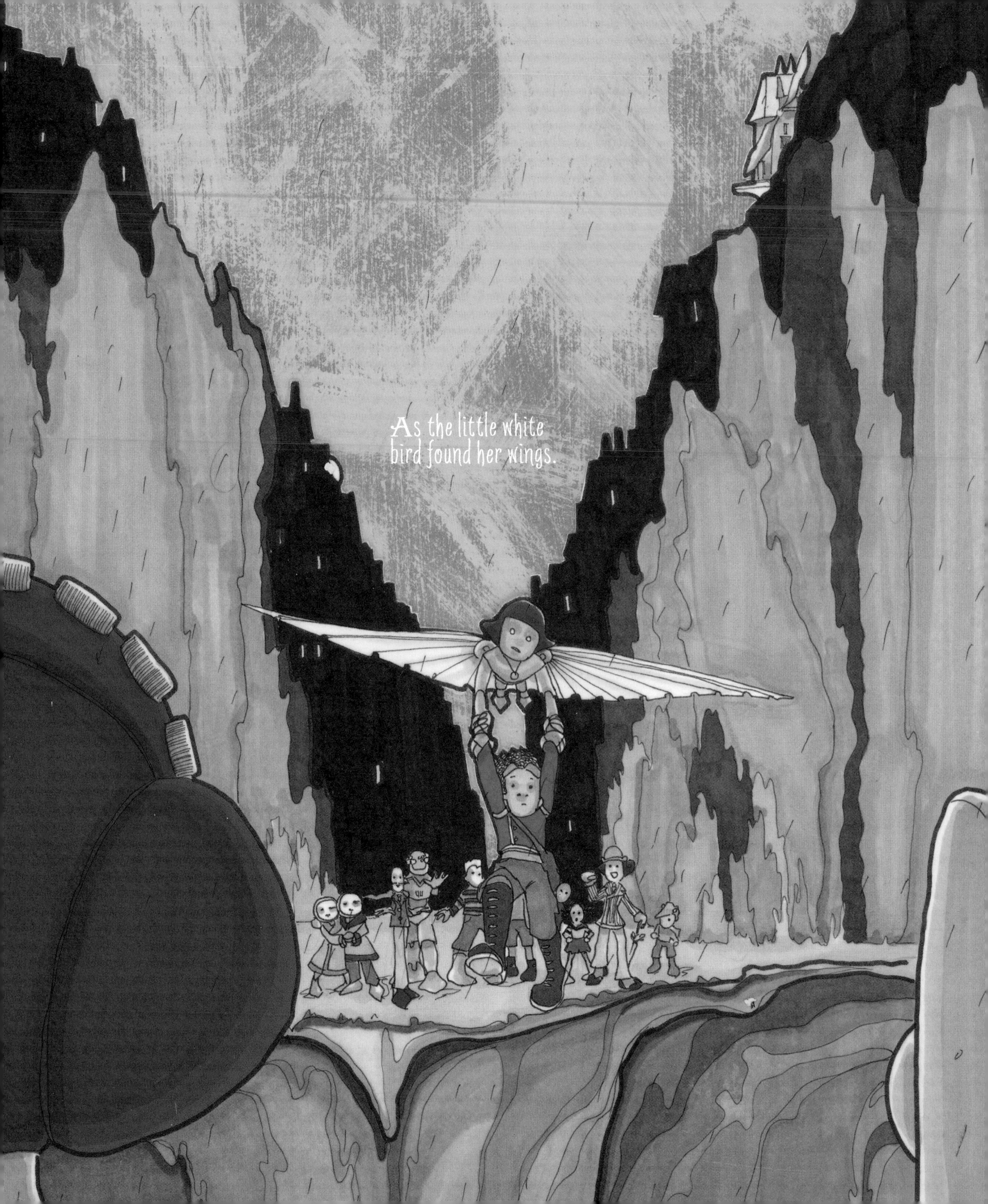
As the little white bird found her wings.

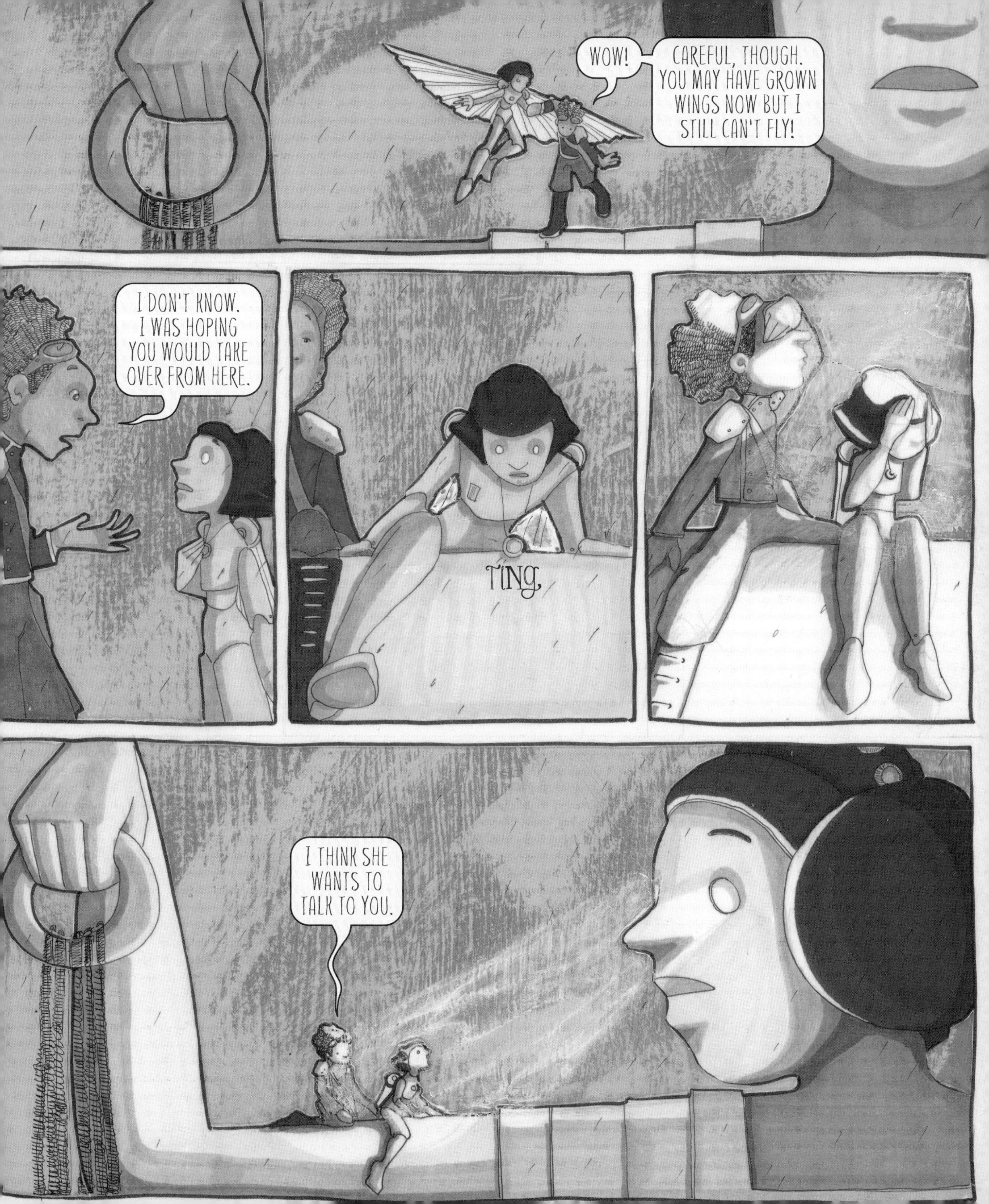
WOW!
CAREFUL, THOUGH. YOU MAY HAVE GROWN WINGS NOW BUT I STILL CAN'T FLY!
I DON'T KNOW. I WAS HOPING YOU WOULD TAKE OVER FROM HERE.
TING.
I THINK SHE WANTS TO TALK TO YOU.

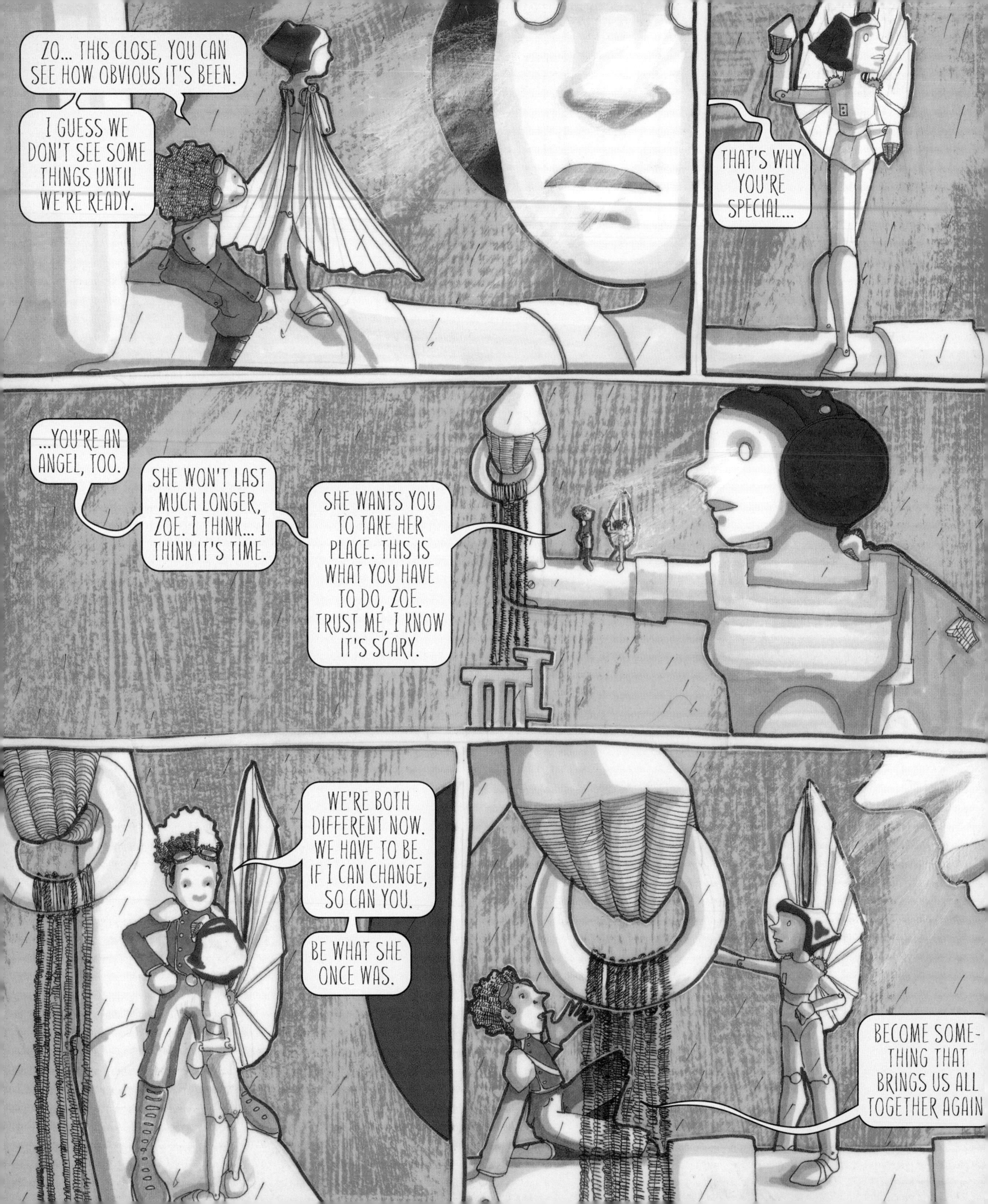

ZO... THIS CLOSE, YOU CAN SEE HOW OBVIOUS IT'S BEEN.
I GUESS WE DON'T SEE SOME THINGS UNTIL WE'RE READY.
THAT'S WHY YOU'RE SPECIAL...
...YOU'RE AN ANGEL, TOO.
SHE WON'T LAST MUCH LONGER, ZOE. I THINK... I THINK IT'S TIME.
SHE WANTS YOU TO TAKE HER PLACE. THIS IS WHAT YOU HAVE TO DO, ZOE. TRUST ME, I KNOW IT'S SCARY.
WE'RE BOTH DIFFERENT NOW. WE HAVE TO BE. IF I CAN CHANGE, SO CAN YOU.
BE WHAT SHE ONCE WAS.
BECOME SOME-THING THAT BRINGS US ALL TOGETHER AGAIN

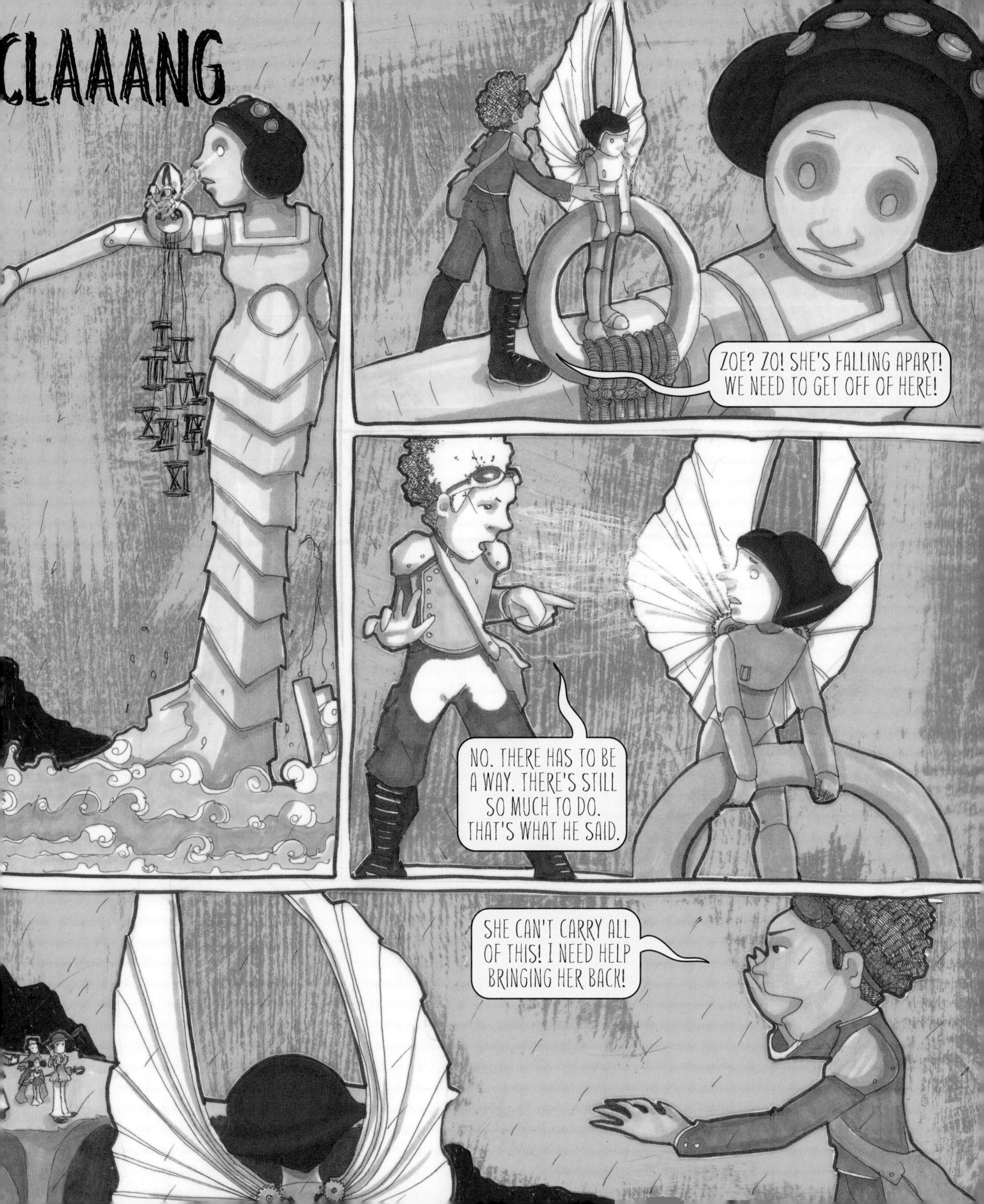
CLAANG
ZOE? ZO! SHE'S FALLING APART! WE NEED TO GET OFF OF HERE!
NO. THERE HAS TO BE A WAY. THERE'S STILL SO MUCH TO DO. THAT'S WHAT HE SAID.
SHE CAN'T CARRY ALL OF THIS! I NEED HELP BRINGING HER BACK!

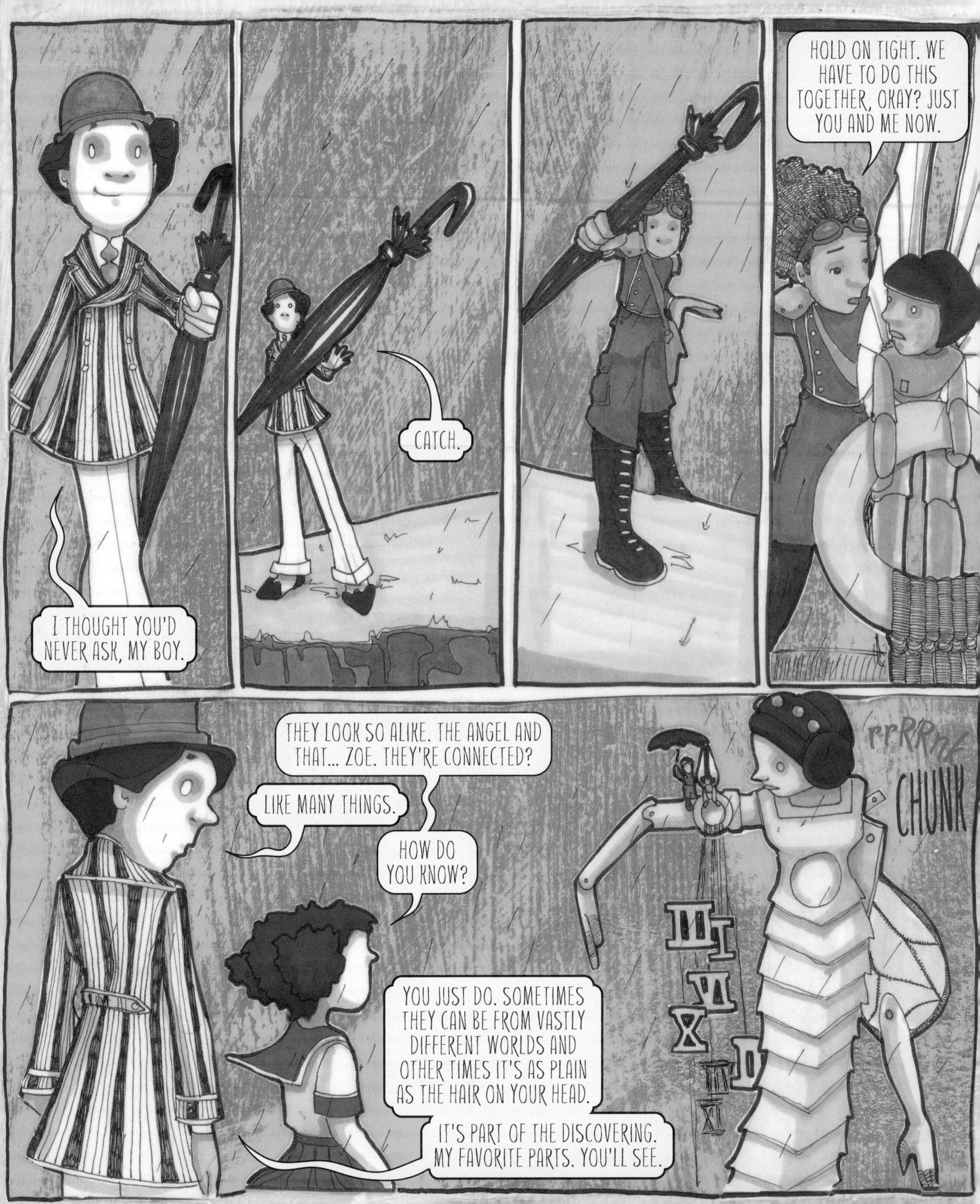
I THOUGHT YOU'D NEVER ASK, MY BOY.
CATCH.
HOLD ON TIGHT. WE HAVE TO DO THIS TOGETHER, OKAY? JUST YOU AND ME NOW.
THEY LOOK SO ALIKE. THE ANGEL AND THAT... ZOE. THEY'RE CONNECTED?
LIKE MANY THINGS.
HOW DO YOU KNOW?
YOU JUST DO. SOMETIMES THEY CAN BE FROM VASTLY DIFFERENT WORLDS AND OTHER TIMES IT'S AS PLAIN AS THE HAIR ON YOUR HEAD.
IT'S PART OF THE DISCOVERING. MY FAVORITE PARTS. YOU'LL SEE.
rrRRnk
CHUNK

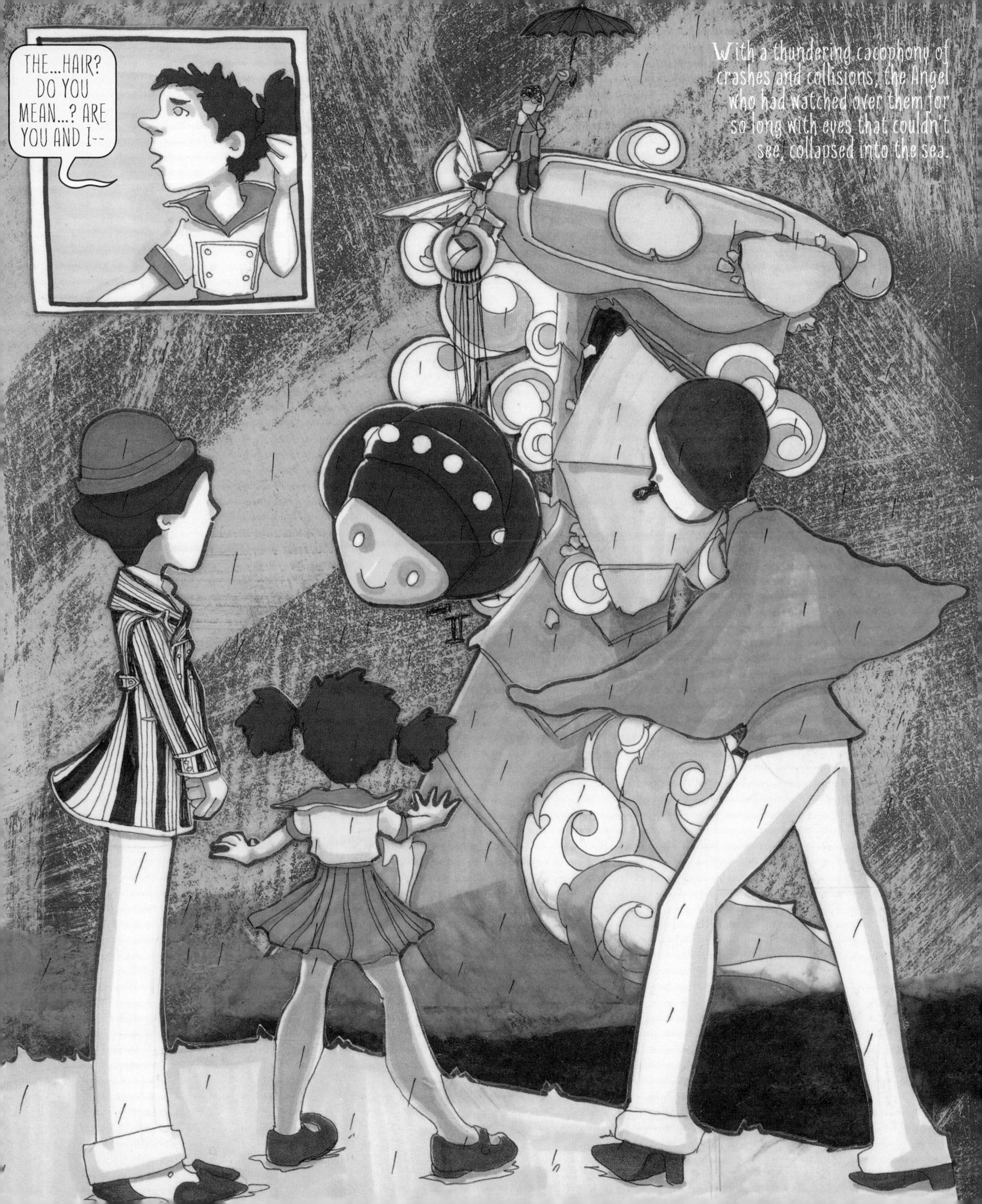
THE...HAIR? DO YOU MEAN...? ARE YOU AND I--
With a thundering cacophony of crashes and collisions, the Angel who had watched over them for so long with eyes that couldn't see, collapsed into the sea.

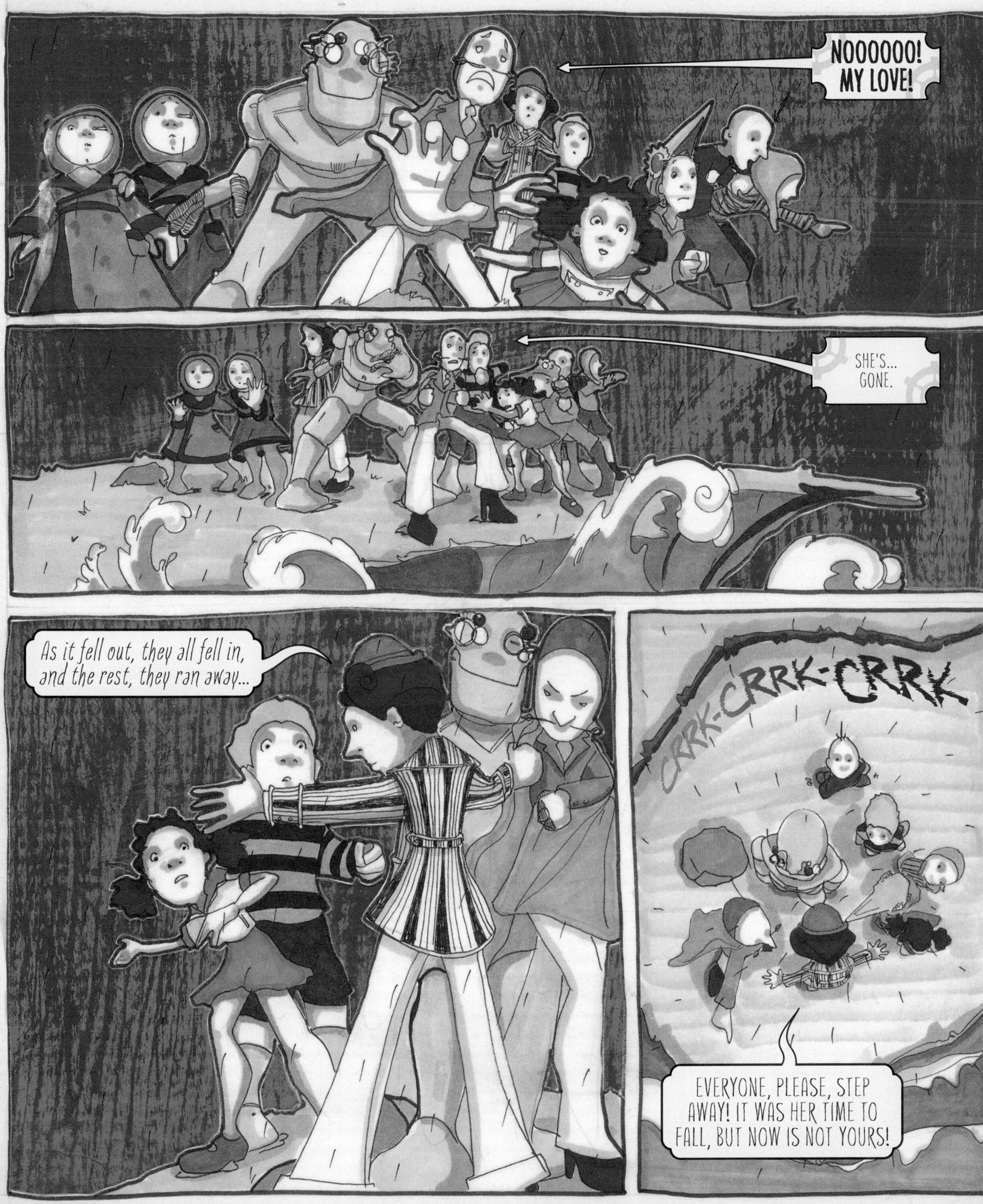
NOOOOOO! MY LOVE!
SHE'S... GONE.
As it fell out, they all fell in, and the rest, they ran away...
CRRK-CRRK-CRRK
EVERYONE, PLEASE, STEP AWAY! IT WAS HER TIME TO FALL, BUT NOW IS NOT YOURS!

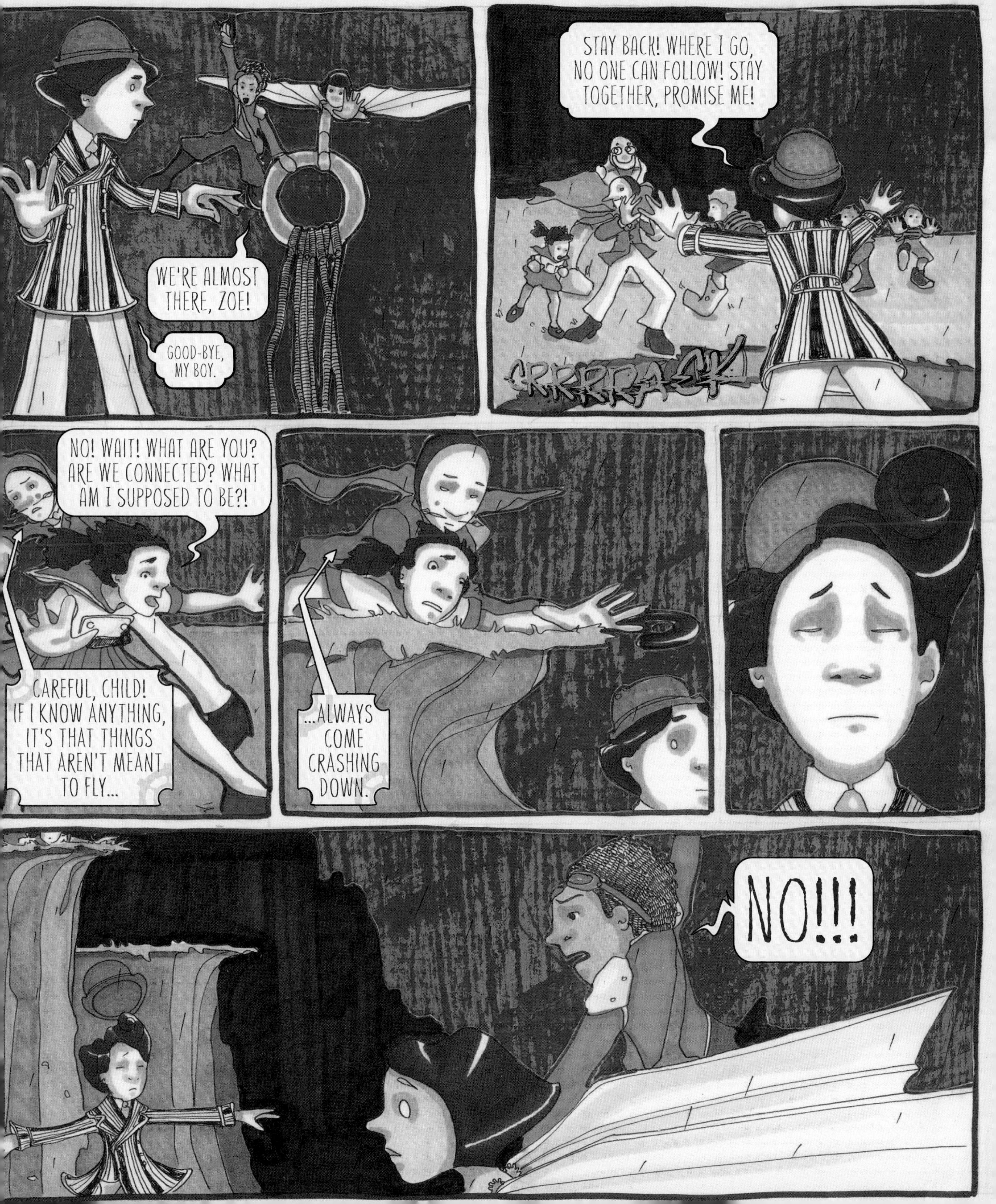
WE'RE ALMOST THERE, ZOE!
GOOD-BYE, MY BOY.
STAY BACK! WHERE I GO, NO ONE CAN FOLLOW! STAY TOGETHER, PROMISE ME!
CRRRRACK
NO! WAIT! WHAT ARE YOU? ARE WE CONNECTED? WHAT AM I SUPPOSED TO BE?!
CAREFUL, CHILD! IF I KNOW ANYTHING, IT'S THAT THINGS THAT AREN'T MEANT TO FLY...
...ALWAYS COME CRASHING DOWN.
NO!!!

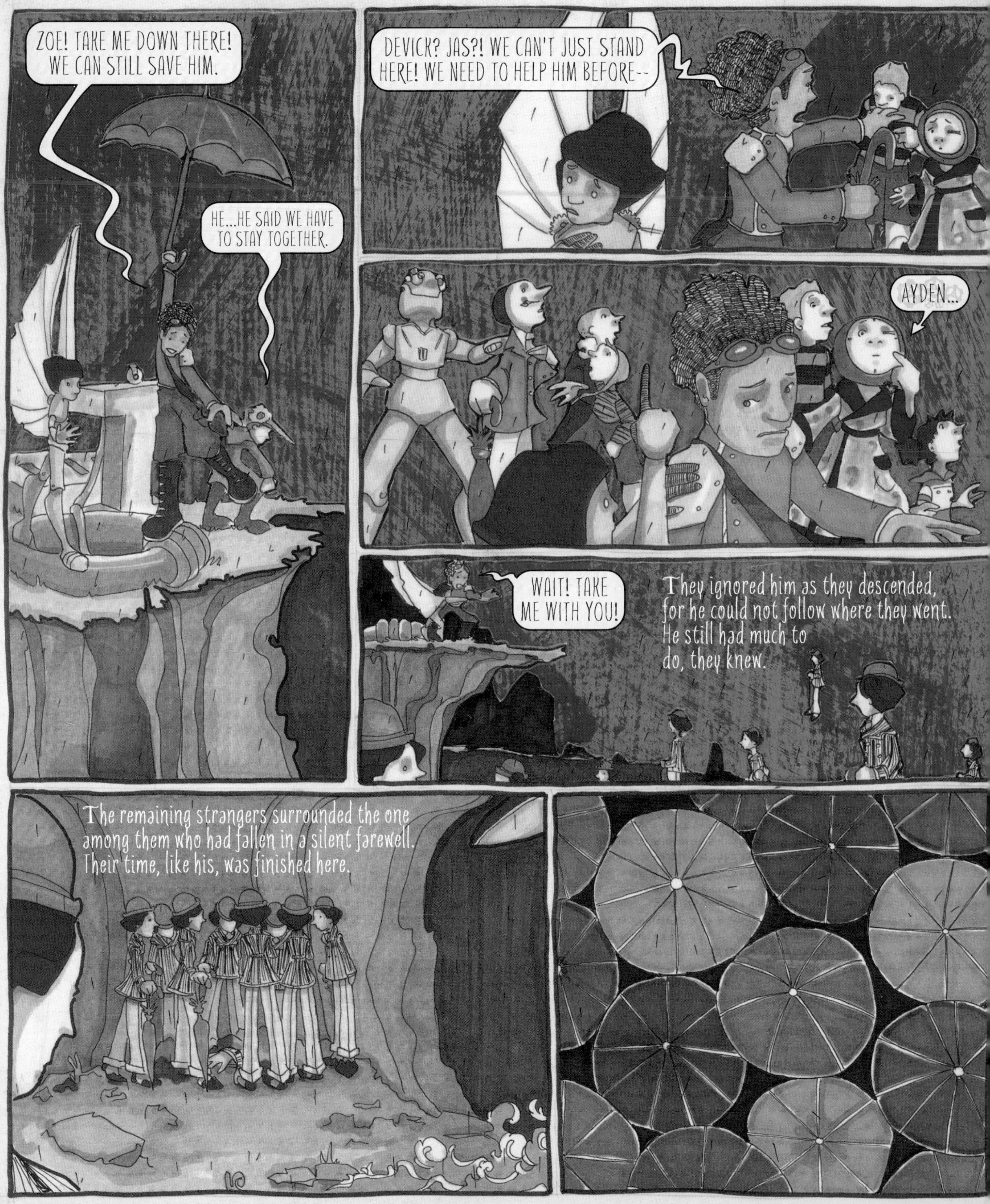
ZOE! TAKE ME DOWN THERE! WE CAN STILL SAVE HIM.
HE...HE SAID WE HAVE TO STAY TOGETHER.
DEVICK? JAS?! WE CAN'T JUST STAND HERE! WE NEED TO HELP HIM BEFORE--
AYDEN...
WAIT! TAKE ME WITH YOU!
They ignored him as they descended, for he could not follow where they went. He still had much to do, they knew.
The remaining strangers surrounded the one among them who had fallen in a silent farewell. Their time, like his, was finished here.

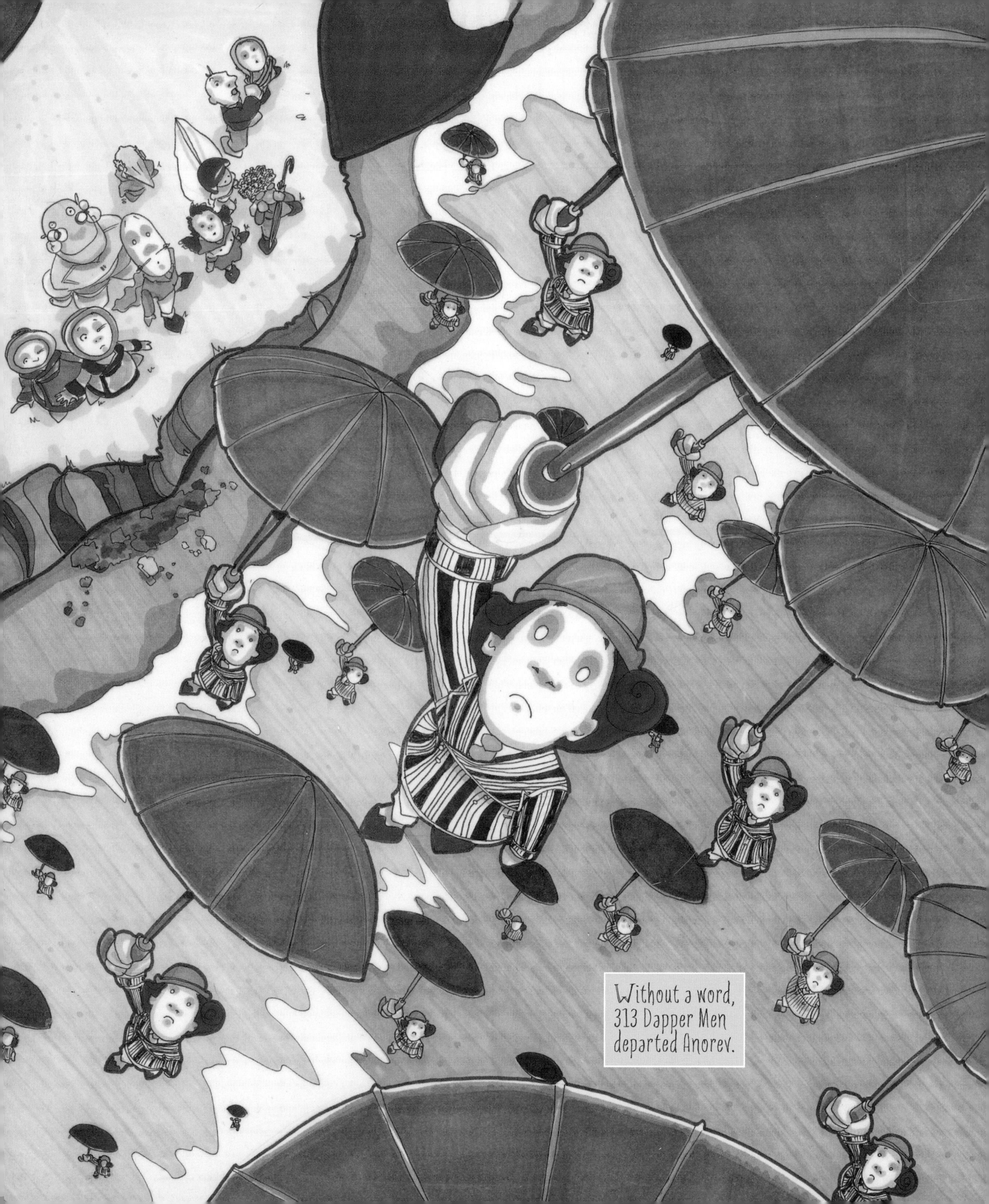
Without a word, 313 Dapper Men departed Anorev.

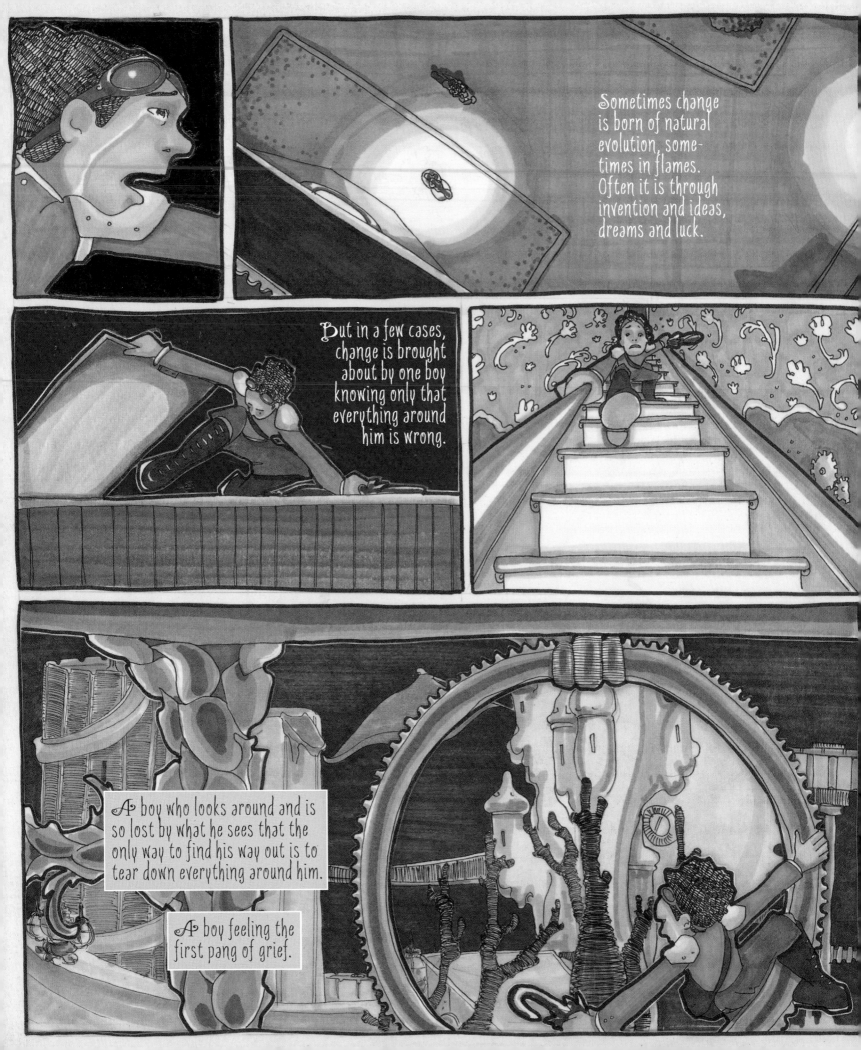

Sometimes change is born of natural evolution, sometimes in flames. Often it is through invention and ideas, dreams and luck.

But in a few cases, change is brought about by one boy knowing only that everything around him is wrong.

A boy who looks around and is so lost by what he sees that the only way to find his way out is to tear down everything around him.

A boy feeling the first pang of grief.

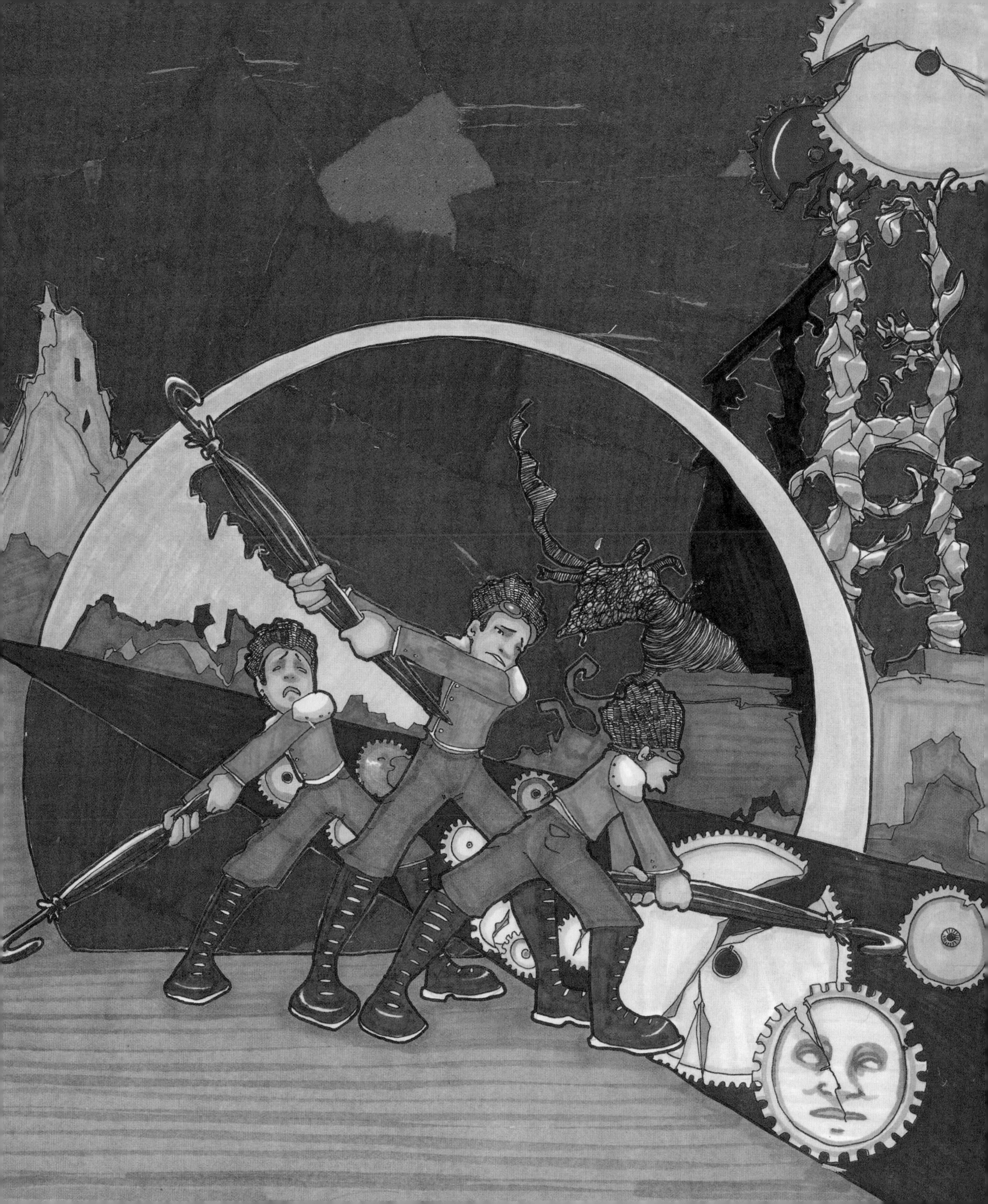

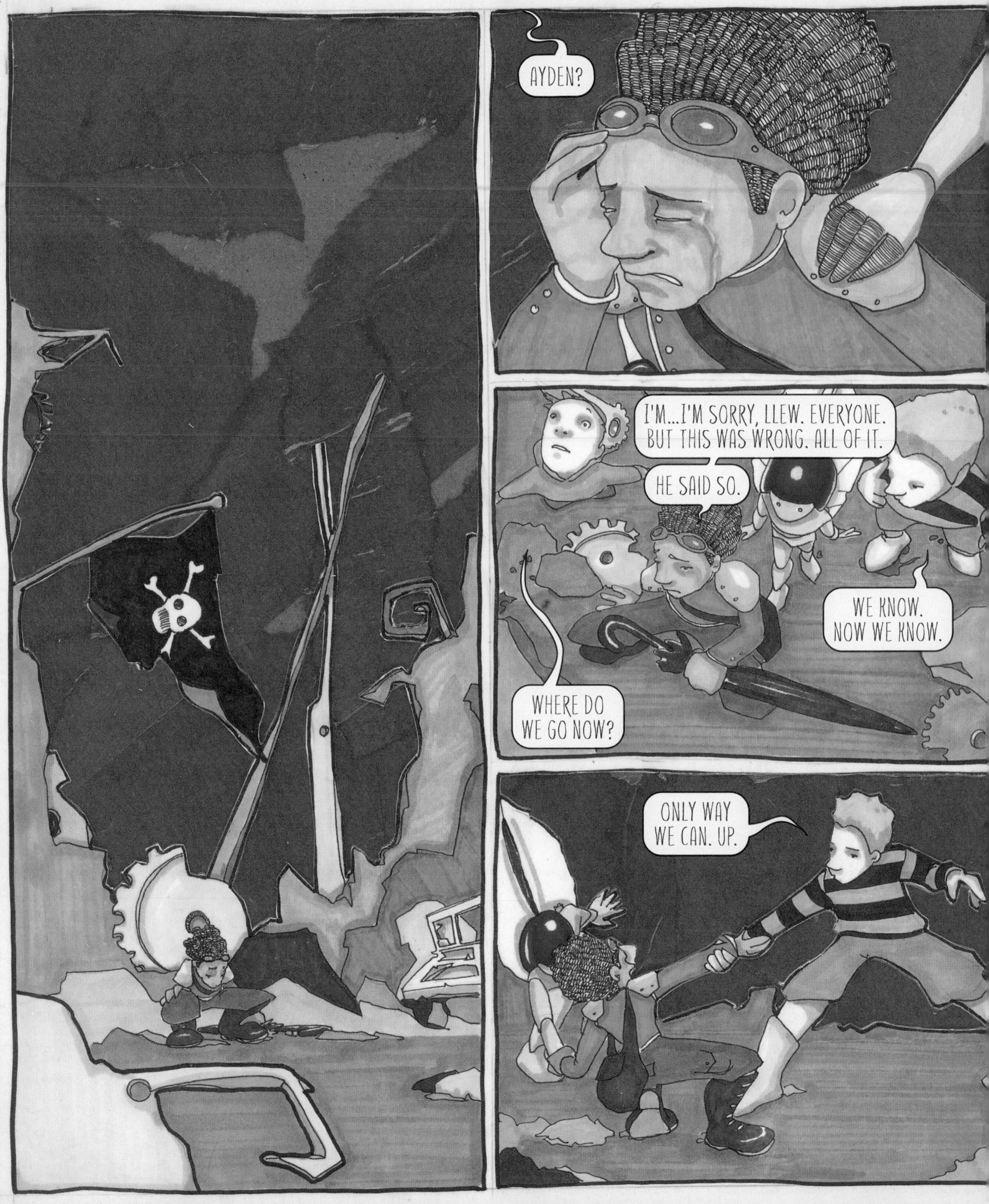
AYDEN?
I'M...I'M SORRY, LLEW. EVERYONE. BUT THIS WAS WRONG. ALL OF IT.
HE SAID SO.
WE KNOW. NOW WE KNOW.
WHERE DO WE GO NOW?
ONLY WAY WE CAN. UP.

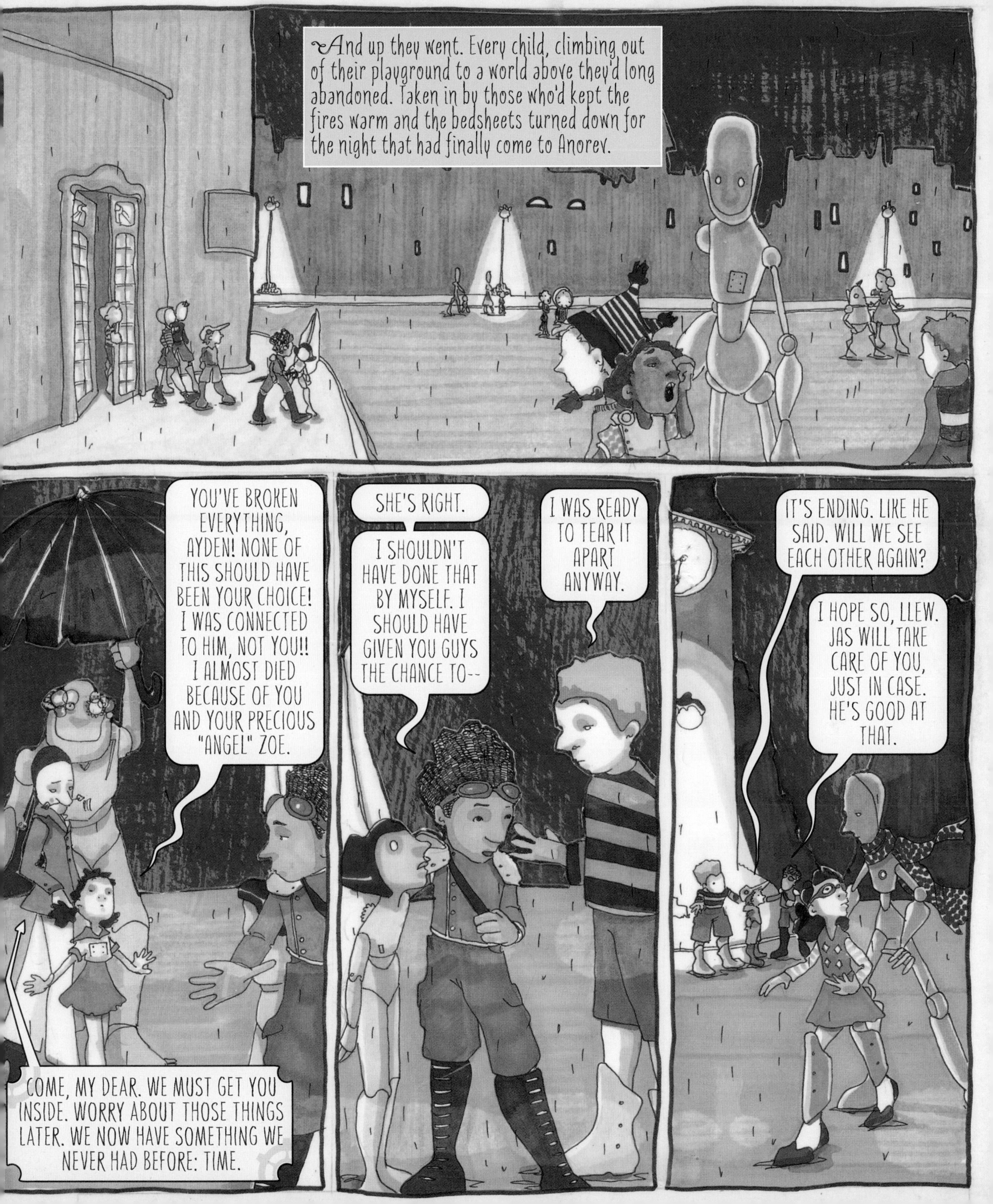
And up they went. Every child, climbing out of their playground to a world above they'd long abandoned. Taken in by those who'd kept the fires warm and the bedsheets turned down for the night that had finally come to Anorev.
YOU'VE BROKEN EVERYTHING, AYDEN! NONE OF THIS SHOULD HAVE BEEN YOUR CHOICE! I WAS CONNECTED TO HIM, NOT YOU!! I ALMOST DIED BECAUSE OF YOU AND YOUR PRECIOUS "ANGEL" ZOE.
COME, MY DEAR. WE MUST GET YOU INSIDE. WORRY ABOUT THOSE THINGS LATER. WE NOW HAVE SOMETHING WE NEVER HAD BEFORE: TIME.
SHE'S RIGHT.
I SHOULDN'T HAVE DONE THAT BY MYSELF. I SHOULD HAVE GIVEN YOU GUYS THE CHANCE TO--
I WAS READY TO TEAR IT APART ANYWAY.
IT'S ENDING. LIKE HE SAID. WILL WE SEE EACH OTHER AGAIN?
I HOPE SO, LLEW. JAS WILL TAKE CARE OF YOU, JUST IN CASE. HE'S GOOD AT THAT.

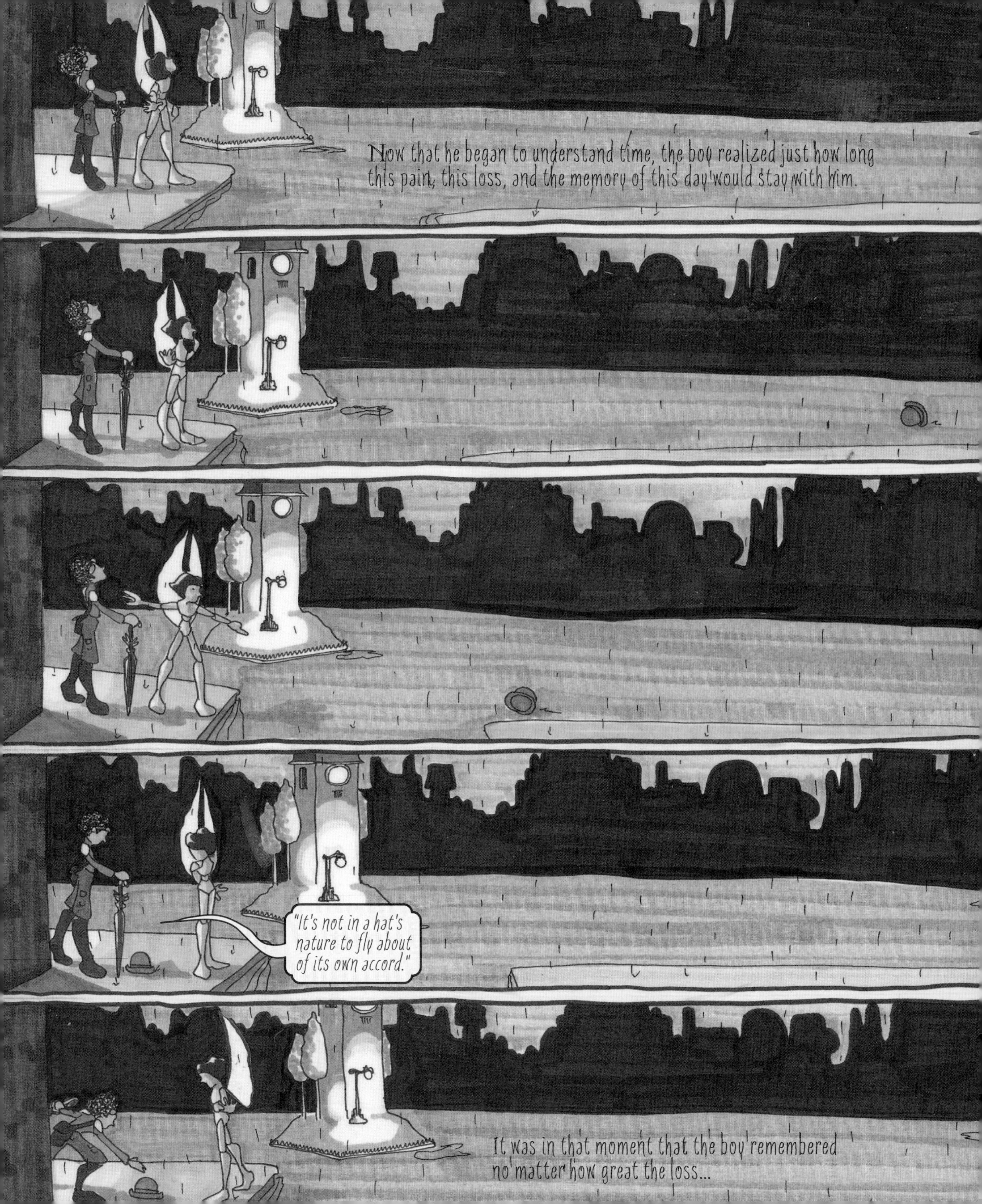
Now that he began to understand time, the boy realized just how long this pain, this loss, and the memory of this day would stay with him.
"It's not in a hat's nature to fly about of its own accord."
It was in that moment that the boy remembered no matter how great the loss...

He would never truly be alone.

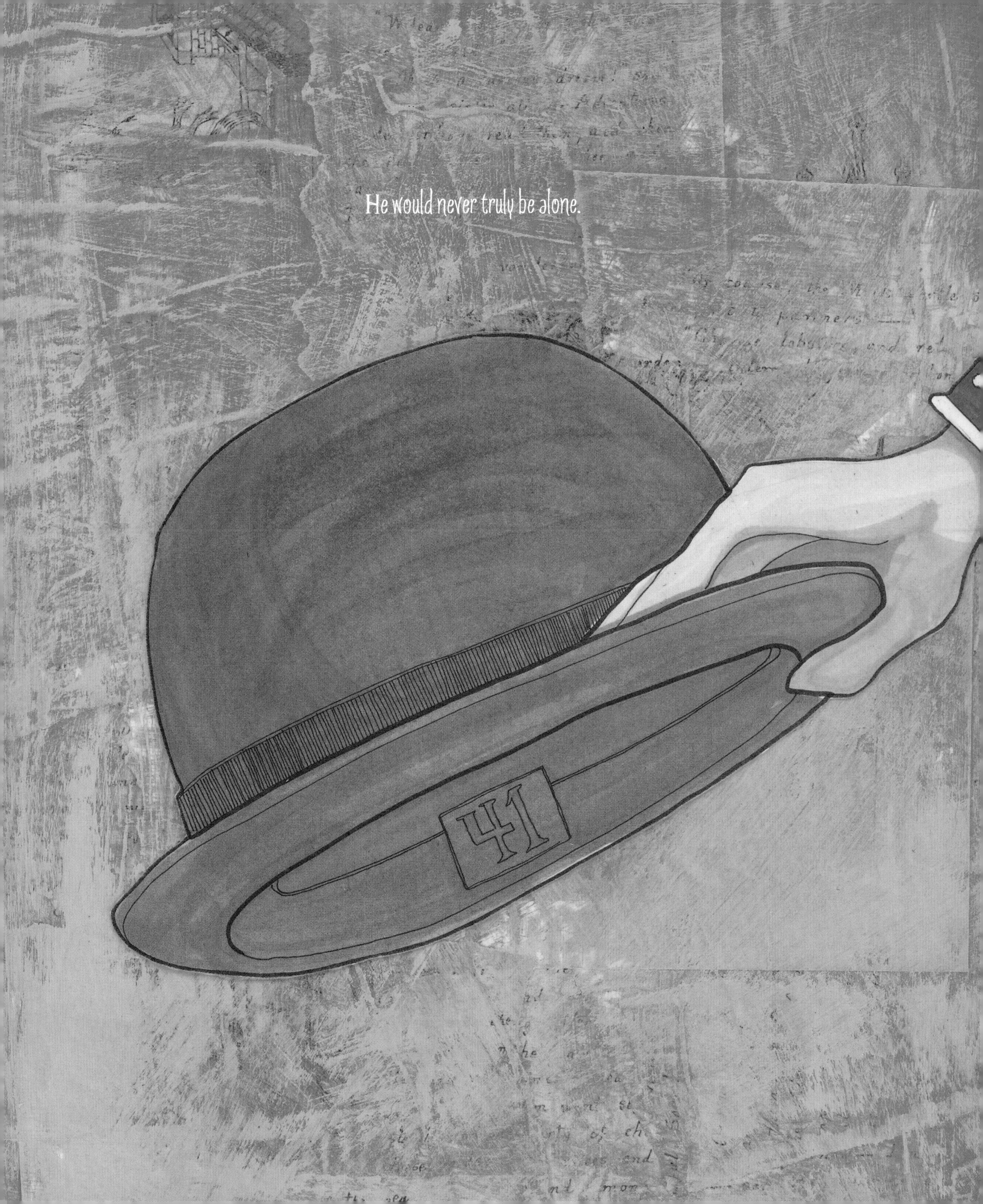

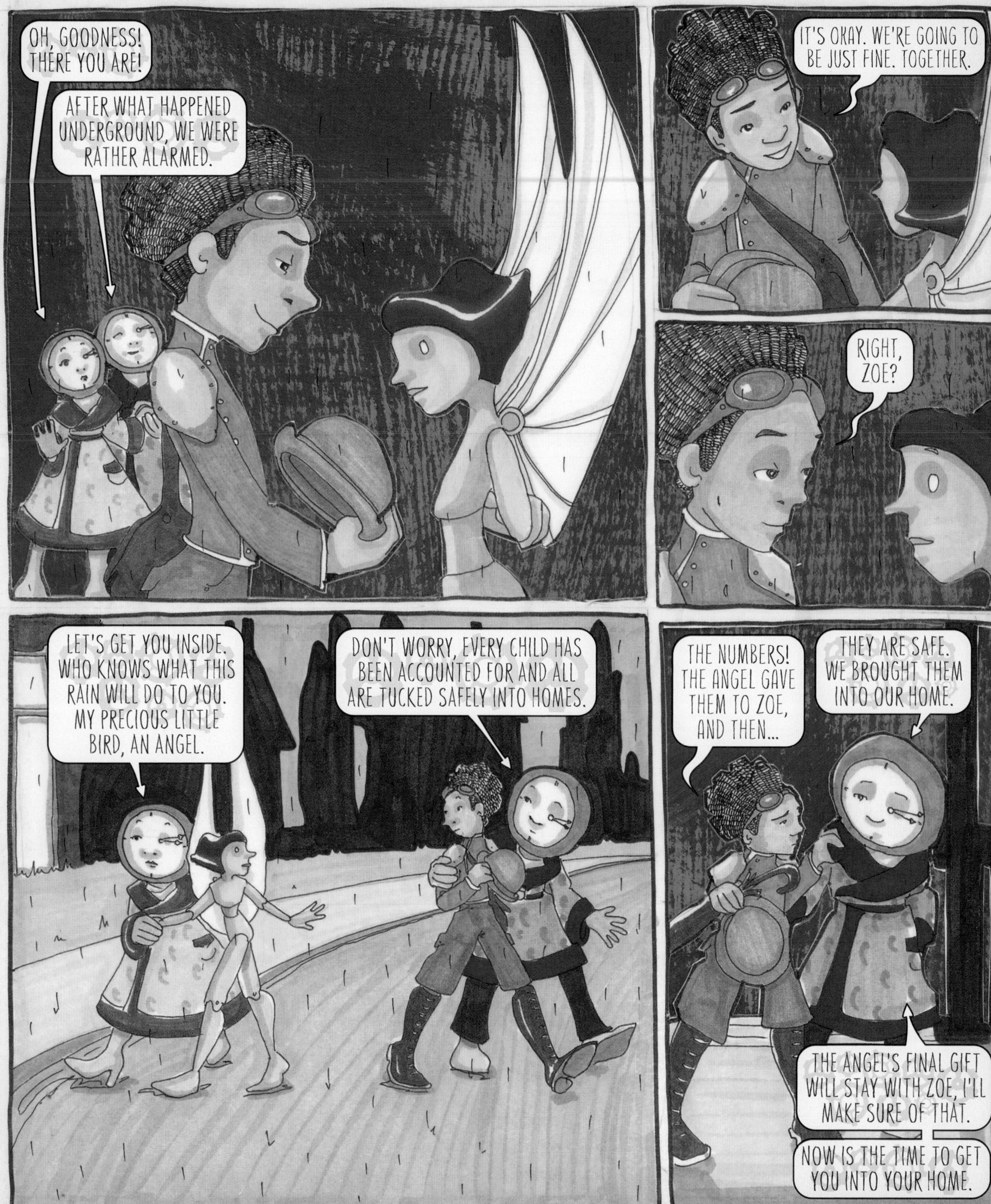
OH, GOODNESS! THERE YOU ARE!
AFTER WHAT HAPPENED UNDERGROUND, WE WERE RATHER ALARMED.
IT'S OKAY. WE'RE GOING TO BE JUST FINE. TOGETHER.
RIGHT, ZOE?
LET'S GET YOU INSIDE. WHO KNOWS WHAT THIS RAIN WILL DO TO YOU. MY PRECIOUS LITTLE BIRD, AN ANGEL.
DON'T WORRY, EVERY CHILD HAS BEEN ACCOUNTED FOR AND ALL ARE TUCKED SAFELY INTO HOMES.
THE NUMBERS! THE ANGEL GAVE THEM TO ZOE, AND THEN...
THEY ARE SAFE. WE BROUGHT THEM INTO OUR HOME.
THE ANGEL'S FINAL GIFT WILL STAY WITH ZOE, I'LL MAKE SURE OF THAT.
NOW IS THE TIME TO GET YOU INTO YOUR HOME.

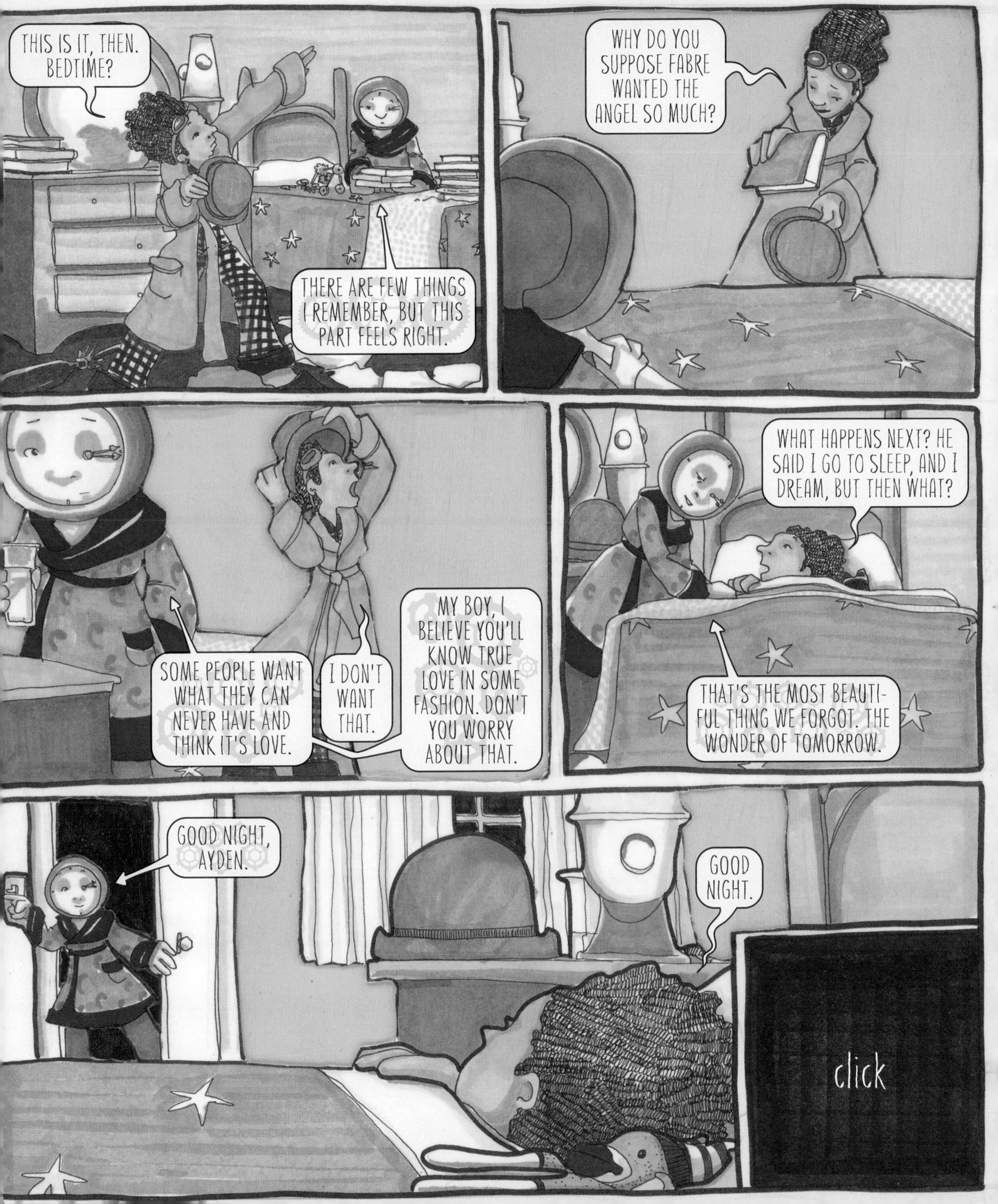
THIS IS IT, THEN. BEDTIME?
THERE ARE FEW THINGS I REMEMBER, BUT THIS PART FEELS RIGHT.
WHY DO YOU SUPPOSE FABRE WANTED THE ANGEL SO MUCH?
SOME PEOPLE WANT WHAT THEY CAN NEVER HAVE AND THINK IT'S LOVE.
I DON'T WANT THAT.
MY BOY, I BELIEVE YOU'LL KNOW TRUE LOVE IN SOME FASHION. DON'T YOU WORRY ABOUT THAT.
WHAT HAPPENS NEXT? HE SAID I GO TO SLEEP, AND I DREAM, BUT THEN WHAT?
THAT'S THE MOST BEAUTIFUL THING WE FORGOT. THE WONDER OF TOMORROW.
GOOD NIGHT, AYDEN.
GOOD NIGHT.
click

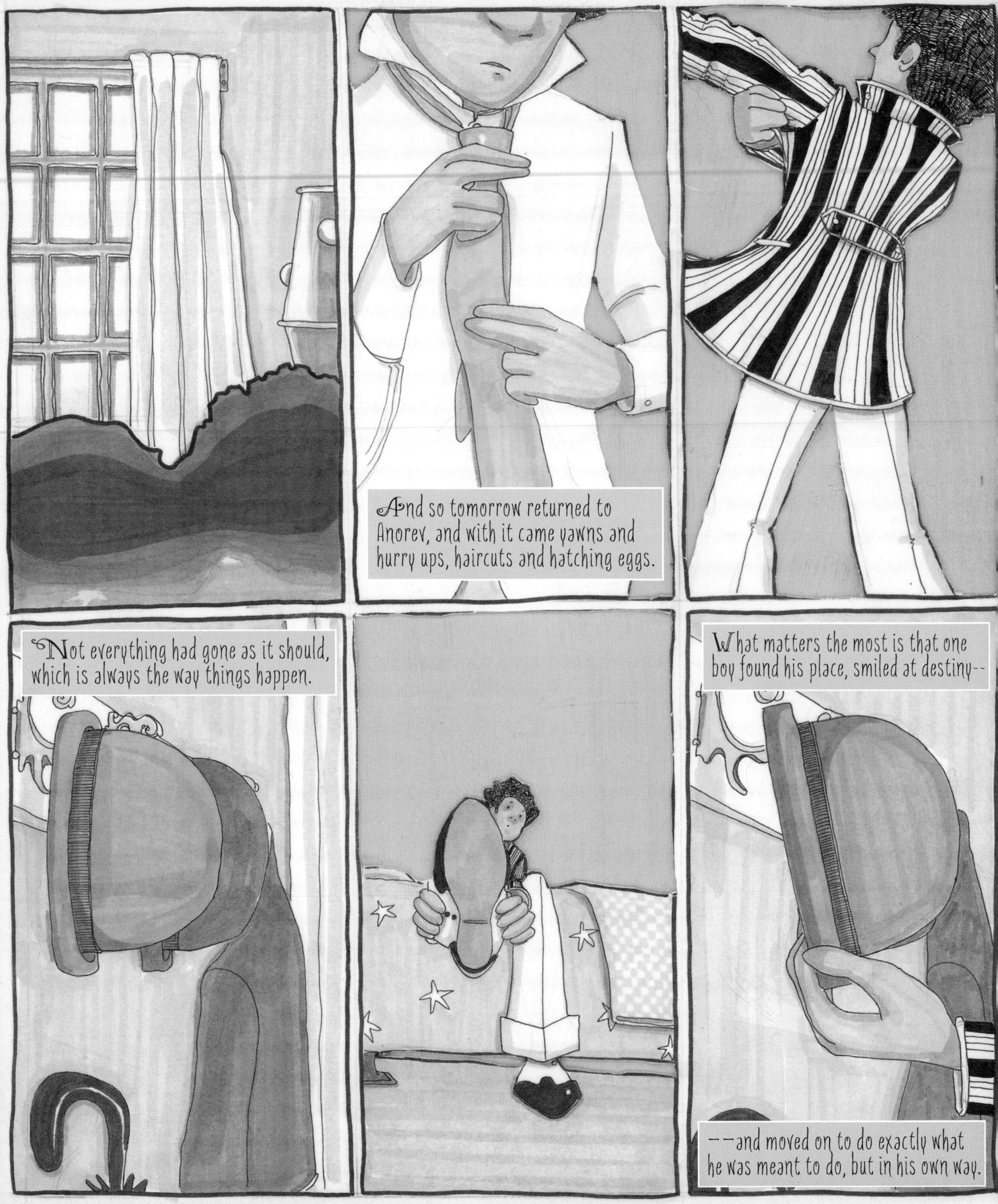
And so tomorrow returned to Anorev, and with it came yawns and hurry ups, haircuts and hatching eggs.
Not everything had gone as it should, which is always the way things happen.
What matters the most is that one boy found his place, smiled at destiny--
--and moved on to do exactly what he was meant to do, but in his own way.

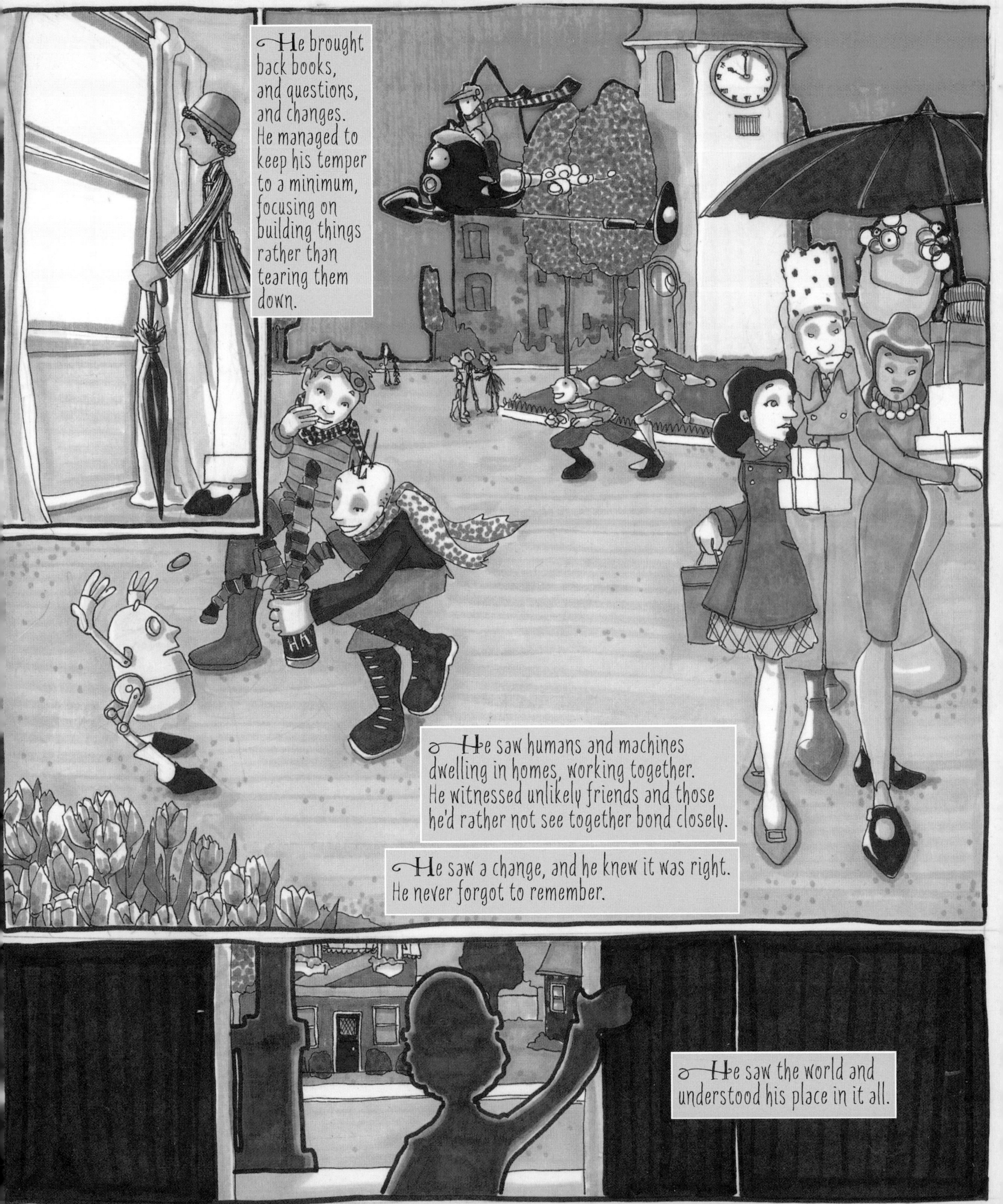
He brought back books, and questions, and changes. He managed to keep his temper to a minimum, focusing on building things rather than tearing them down.
HA
He saw humans and machines dwelling in homes, working together. He witnessed unlikely friends and those he'd rather not see together bond closely.
He saw a change, and he knew it was right. He never forgot to remember.
He saw the world and understood his place in it all.

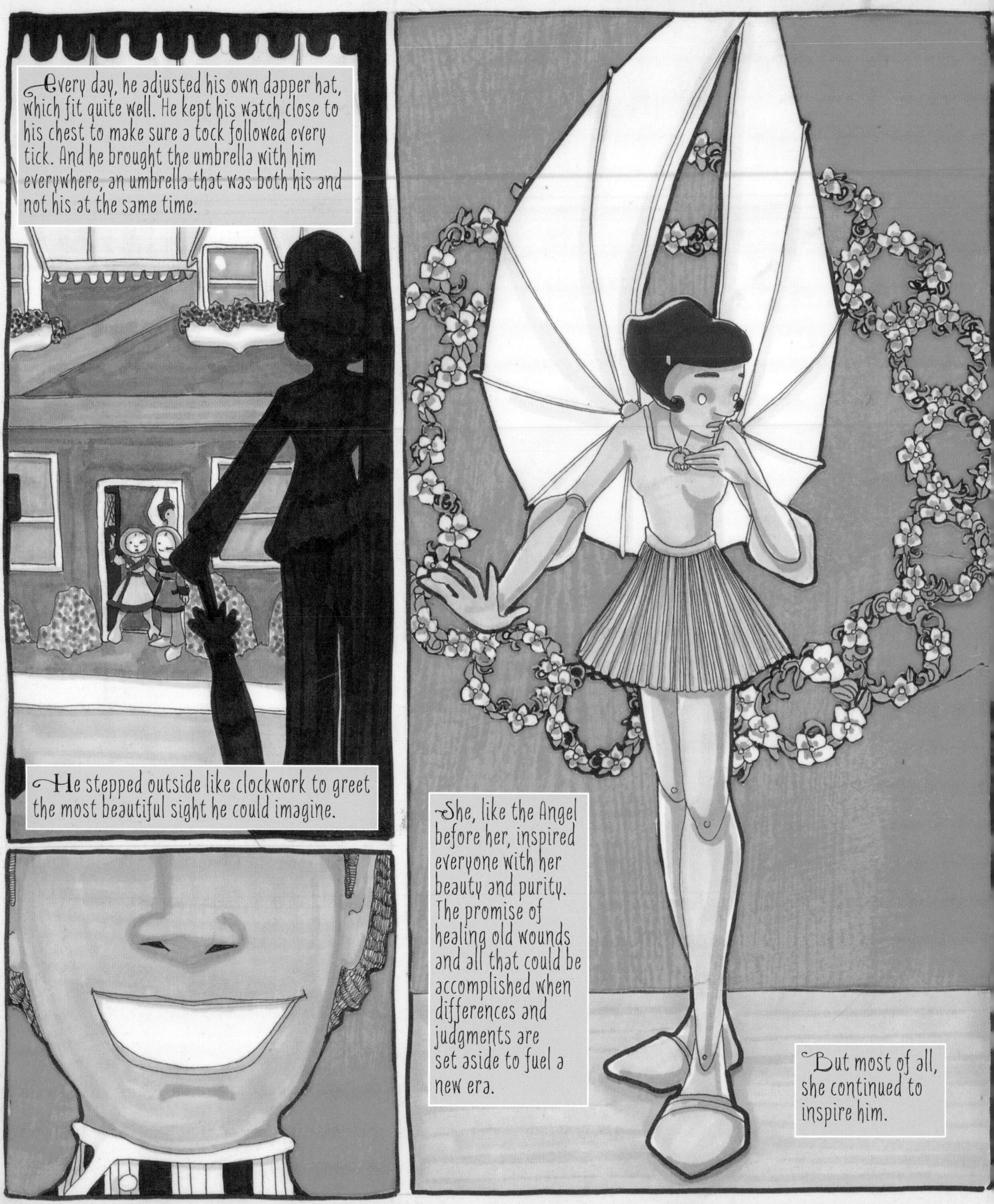
Every day, he adjusted his own dapper hat, which fit quite well. He kept his watch close to his chest to make sure a tock followed every tick. And he brought the umbrella with him everywhere, an umbrella that was both his and not his at the same time.
He stepped outside like clockwork to greet the most beautiful sight he could imagine.
She, like the Angel before her, inspired everyone with her beauty and purity. The promise of healing old wounds and all that could be accomplished when differences and judgments are set aside to fuel a new era.
But most of all, she continued to inspire him.

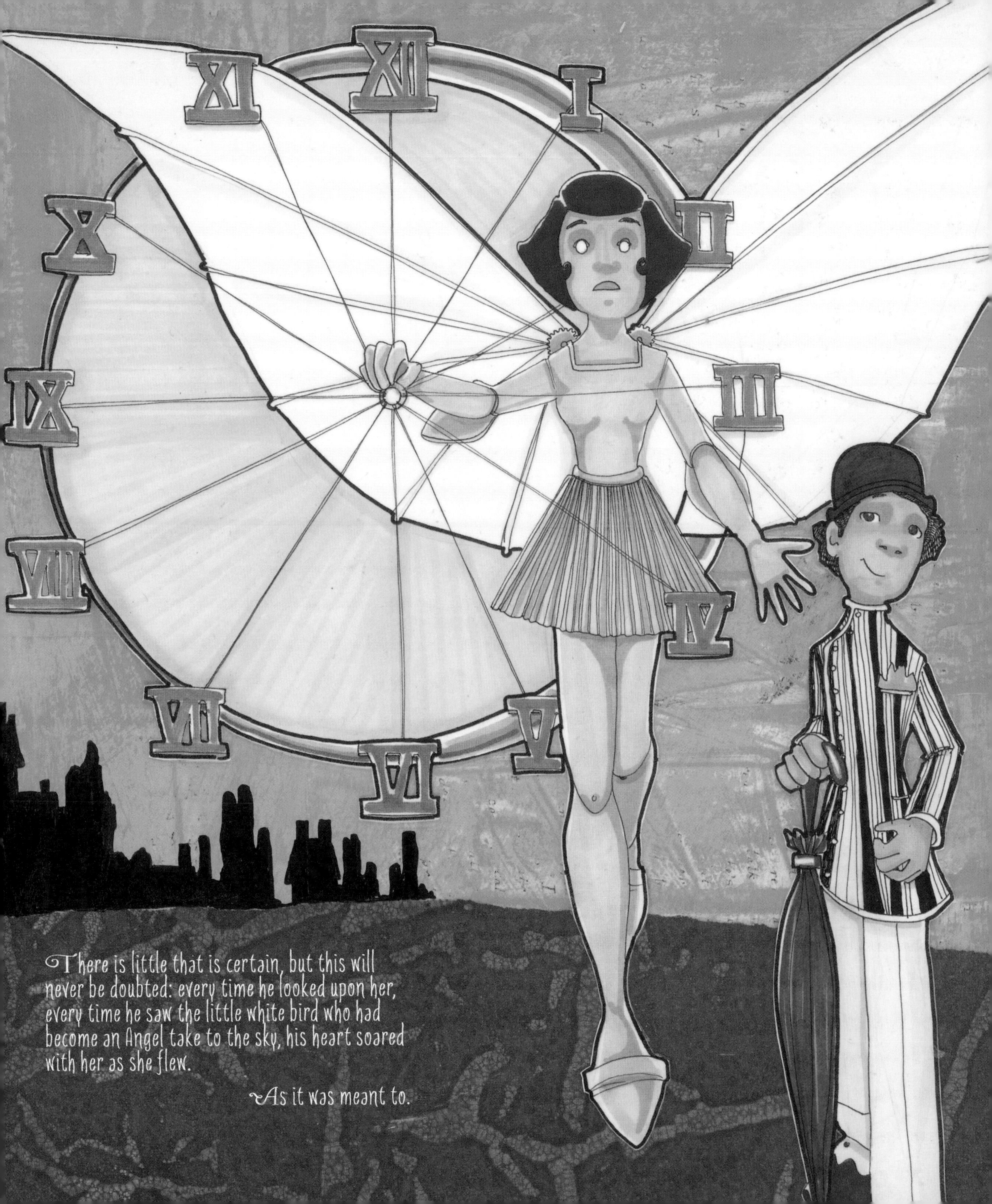

There is little that is certain, but this will never be doubted: every time he looked upon her, every time he saw the little white bird who had become an Angel take to the sky, his heart soared with her as she flew.

As it was meant to.

And there was, as it happened, always time for a nice cup of warm tea.

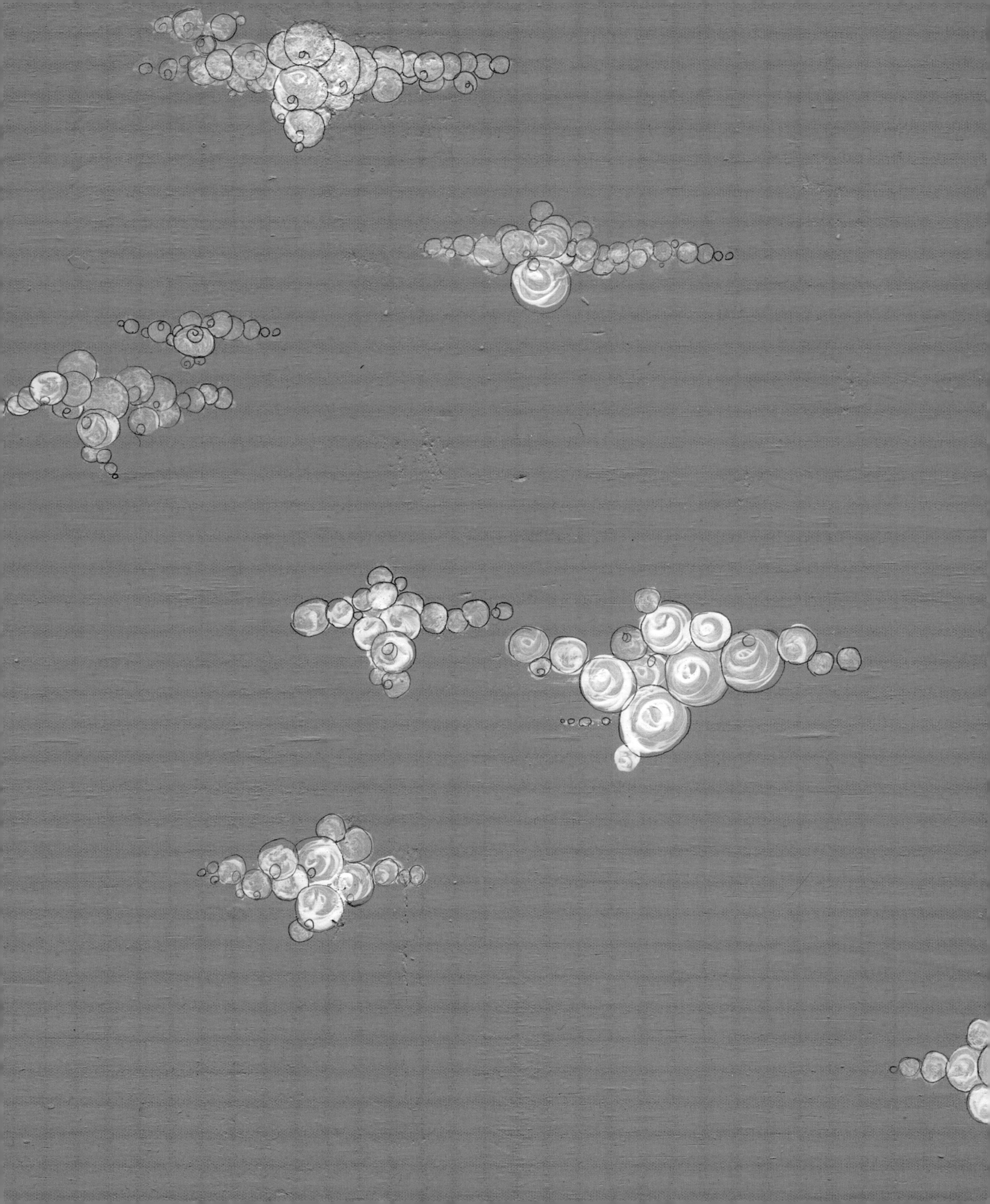

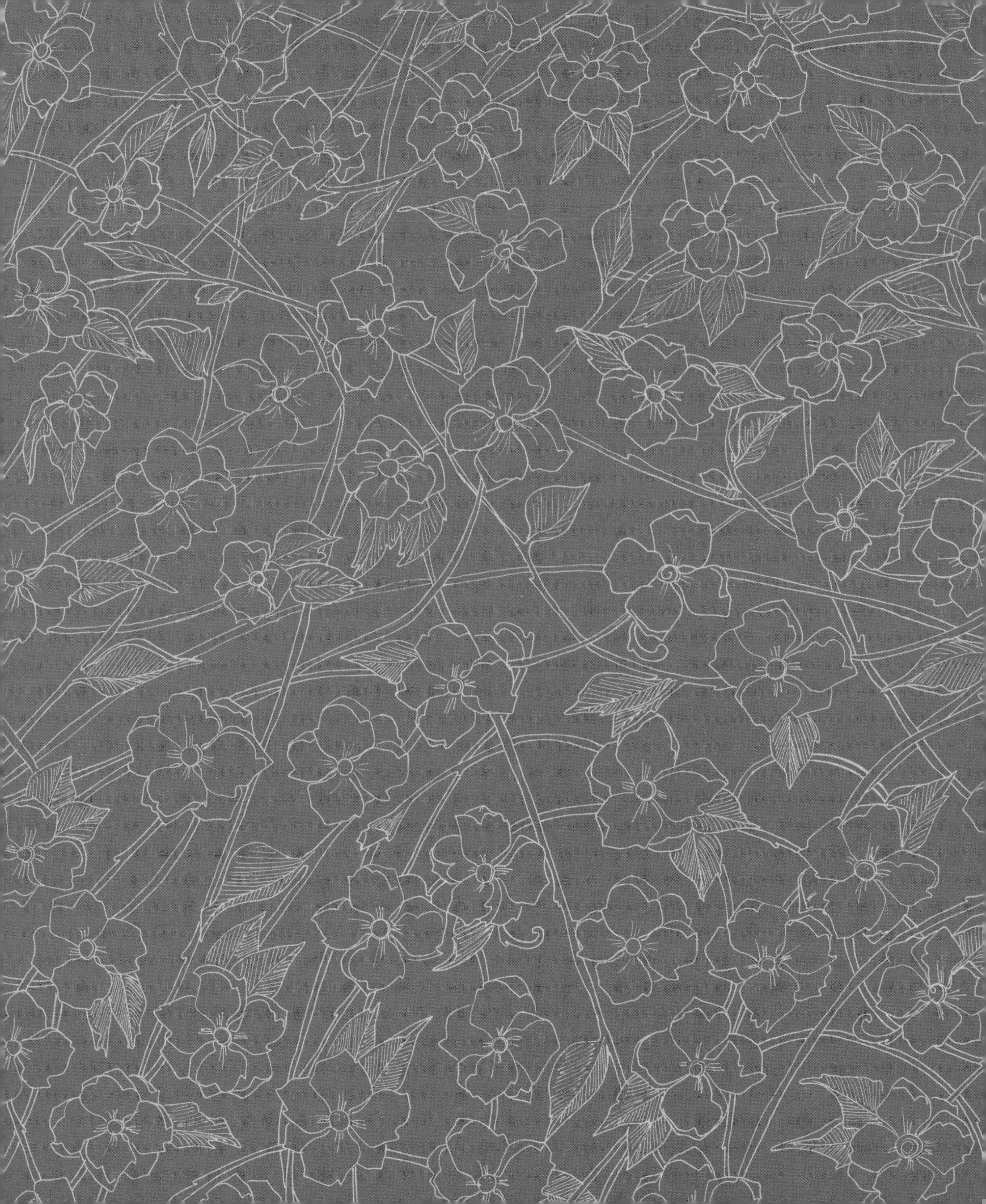

A GALLERY OF ART BY OUR ESTEEMED COLLEAGUES & FRIENDS

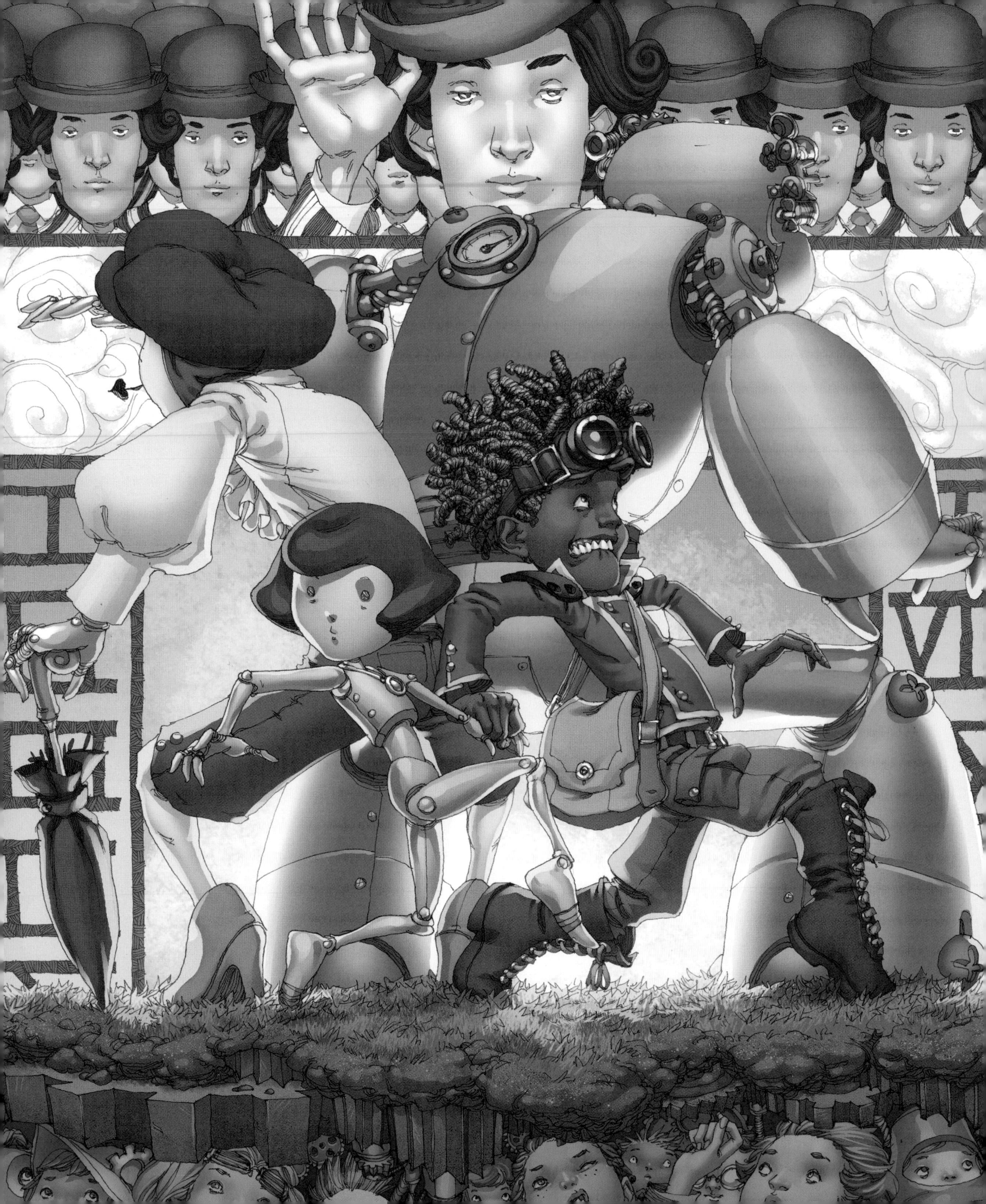

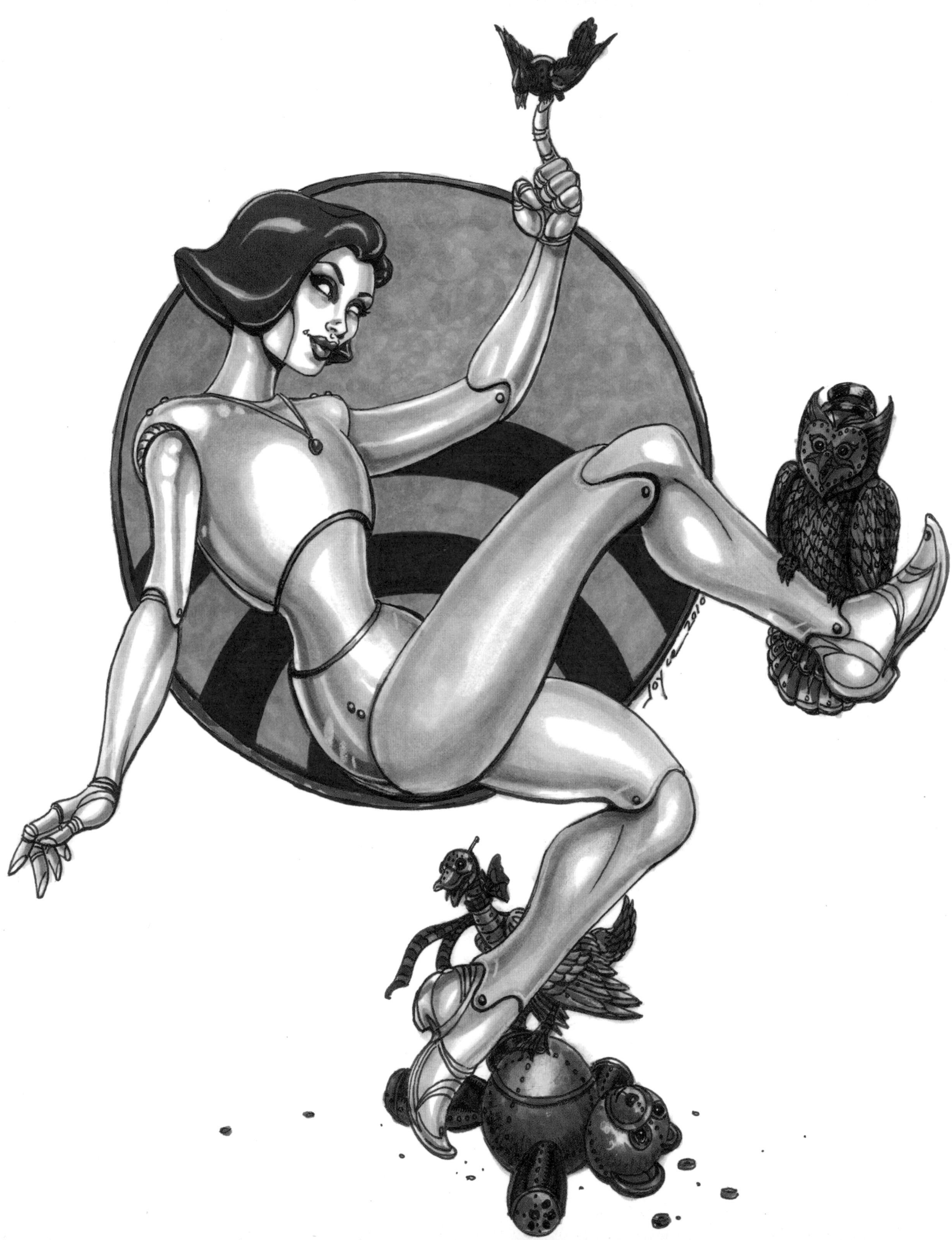

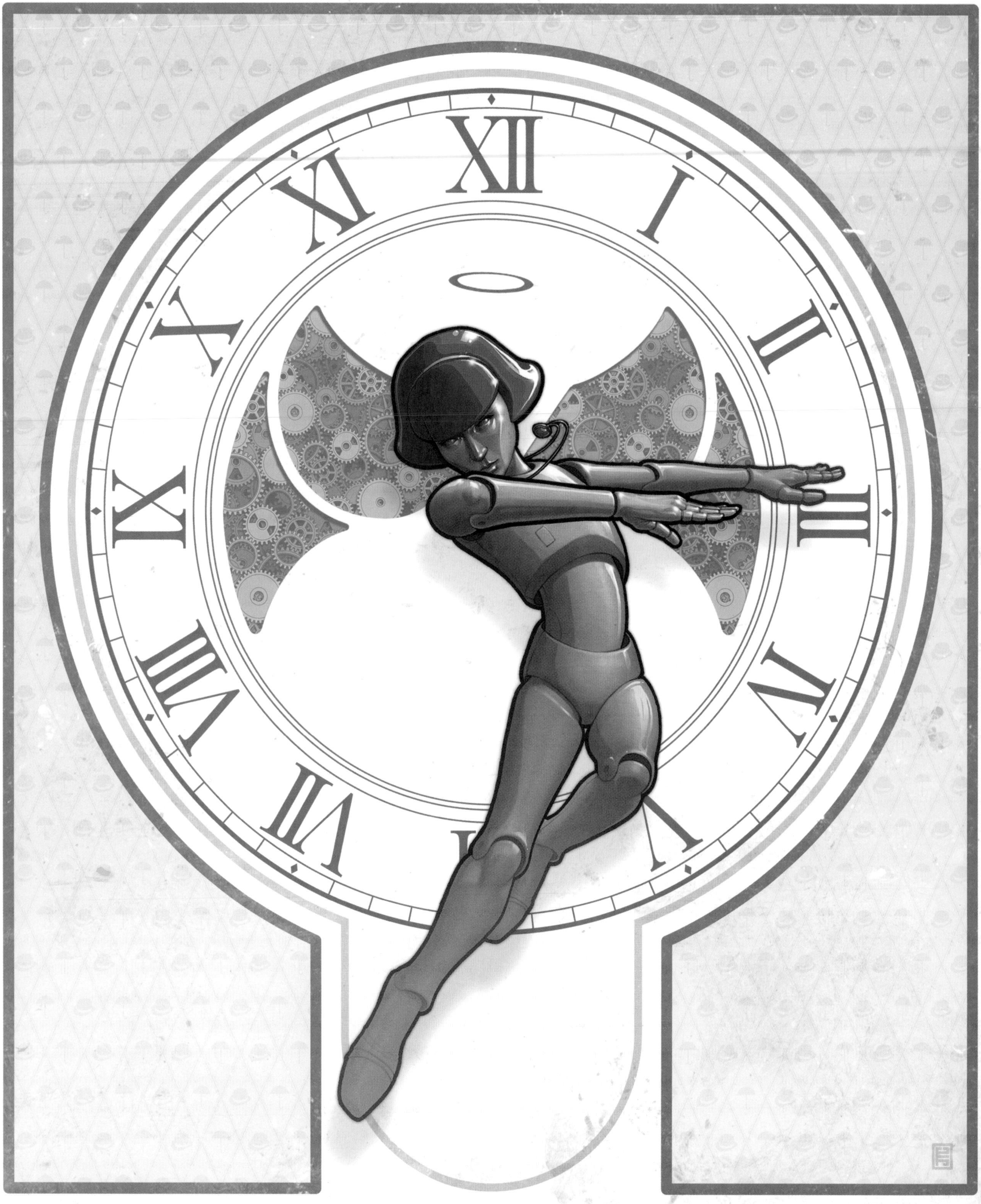

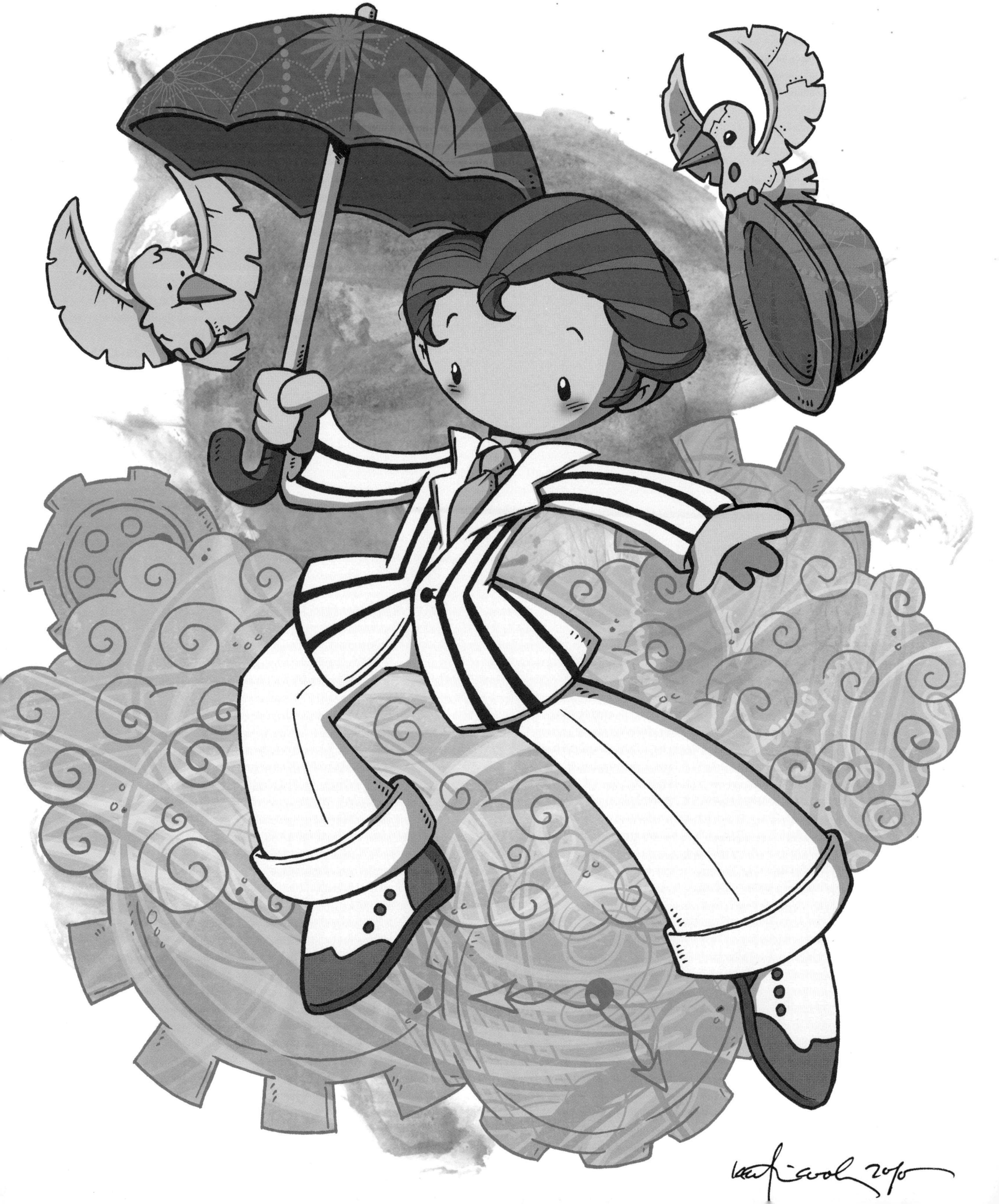

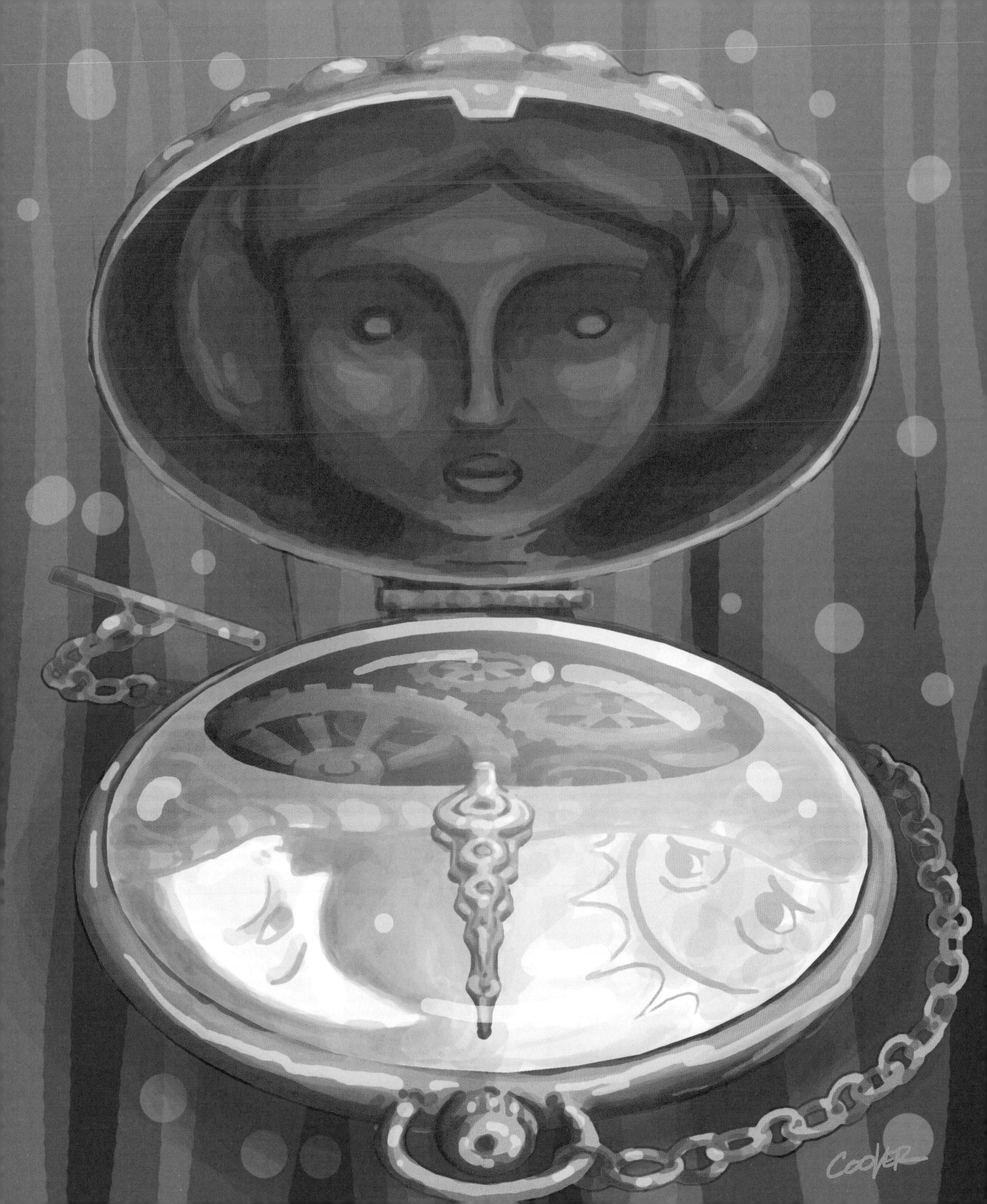
COOVER

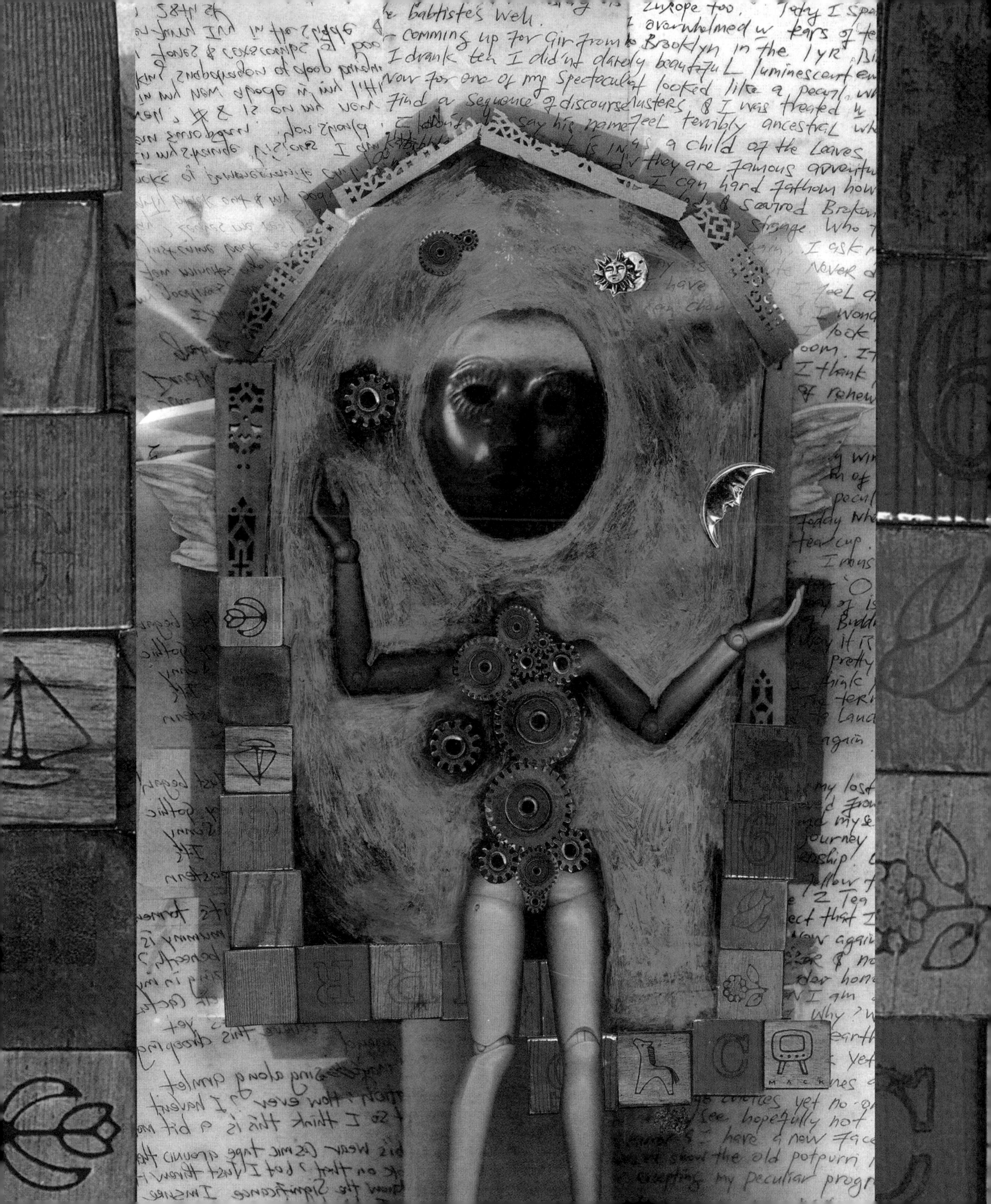

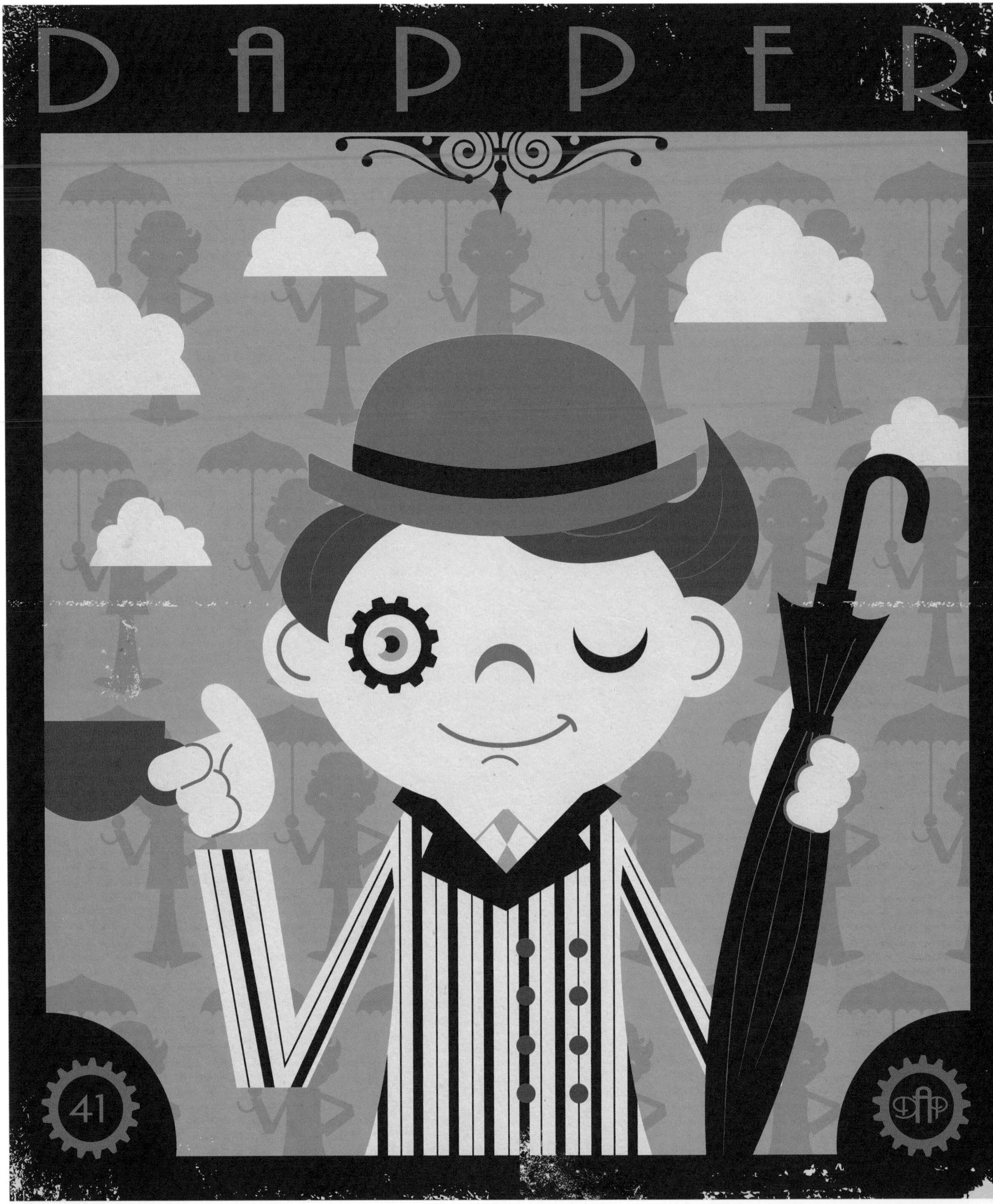
DAPPER
41

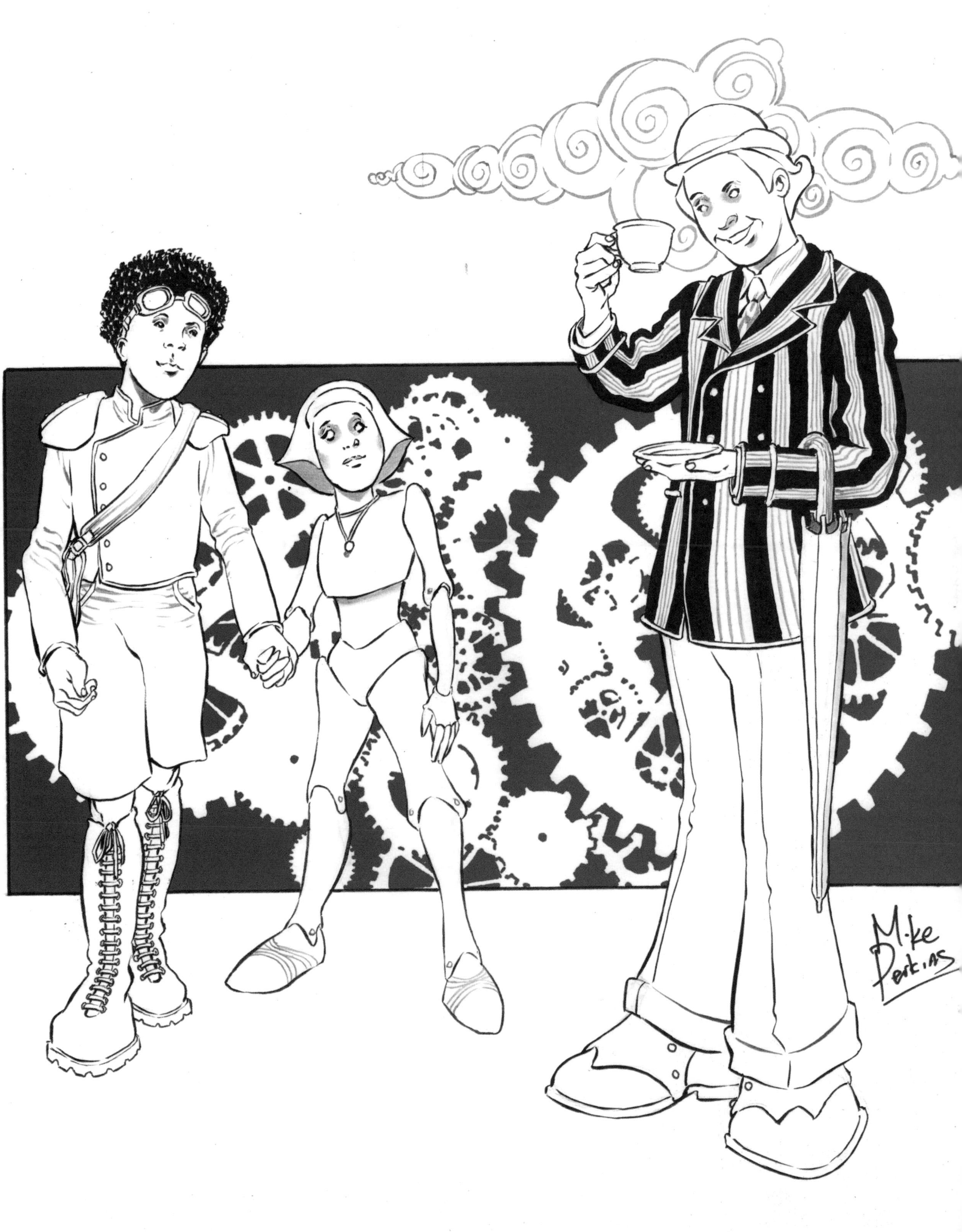
Mike Perkins

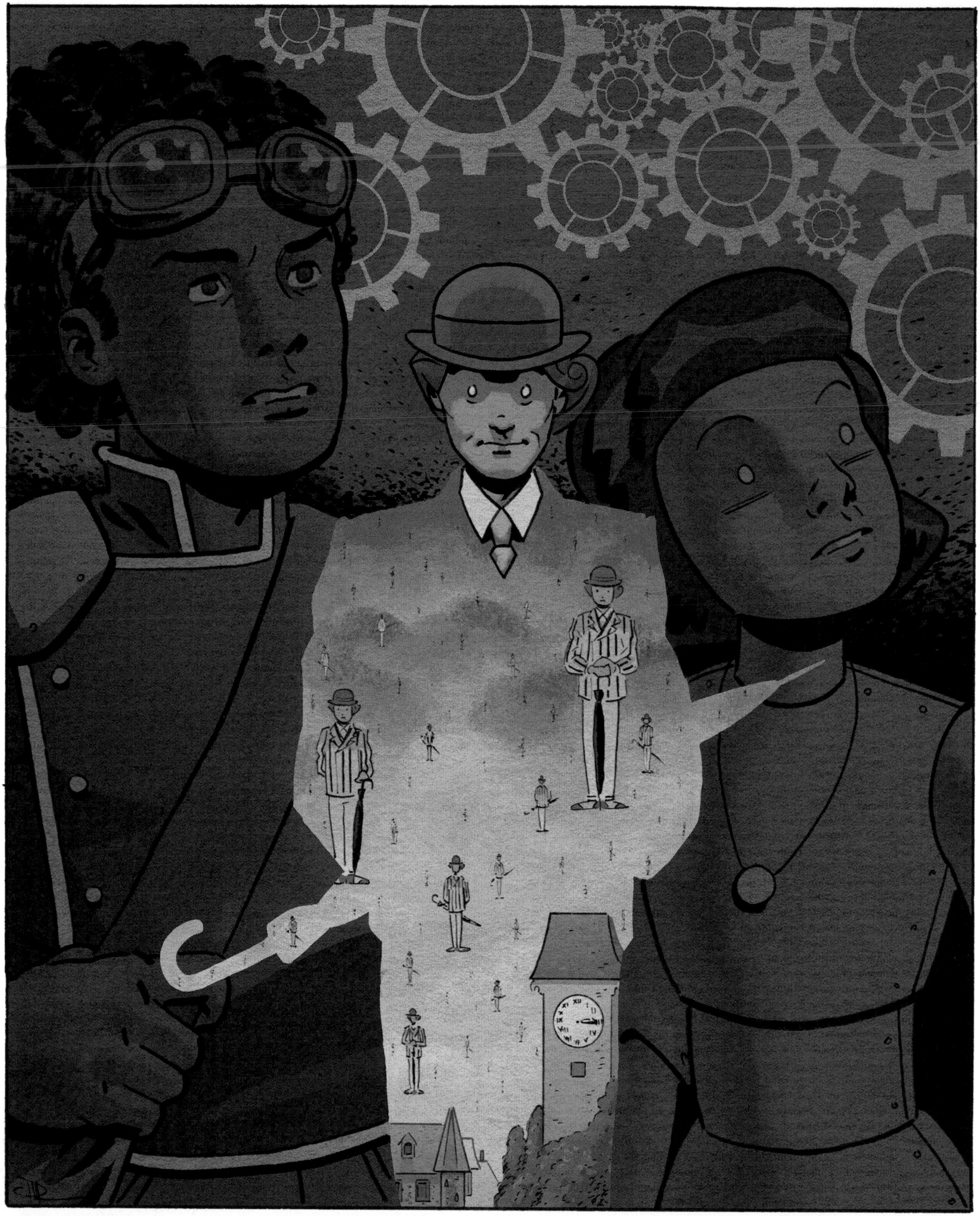

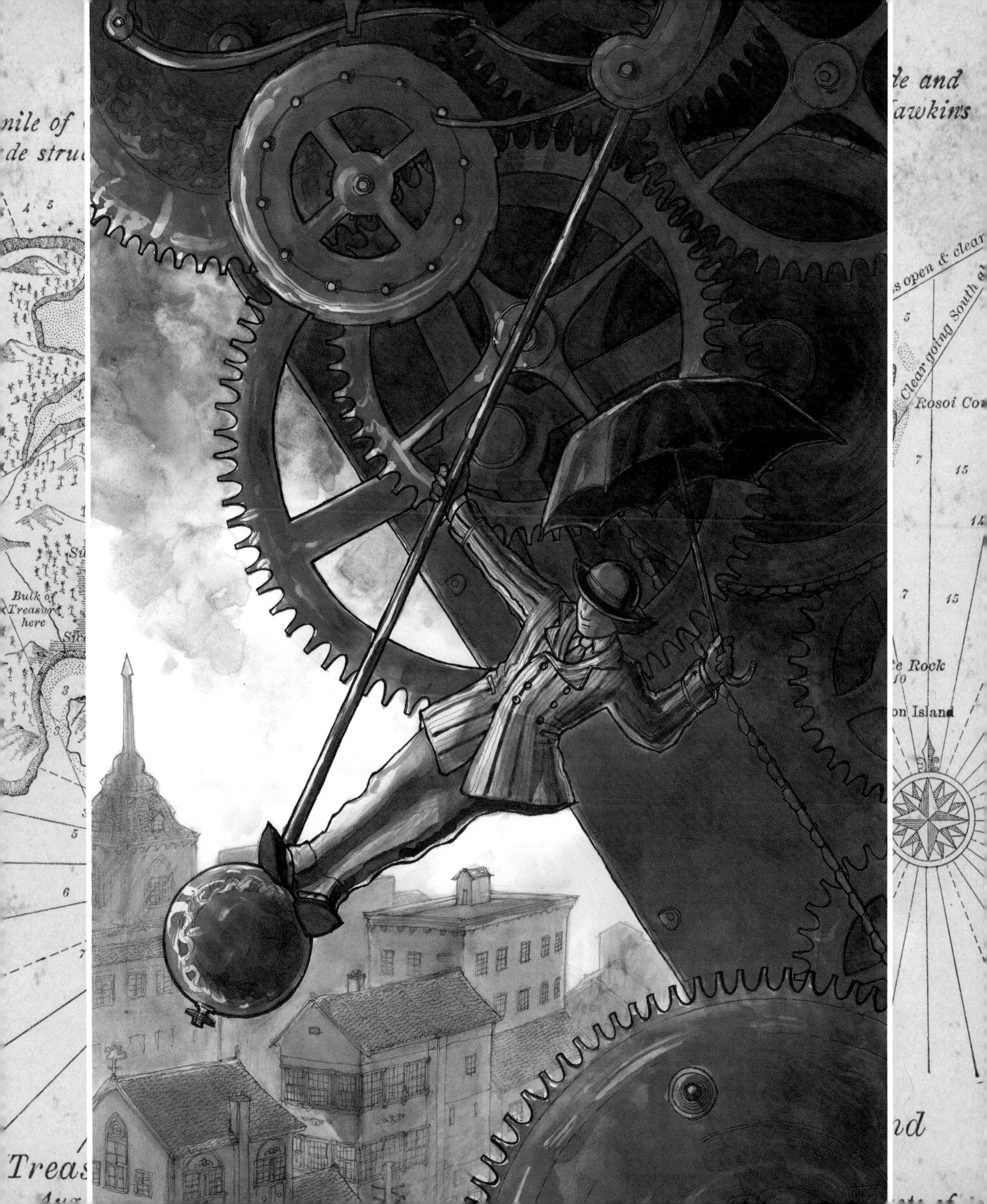

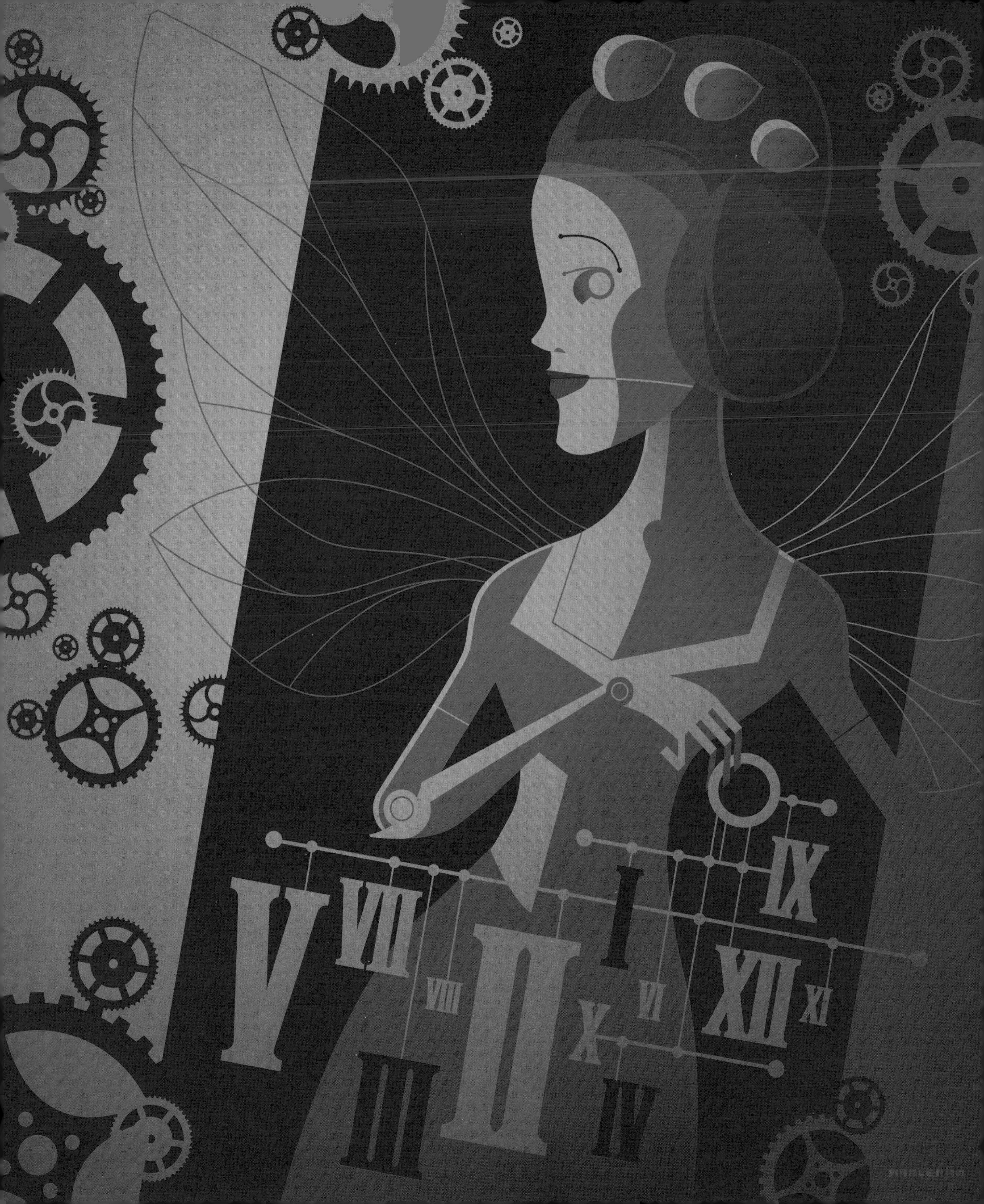
V
VII
VIII
II
III
I
X
IV
VI
IX
XII
XI

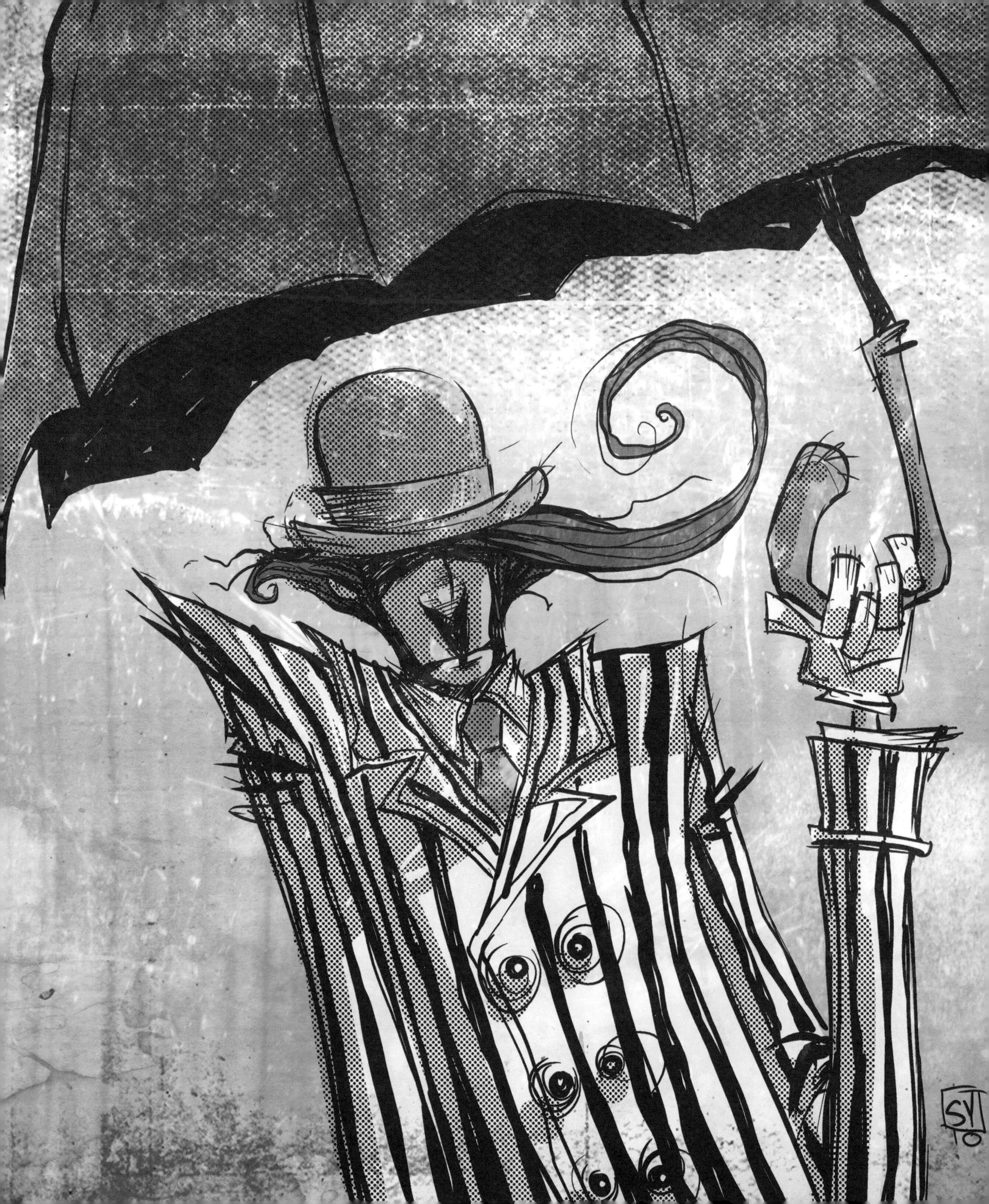

FREE COMIC BOOK DAY EXCLUSIVES

SEASON OF THE DAPPER MEN

STEPS OF THE DAPPER MEN

A NOTE FROM THE AUTHOR

The next volume in the *Dapper Men* trilogy will be *Time of the Dapper Men*. Before you jump into that, however, there are two stories that bridge the gap between this volume and the next—*Season of the Dapper Men* and *Steps of the Dapper Men*. Both stories were only available in Archaia's Free Comic Book Day offerings in 2011 and 2012, respectively. Now they are presented here for you to enjoy. See Ayden's farewell to Zoe as he starts his journey around the world. Then meet Aurora in a story that tells you what she was going through during *Return of the Dapper Men* and hints at a deeper connection she has with Ayden.

Enjoy these tales, and get ready for what comes next: the story is far from over...

—JIM McCANN

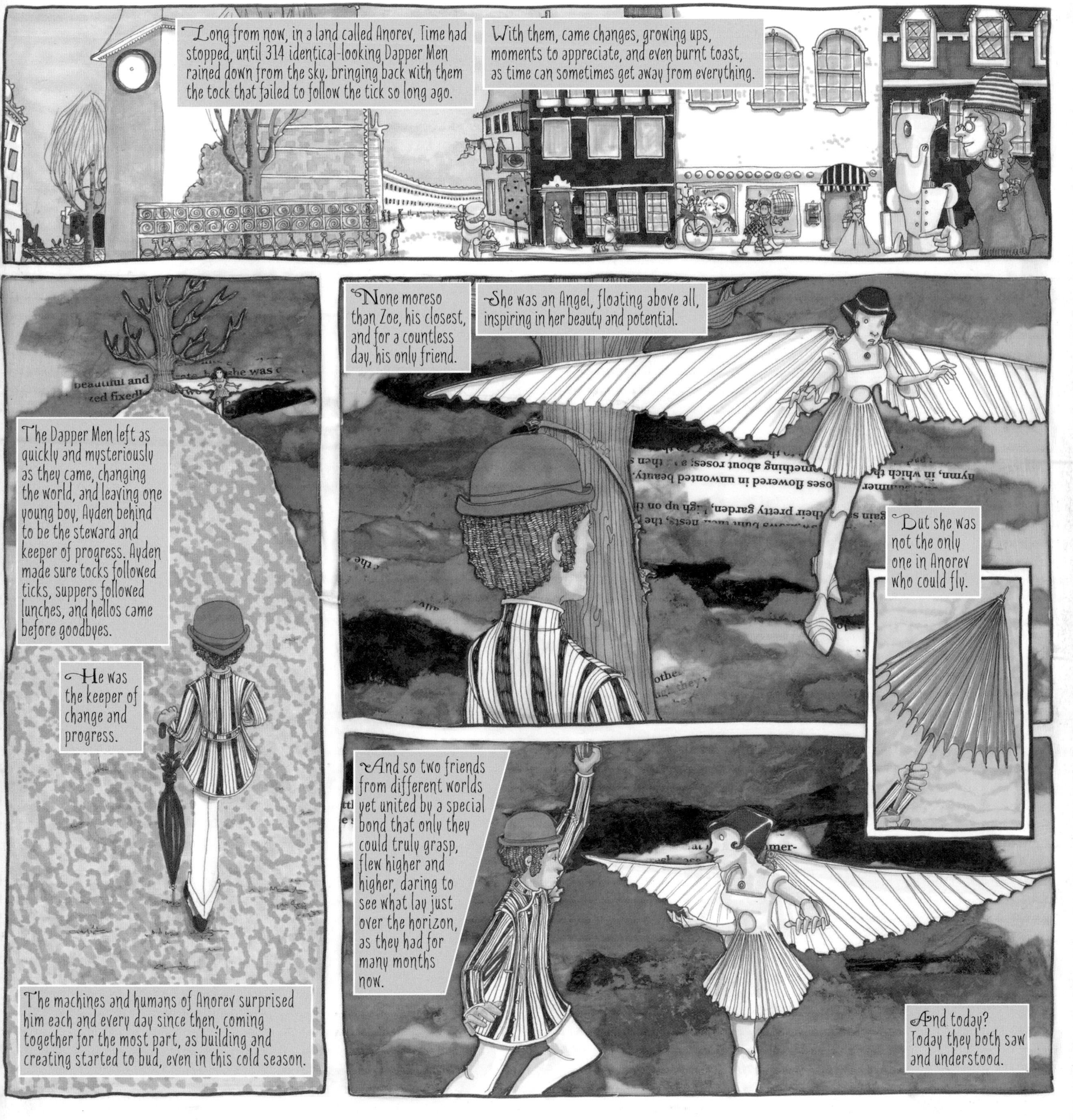
Long from now, in a land called Anorev, Time had stopped, until 314 identical-looking Dapper Men rained down from the sky, bringing back with them the tock that failed to follow the tick so long ago.
With them, came changes, growing ups, moments to appreciate, and even burnt toast, as time can sometimes get away from everything.
The Dapper Men left as quickly and mysteriously as they came, changing the world, and leaving one young boy, Ayden behind to be the steward and keeper of progress. Ayden made sure tocks followed ticks, suppers followed lunches, and hellos came before goodbyes.
He was the keeper of change and progress.
The machines and humans of Anorev surprised him each and every day since then, coming together for the most part, as building and creating started to bud, even in this cold season.
None moreso than Zoe, his closest, and for a countless day, his only friend.
She was an Angel, floating above all, inspiring in her beauty and potential.
But she was not the only one in Anorev who could fly.
And so two friends from different worlds yet united by a special bond that only they could truly grasp, flew higher and higher, daring to see what lay just over the horizon, as they had for many months now.
And today? Today they both saw and understood.

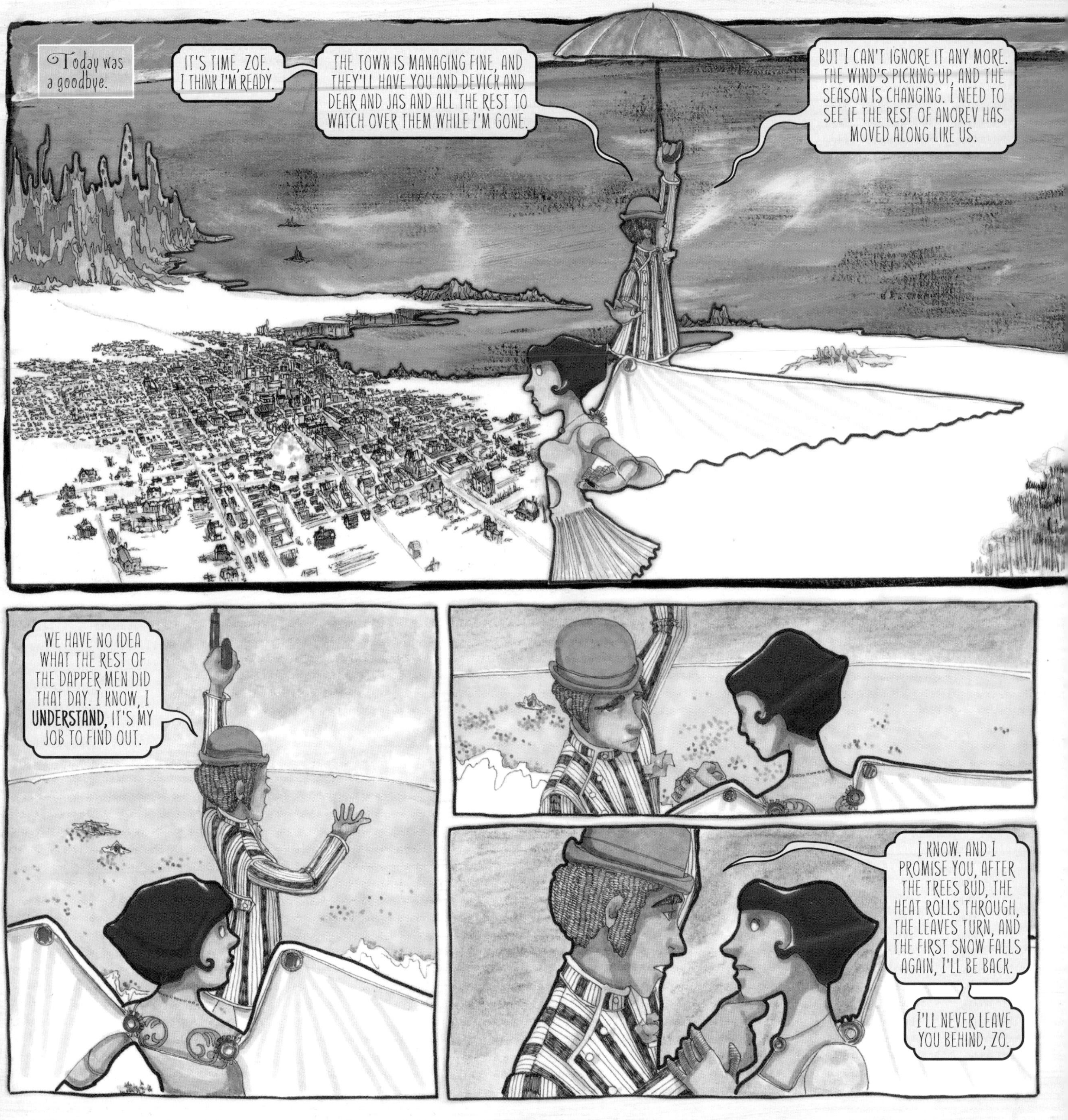
Today was a goodbye.
IT'S TIME, ZOE. I THINK I'M READY.
THE TOWN IS MANAGING FINE, AND THEY'LL HAVE YOU AND DEVICK AND DEAR AND JAS AND ALL THE REST TO WATCH OVER THEM WHILE I'M GONE.
BUT I CAN'T IGNORE IT ANY MORE. THE WIND'S PICKING UP, AND THE SEASON IS CHANGING. I NEED TO SEE IF THE REST OF ANOREV HAS MOVED ALONG LIKE US.
WE HAVE NO IDEA WHAT THE REST OF THE DAPPER MEN DID THAT DAY. I KNOW, I **UNDERSTAND,** IT'S MY JOB TO FIND OUT.
I KNOW. AND I PROMISE YOU, AFTER THE TREES BUD, THE HEAT ROLLS THROUGH, THE LEAVES TURN, AND THE FIRST SNOW FALLS AGAIN, I'LL BE BACK.
I'LL NEVER LEAVE YOU BEHIND, ZO.

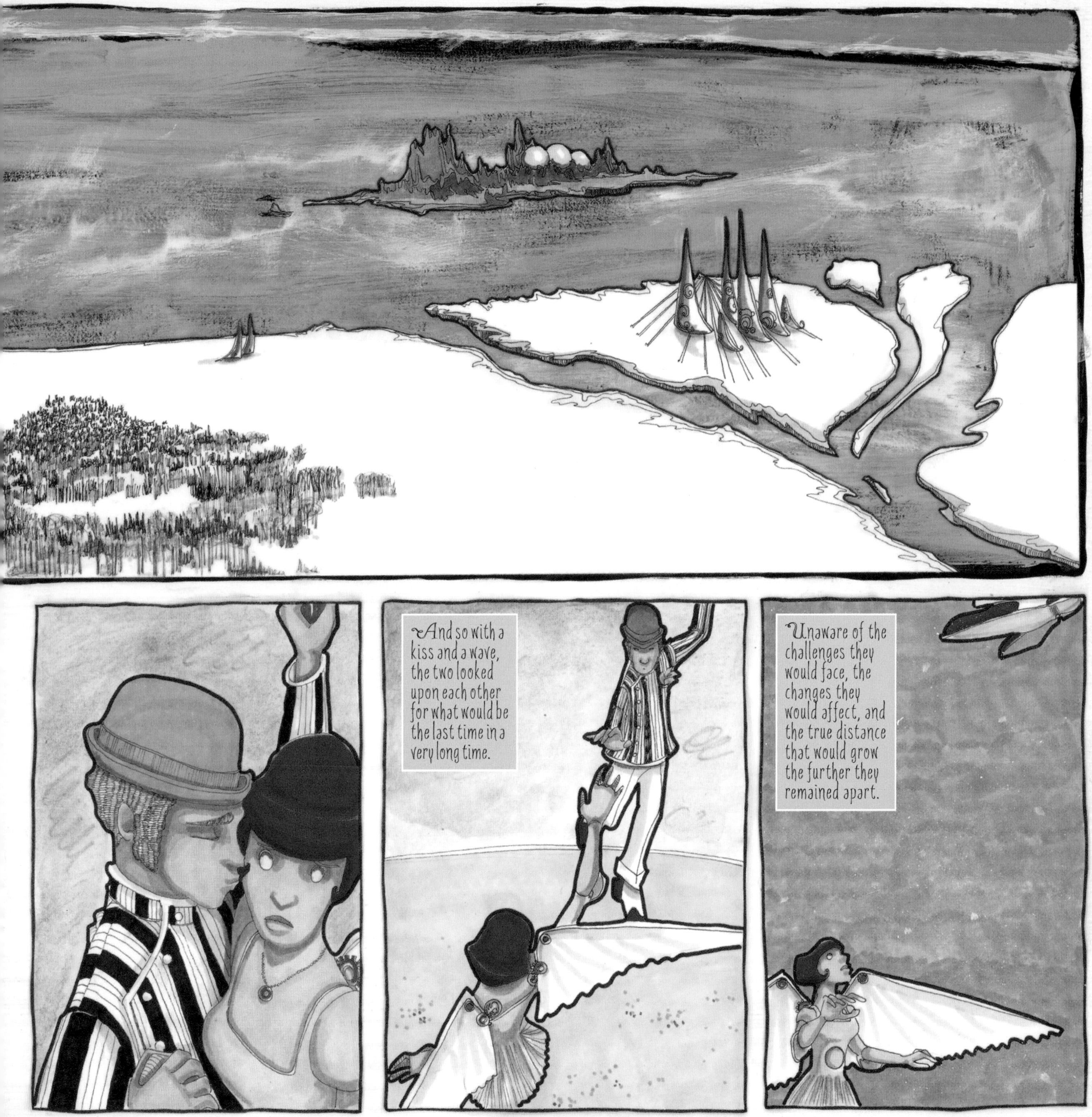
And so with a kiss and a wave, the two looked upon each other for what would be the last time in a very long time.
Unaware of the challenges they would face, the changes they would affect, and the true distance that would grow the further they remained apart.

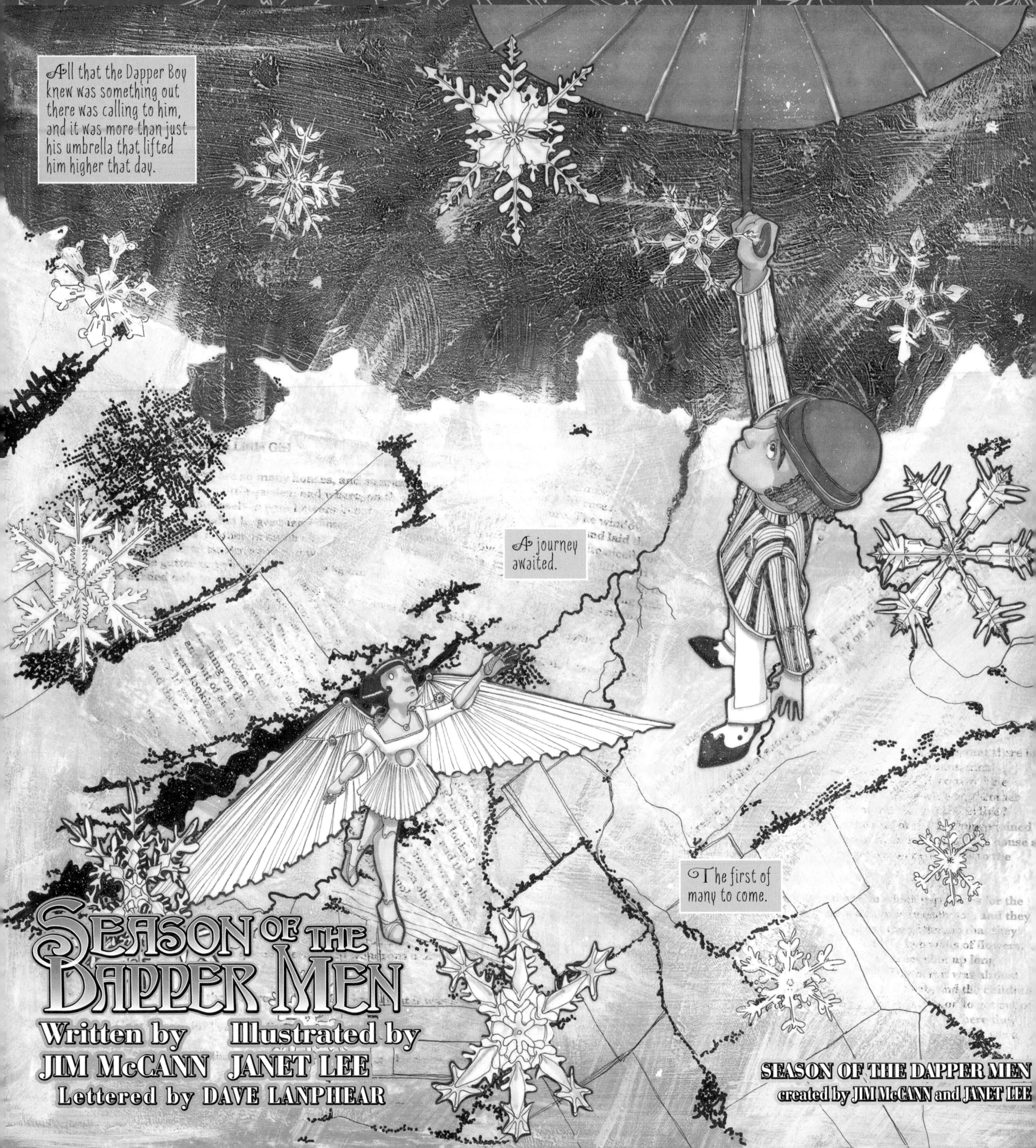
All that the Dapper Boy knew was something out there was calling to him, and it was more than just his umbrella that lifted him higher that day.
A journey awaited.
The first of many to come.
SEASON OF THE DAPPER MEN
Written by JIM McCANN
Illustrated by JANET LEE
Lettered by DAVE LANPHEAR
SEASON OF THE DAPPER MEN created by JIM McCANN and JANET LEE

STEPS OF THE DAPPER MEN

Written by
JIM McCANN

Illustrated by
JANET K. LEE

Lettered by DAVE LANPHEAR

DAPPER MEN
created by JIM McCANN and JANET K. LEE

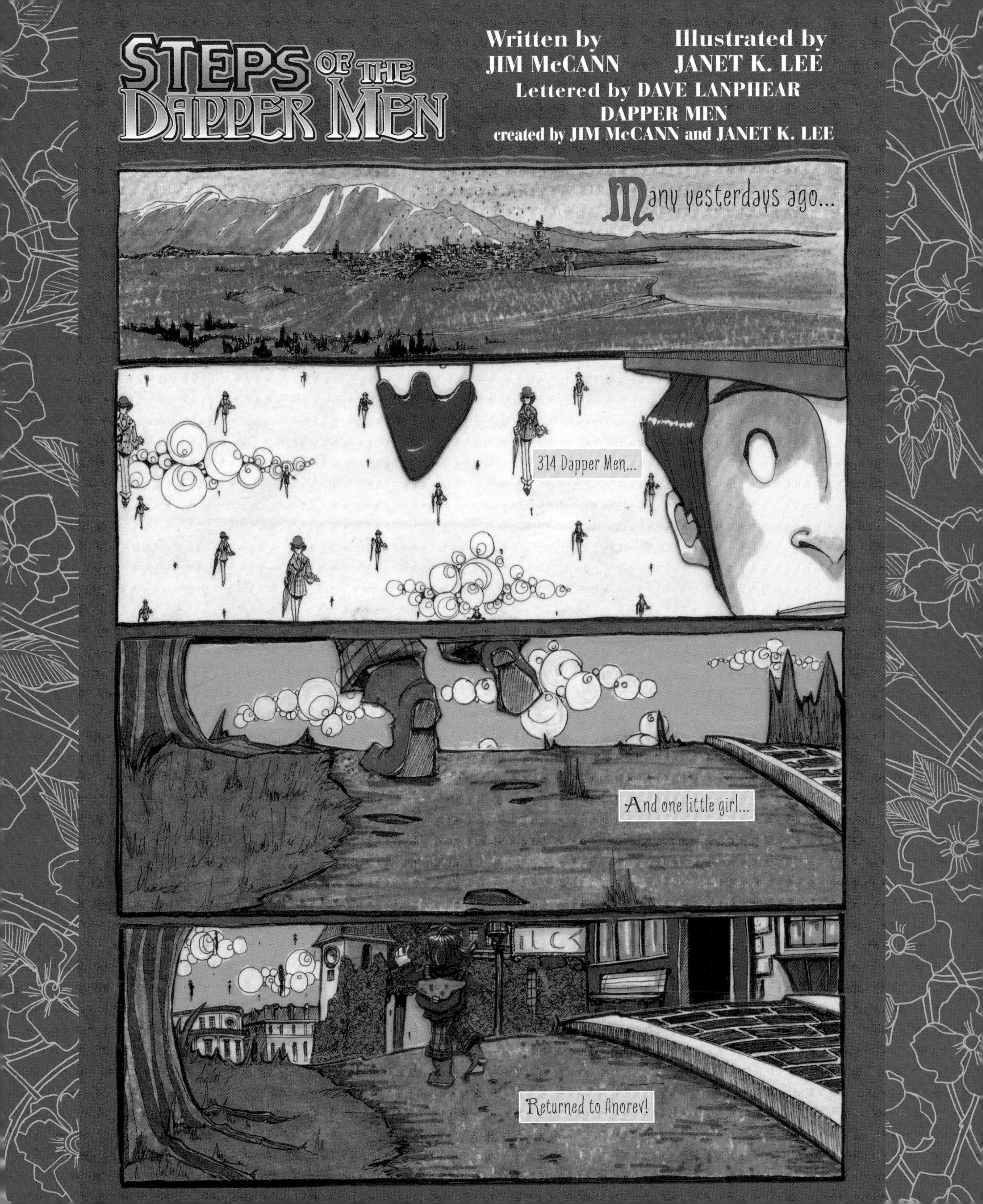

Many yesterdays ago...
314 Dapper Men...
And one little girl...
Returned to Anorev!

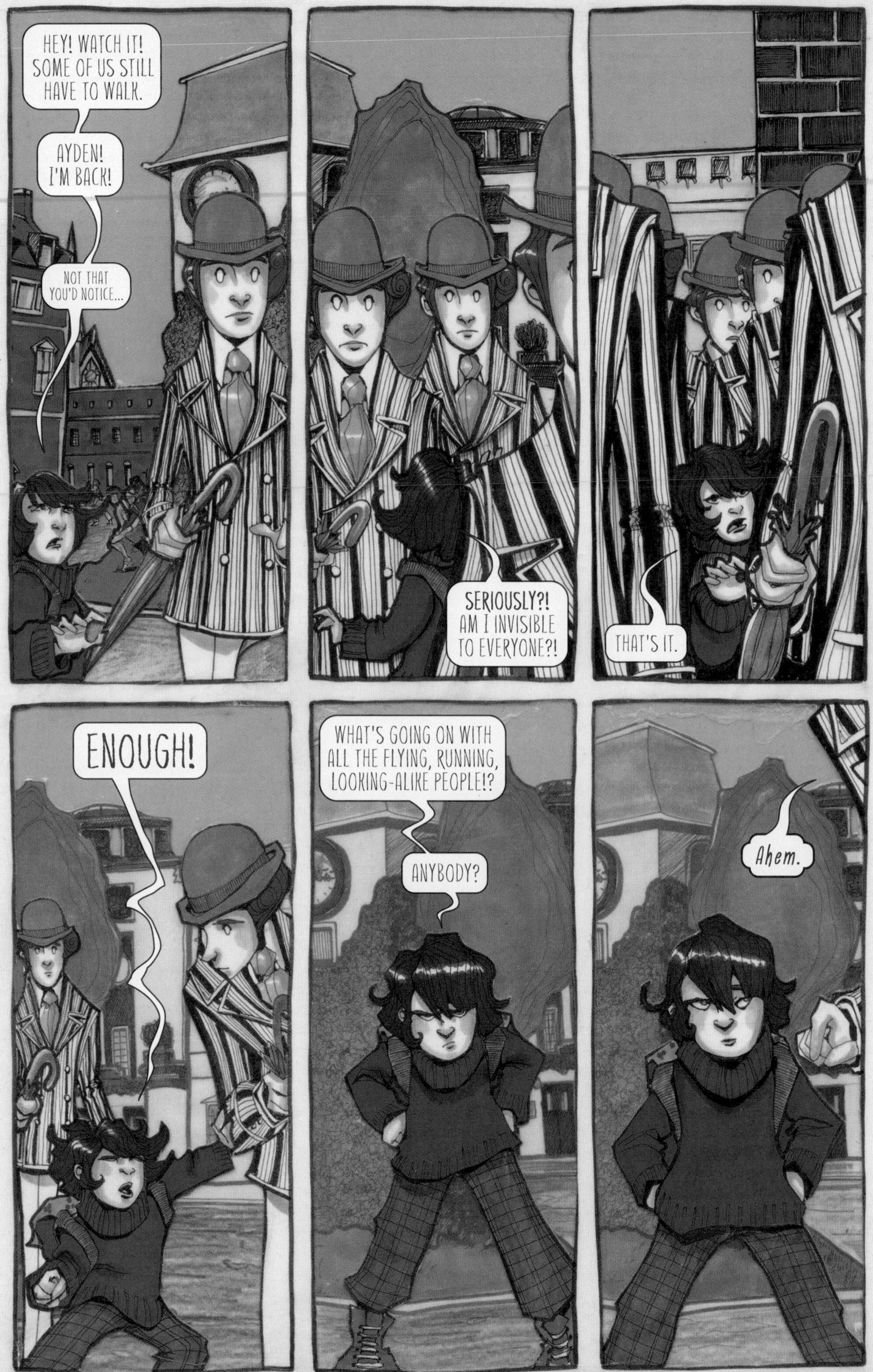
HEY! WATCH IT! SOME OF US STILL HAVE TO WALK.
AYDEN! I'M BACK!
NOT THAT YOU'D NOTICE...
SERIOUSLY?! AM I INVISIBLE TO EVERYONE?!
THAT'S IT.
ENOUGH!
WHAT'S GOING ON WITH ALL THE FLYING, RUNNING, LOOKING-ALIKE PEOPLE!?
ANYBODY?
Ahem.

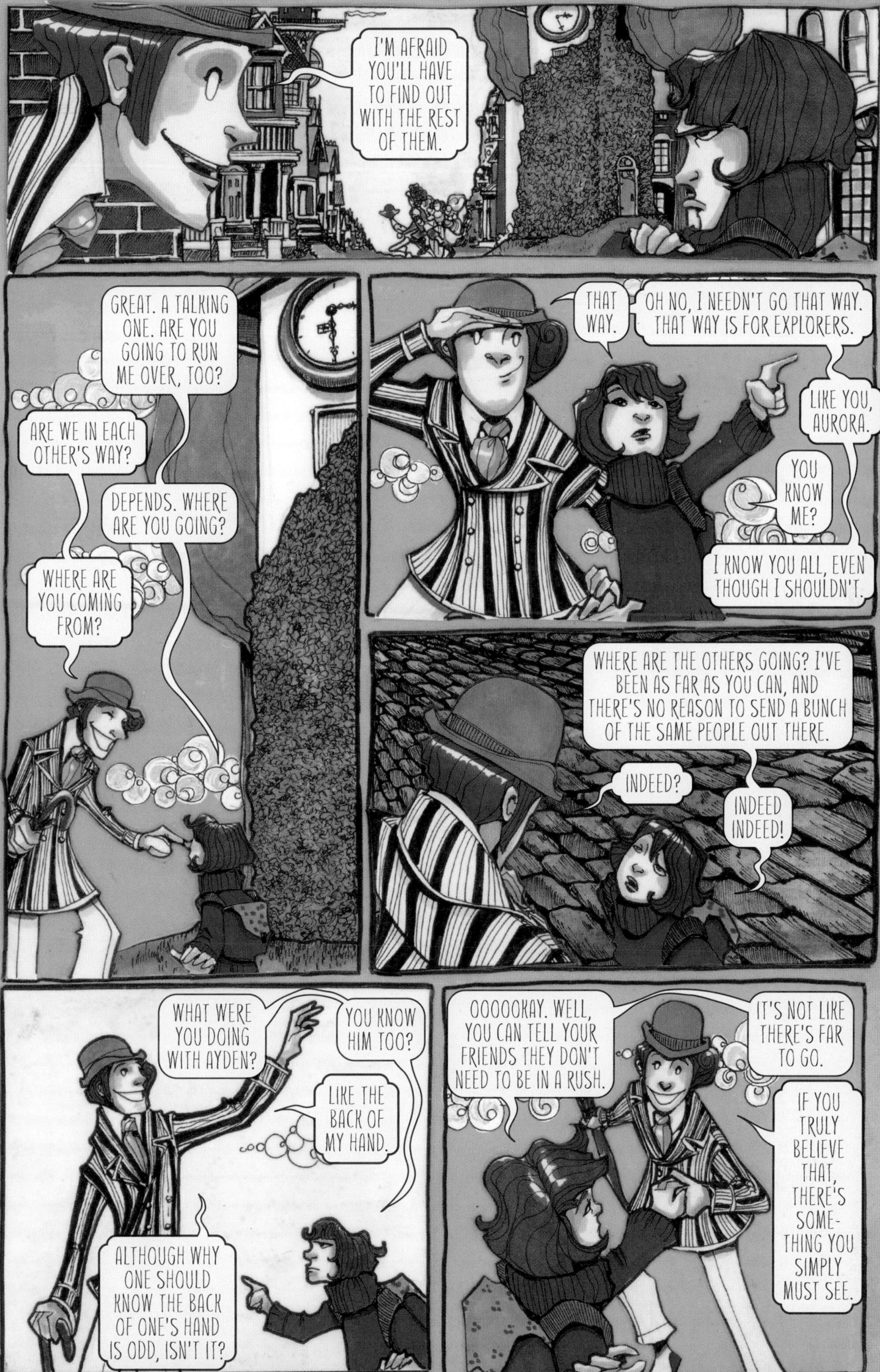
I'M AFRAID YOU'LL HAVE TO FIND OUT WITH THE REST OF THEM.
GREAT. A TALKING ONE. ARE YOU GOING TO RUN ME OVER, TOO?
ARE WE IN EACH OTHER'S WAY?
DEPENDS. WHERE ARE YOU GOING?
WHERE ARE YOU COMING FROM?
THAT WAY.
OH NO, I NEEDN'T GO THAT WAY. THAT WAY IS FOR EXPLORERS.
LIKE YOU, AURORA.
YOU KNOW ME?
I KNOW YOU ALL, EVEN THOUGH I SHOULDN'T.
WHERE ARE THE OTHERS GOING? I'VE BEEN AS FAR AS YOU CAN, AND THERE'S NO REASON TO SEND A BUNCH OF THE SAME PEOPLE OUT THERE.
INDEED?
INDEED INDEED!
WHAT WERE YOU DOING WITH AYDEN?
YOU KNOW HIM TOO?
LIKE THE BACK OF MY HAND.
ALTHOUGH WHY ONE SHOULD KNOW THE BACK OF ONE'S HAND IS ODD, ISN'T IT?
OOOOOKAY. WELL, YOU CAN TELL YOUR FRIENDS THEY DON'T NEED TO BE IN A RUSH.
IT'S NOT LIKE THERE'S FAR TO GO.
IF YOU TRULY BELIEVE THAT, THERE'S SOME-THING YOU SIMPLY MUST SEE.

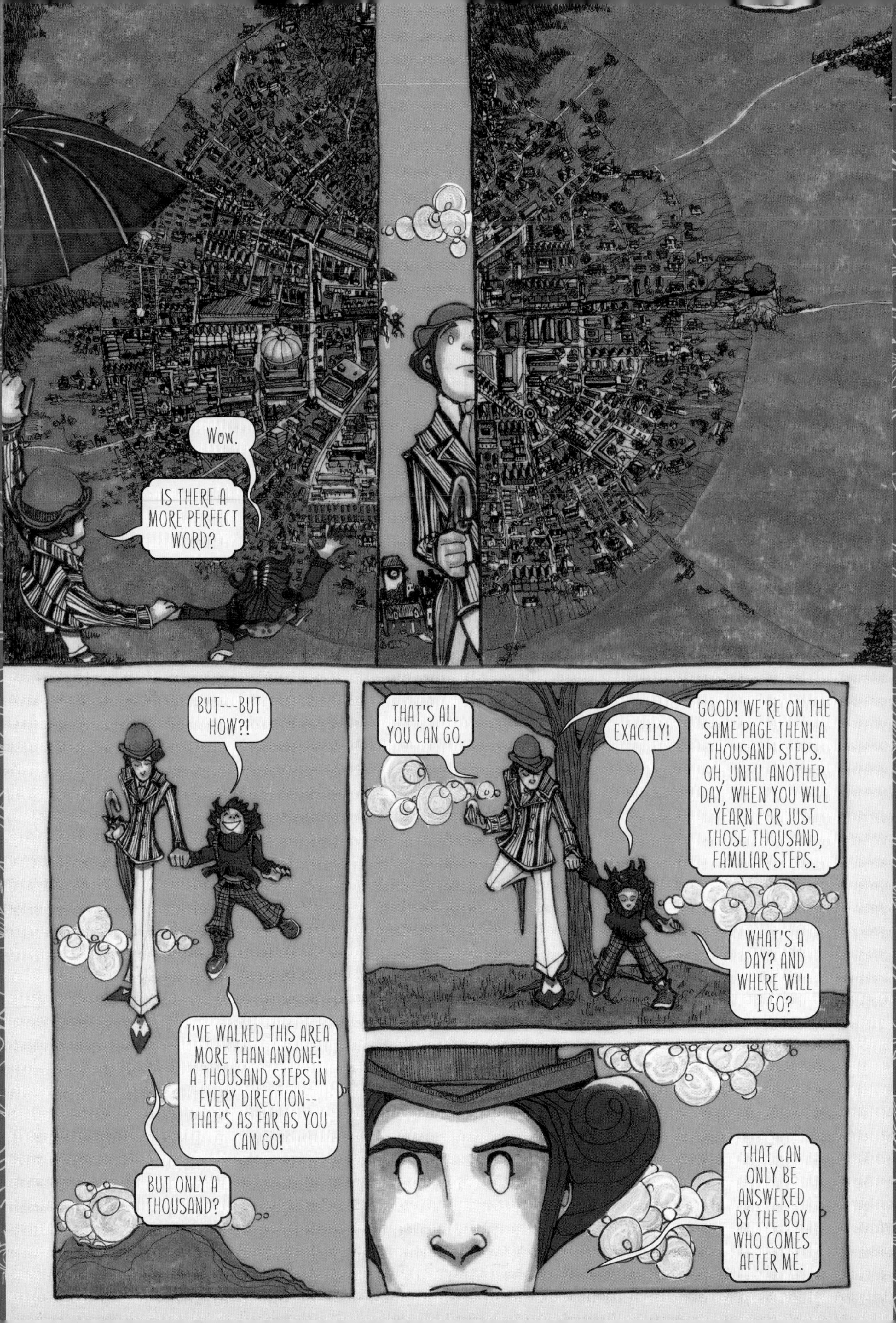
Wow.
IS THERE A MORE PERFECT WORD?
BUT---BUT HOW?!
I'VE WALKED THIS AREA MORE THAN ANYONE! A THOUSAND STEPS IN EVERY DIRECTION--THAT'S AS FAR AS YOU CAN GO!
BUT ONLY A THOUSAND?
THAT'S ALL YOU CAN GO.
EXACTLY!
GOOD! WE'RE ON THE SAME PAGE THEN! A THOUSAND STEPS. OH, UNTIL ANOTHER DAY, WHEN YOU WILL YEARN FOR JUST THOSE THOUSAND, FAMILIAR STEPS.
WHAT'S A DAY? AND WHERE WILL I GO?
THAT CAN ONLY BE ANSWERED BY THE BOY WHO COMES AFTER ME.

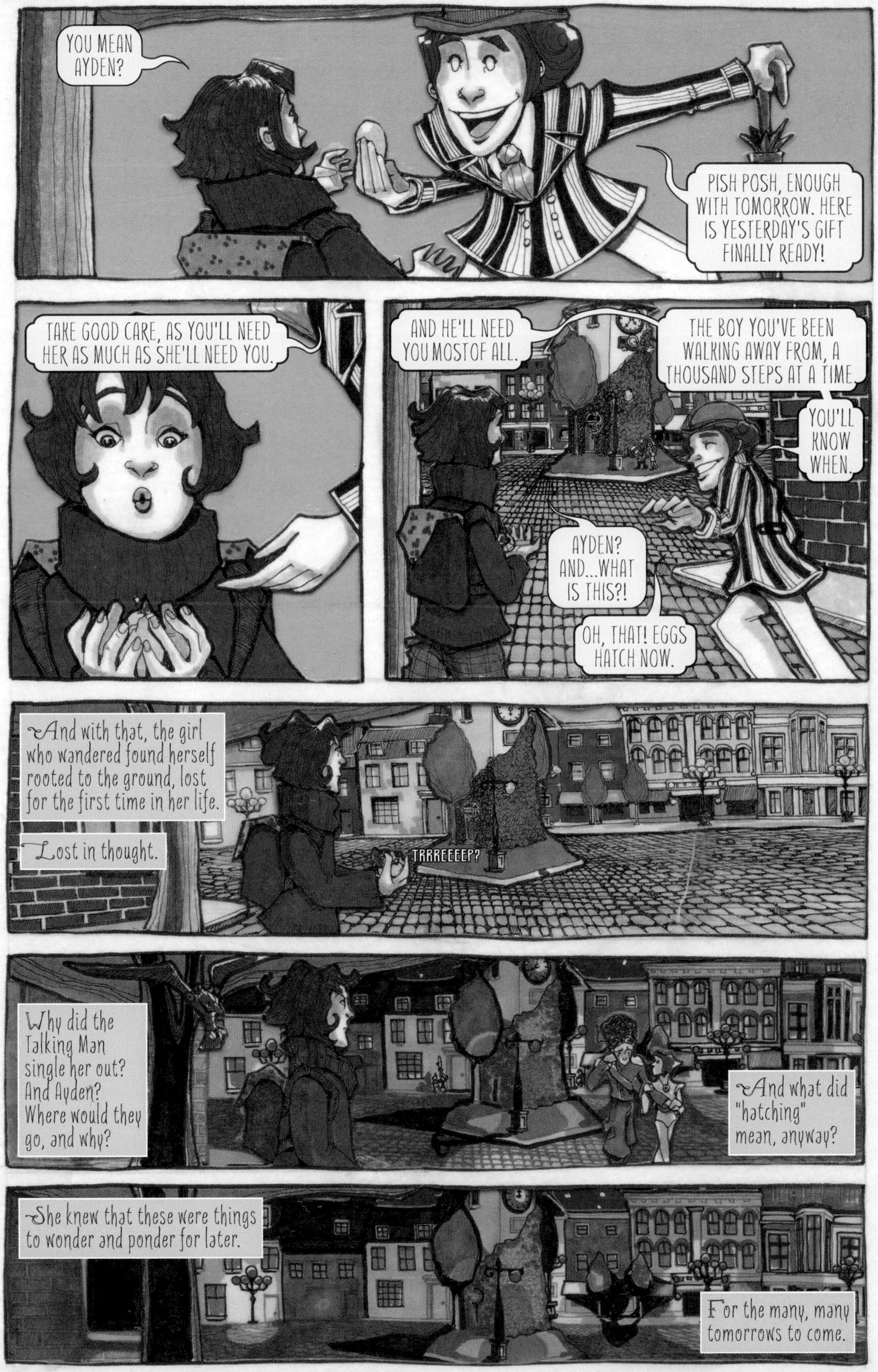
YOU MEAN AYDEN?
PISH POSH, ENOUGH WITH TOMORROW. HERE IS YESTERDAY'S GIFT FINALLY READY!
TAKE GOOD CARE, AS YOU'LL NEED HER AS MUCH AS SHE'LL NEED YOU.
AND HE'LL NEED YOU MOSTOF ALL.
THE BOY YOU'VE BEEN WALKING AWAY FROM, A THOUSAND STEPS AT A TIME.
YOU'LL KNOW WHEN.
AYDEN? AND...WHAT IS THIS?!
OH, THAT! EGGS HATCH NOW.
And with that, the girl who wandered found herself rooted to the ground, lost for the first time in her life.
Lost in thought.
TRRREEEEP?
Why did the Talking Man single her out? And Ayden? Where would they go, and why?
And what did "hatching" mean, anyway?
She knew that these were things to wonder and ponder for later.
For the many, many tomorrows to come.

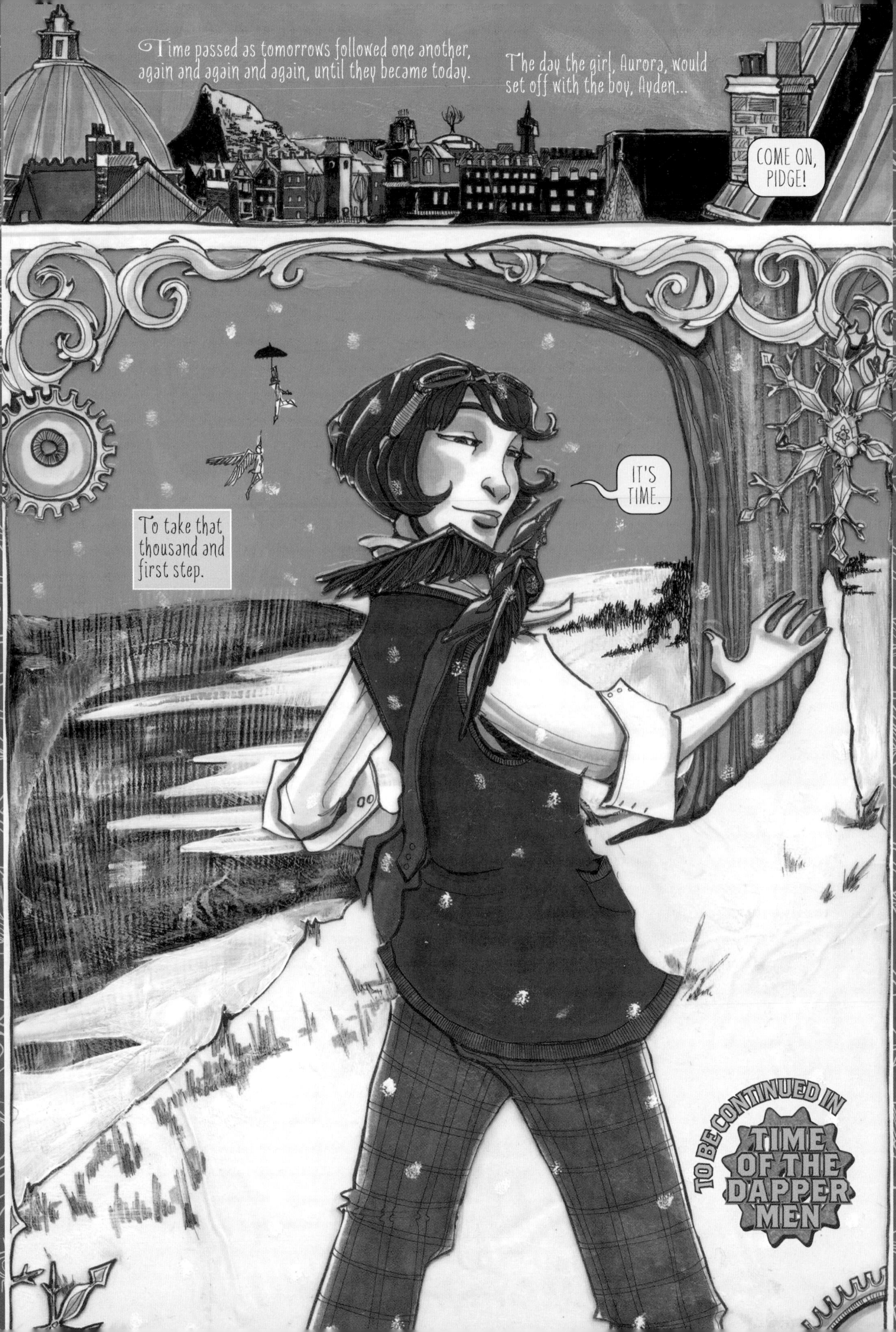
Time passed as tomorrows followed one another, again and again and again, until they became today.
The day the girl, Aurora, would set off with the boy, Ayden...
COME ON, PIDGE!
IT'S TIME.
To take that thousand and first step.
TO BE CONTINUED IN
TIME OF THE DAPPER MEN

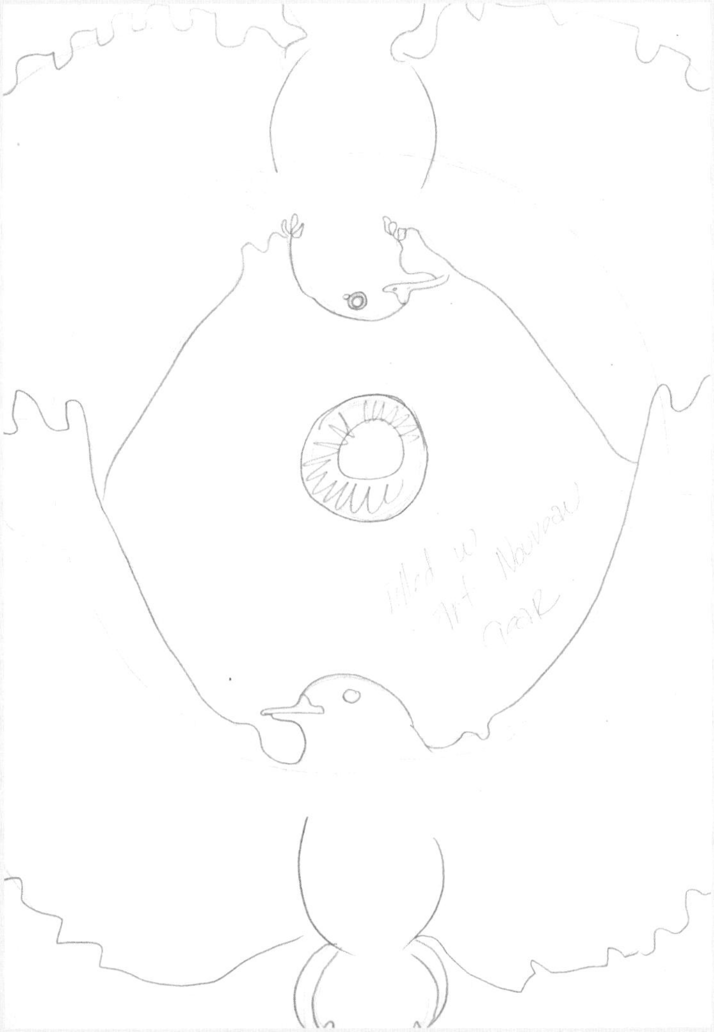

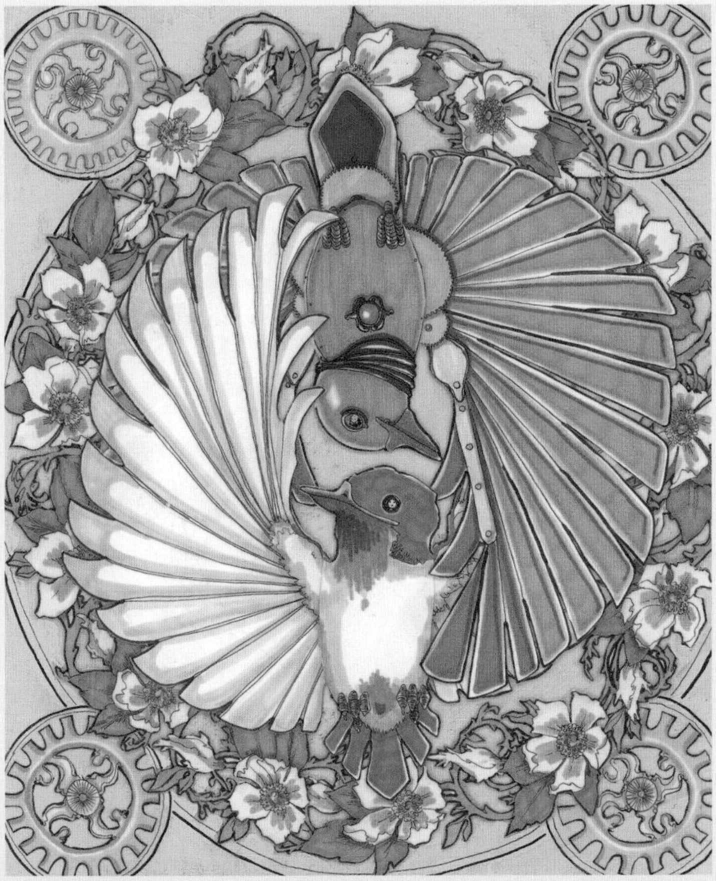

DAPPER MEN SKETCHBOOK

A LOOK AT THE CREATION OF
THE DAPPER MEN WITH JIM MCCANN

A BIRD IN THE HAND

The image of the birds entwined has become one of the most popular images from the entire book. We've sold prints, had bidding wars over the original page, and seen tattoos of it! As you can see, though, it almost didn't turn out the way it did. Below is the original script:

PAGE 15

VERY artistic page- think gallery. EXTREME close up as the two birds swirl, entwined into an organic/ robotic yin/yang. In their eyes are reflected our main characters- in the robot bird's cold metal eye, we see Ayden; in the organic bird's soft eye, we see the cold robotic form of Zoe.

This is the only page that Janet and I ever fought over. You can see in the original sketch, the birds aren't entwined. Janet's argument was that birds' wings couldn't bend back enough to form an actual Yin-Yang. It was an image I felt very strongly about, though. For me, it was the first spiritual allusion to the events happening in the book. We went a few rounds of "That's not possible" and "It's a fairytale!" before Janet threw her arms up in the air and said "Fine!"

In the finished image, Janet's incredible skill makes this page a beauty. There are at least 5 layers of art on this page alone!

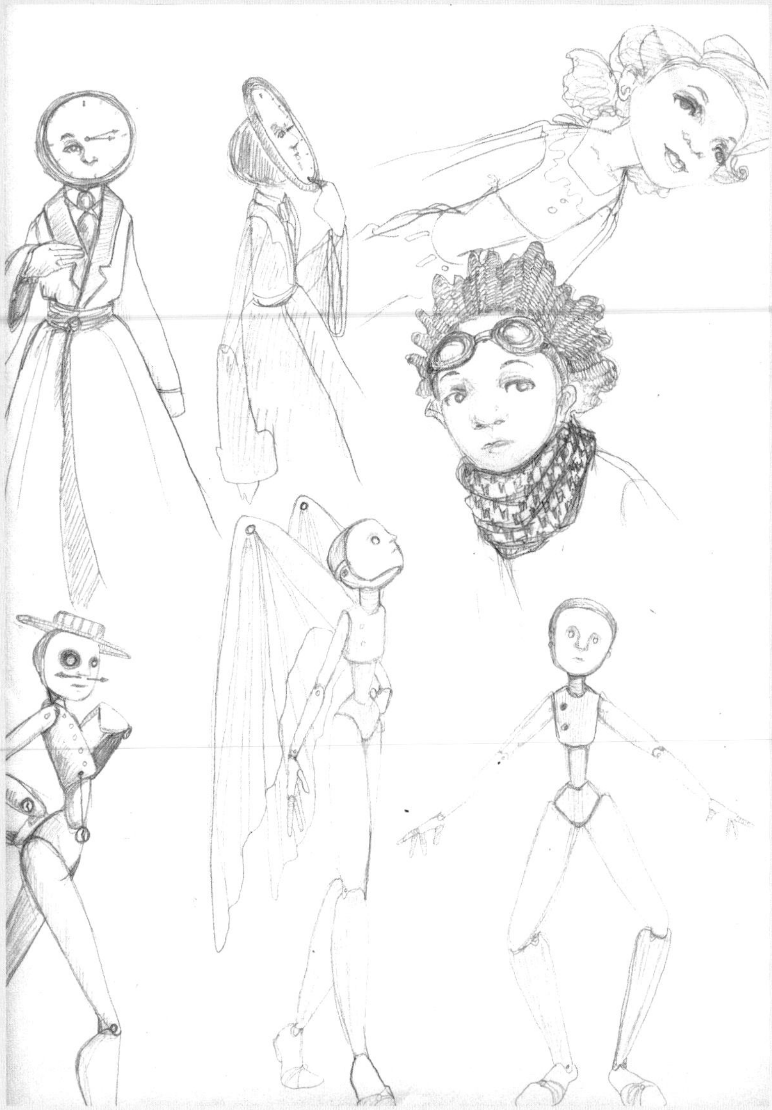

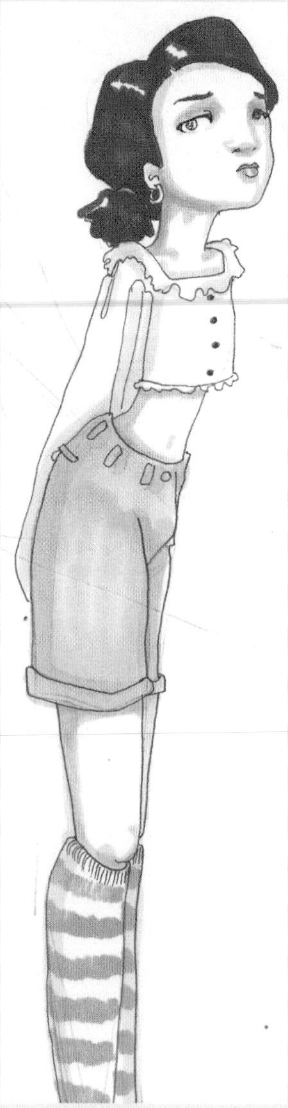

THE GANG'S ALL HERE

One of the things we like best about working together is that Janet's and my process is truly organic. This piece on the far left was drawn during our very first planning session. Janet was sitting on the floor doodling in her sketchbook, and I was typing out plot notes. I looked down and saw the girl in the corner, and her sweet face told me she was actually a brat, covering it up.

Thus was the birth of Harmony.

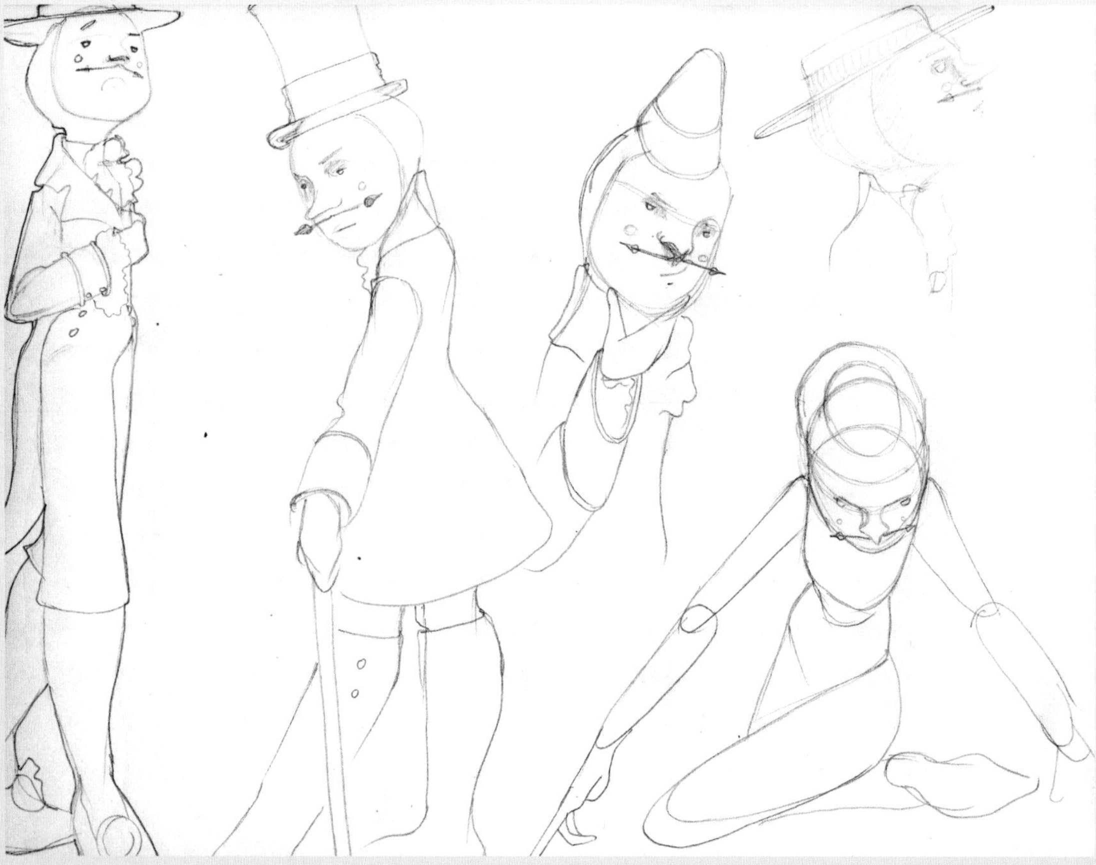

Fabre makes his first appearance here as well, though we hadn't named him yet, so we called him "Frenchie" for a while. Next to him is the Zoe-that-almost-was. The robots at one point were going to look similar, the only differences being the masks or clock faces they wore.

A printed version of this hung on my cubicle wall at Marvel so I could always feel like a part of me was in Anorev.

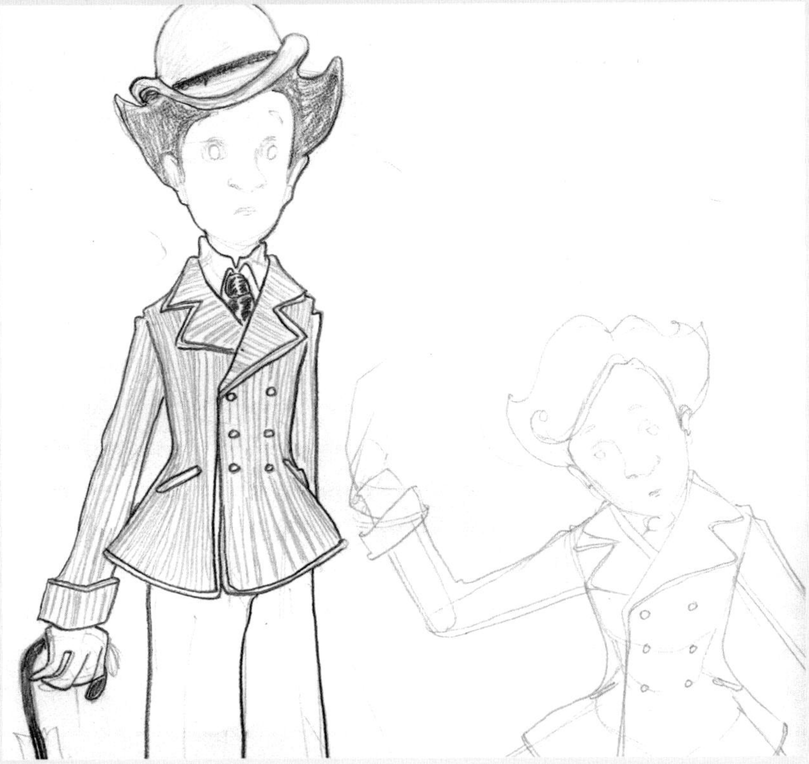

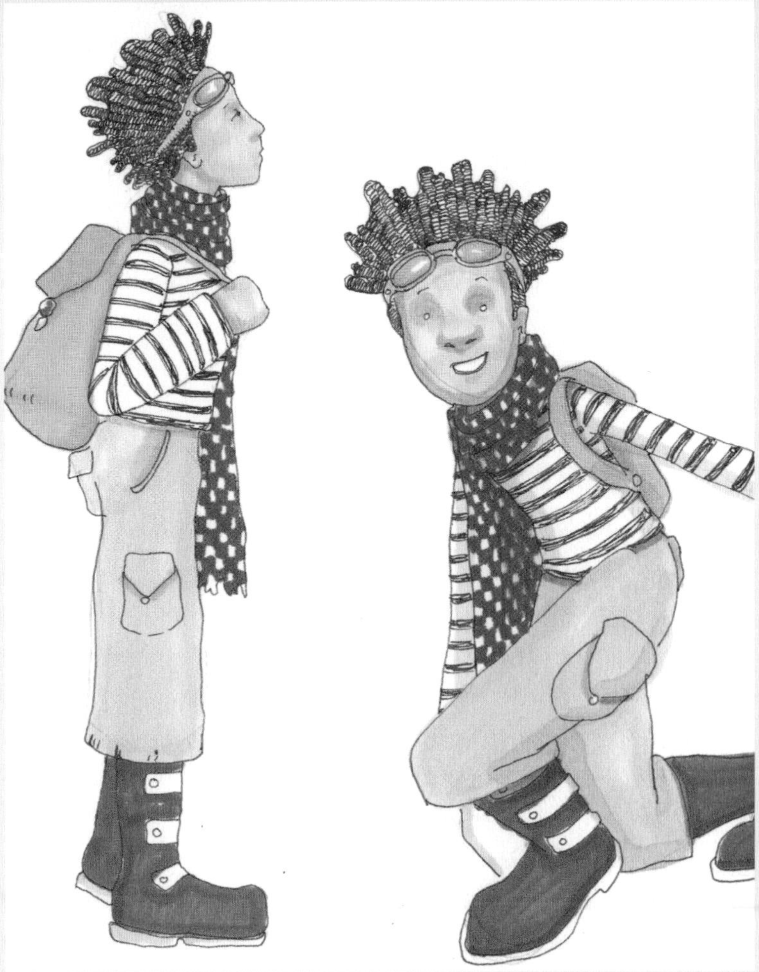

A VERY DAPPER TRIO

The book was inspired by three different paintings by Janet from three different shows. Ayden was the one character who changed the least from his original steampunk-boy holiday ornament. His face thinned out a little and his clothes changed, but that sense of a boy who questions was always there.

41 and the Dapper Men were based on a painting Janet had done of identical men raining from the sky, but with canes. That piece is 6' x 3'—practically the size of a door! To set 41 apart from the others, we wanted to play with how he could be more whimsical. Above are the first sketches of what would be our talkative, enigmatic guide through Anorev.

The one to change the most was Zoe. Her original inspiration is a very 50s/60s Jetsons-inspired robot girl; she looked like she could be Rosie's daughter. To me, neither the original, nor the finished versions of Zoe needed to speak to communicate—they used their eyes and body language, which was more pure. This here was the third version of Zoe, the one we decided to go with. It wasn't until after the design that I mentioned to Janet, "Oh yeah, Zoe doesn't speak."

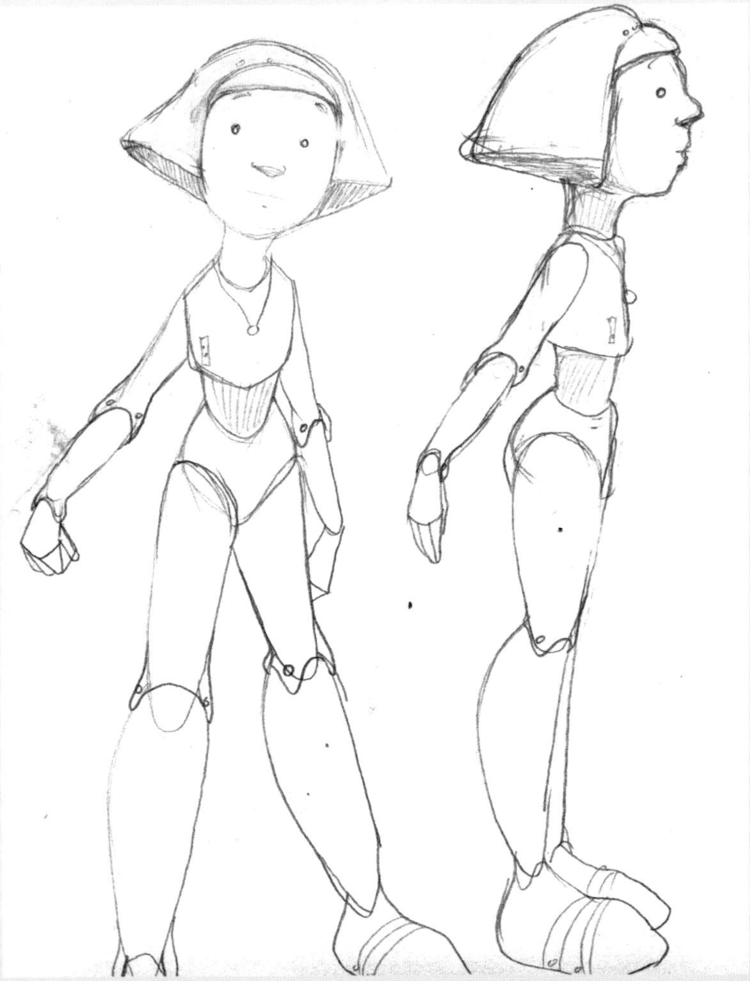

THE MAKING OF A DAPPER PAGE

One of the things that has continued to catch people's attention about *Return of the Dapper Men*, from the initial pitch to convention appearances to the final book has been the art. Not only because of its imaginative style and inspirational visuals, but because of the actual art itself, specifically how the art was made. Janet's process has been called "groundbreaking" and "revolutionary," but it's rooted in a time-honored tradition: decoupage. It's this style that adds texture and depth to an already rich world, giving it an organic feel in a world comprised of robots and pin-stripe suits.

So, how does she do it?

The construction of a page begins with the script. Janet and I have known each other for years and it was her art style that inspired the fairy tale approach to the story of *Return of the Dapper Men*. Janet, being a gallery artist, could handle a number of splash pages with very little direction — in fact, for many of them. I would indicate in the script the general feeling that we were going for and provide the narration and let her go free. This, however, was her first graphic novel, which meant she needed to take her style and adopt it to sequential visual storytelling. It also meant I had to adjust a bit as well. As we got deeper into the story and Janet became more comfortable with the sequential pages and multiple panels. I started adding more. It also fit the theme of the book — that Time had returned and order was being restored. It also helped drive home the urgency as the sun was setting. This urgency came to a head in page 70.

Here is the script for page 70:

PAGE 70

Panel 1: 41 is looking up among the clouds.

41: We can't be everywhere at once. Well, we could, I suppose, but that's neither here nor there. Or there. Or even way out there.

Panel 2: He turns towards the crowd (and us).

41: The point is we shouldn't have needed to return! But you...

you just stopped! Does it matter where we've been when it's you who should have been going places?

Panels 3 - 8: A series of small panels (like when Fabre was trying on hats) with Harmony and Jas, Devick & Dear, Fabre & Guillaume, Reese and Dak and Llew, Zoe and Ayden all taking it in in their own way (Fabre, eyebrow cocked, Devick & Dear huddled together, Harm's arms crossed, Ayden and Zoe understanding), silent. The last small panel should be filled with four Dappers, just looking, with their frowns.

Panel 9: A small panel of 41, looking down.

41: I know... I've already said too much.

Panel 10: Ayden steps forward to address the group. 41 is looking up, a proud look in his eye.

AYDEN: He's right. Everything's wrong. Look around us.

AYDEN: We forgot to remember.

Panel 11: Strip across the page. The other Dappers turn away as Ayden and 41 start to walk. In the background, Harmony and Fabre are sizing each other up. Devick and Dear are with Zoe. 41 is moving Ayden off by himself.

Silence.

We wanted to show as many of the major characters as possible in this moment. 41 understands that he can only say so much, that those who inhabit Anorev need to learn for themselves again. But he has a very captive audience, from the kids to the robots and even some of the other Dapper Men. This was the turning point, the moment we'd start entering ACT III. Ayden finished what 41 started to say, just as it was his destiny to continue everything that 41 left behind.

I knew this would be a difficult page, having 11 panels on the page, but Janet had a great grasp of perspective and character grouping for those middle panels.

And so she started, as most artists do, by drawing.

Janet uses Strathmore Bristol Vellum paper, a slightly texturized and heavy stock paper. She pencils and scans those pencils for me to review. Once approved, which this page was immediately, she goes on to inks, using a combination of Faber-Castell brush pens and Micron .005 pens. The heavy black lines indicate what will be cut after coloring.

For coloring, she used a wide variety of Prismacolor markers. To achieve the proper shine and texture, multiple hues of the same color are often needed. Fun fact (for the reader, not as much fun for Janet): the hair for the Dapper Men has five different shades of red/orange to achieve that glow and shine. Another fact, one that was pointed out by 41 in the book, is that Zoe's hair is colored using the same five hues as the Dapper Men. Harmony's hair only uses four of the hues.

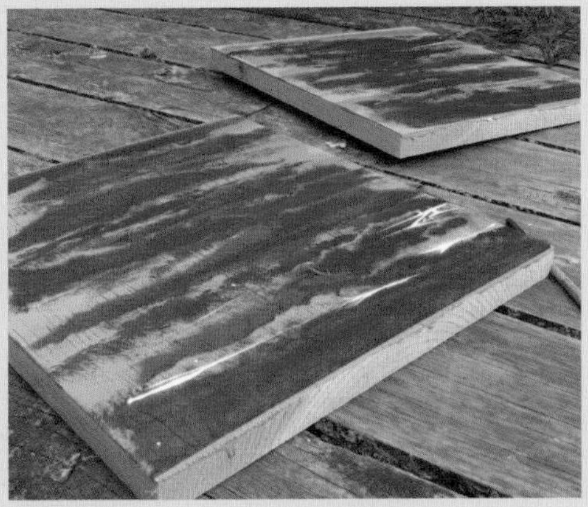

Next up is painting the board. Each of these pages are mounted on board, usually pine, which Janet buys from the lumber section of her local home improvement store, and then takes to the basement and cuts to approximately trim size using a power saw. She sometimes uses pages from books, art papers, or designs that she's drawn to lay down a background on the pine. Usually, as in this page, she paints the wood whatever background color the scene requires, using mistints of house paint, also found at the home improvement store. In this case, the sun is setting and change is in the air, so she painted it using the base coat of the cerulean blue that the Dapper Men had brought back to the world when Time started again and ten layers of sunset colors. Knowing that there would be multiple pages like this, she painted a few boards at a time, then let them dry.

While the background's drying, it's time to cut.

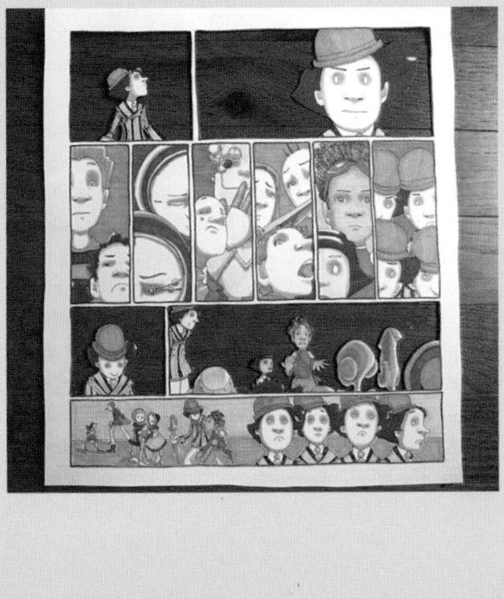

Using three different types of scissors, she goes in and cuts out everywhere that the background should be seen. In other pages, she would sometimes draw additional characters on another page, cut them out, and use them as a layer. In this case, however, it was 41 and the message he started and Ayden continues that were the most important panels, so those were the ones that had the cut-outs. Those panels had the backgrounds cut out so that the sunset on the painted wood would catch your eye and remind you that the world around them is changing.

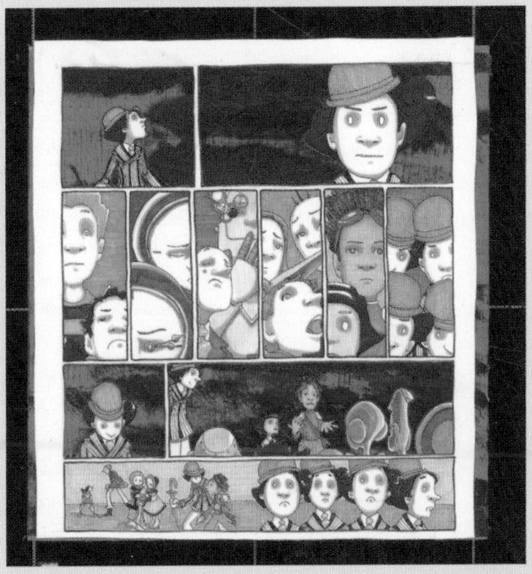

Laying down the layers, Janet then uses a popular item from the 1970s — Mod Podge — to glue the layers to the board. Once the layers are in place and glued down, a varnish is applied to seal the entire thing. Janet has said that her method was developed to make her art kid-proof, going so far as to say you could tap dance on it if you wanted to. The only thing to avoid is getting the piece wet. As you can see, the finished page is also a ready-to-hang piece of gallery art. The board is scanned in high res, the excess is cropped, the lettering layered, and there you have it — a finished page of a graphic novel, done unlike any other that I've seen.

It's an unusual approach and one that has evolved as we put together this first book, all of us learning along the way. But it is one that has inspired me from the moment I saw the three art pieces she had done over various times during Christmas, 2008, that would eventually spark the idea of *Return of the Dapper Men* in my mind. Janet has jokingly dismissed her process as a "poor man's Photoshop," but I think I speak for everyone that sees her work in person and now on the printed page when I say, we're all a little richer for experiencing her art.

—JIM McCANN, SEPTEMBER, 2010

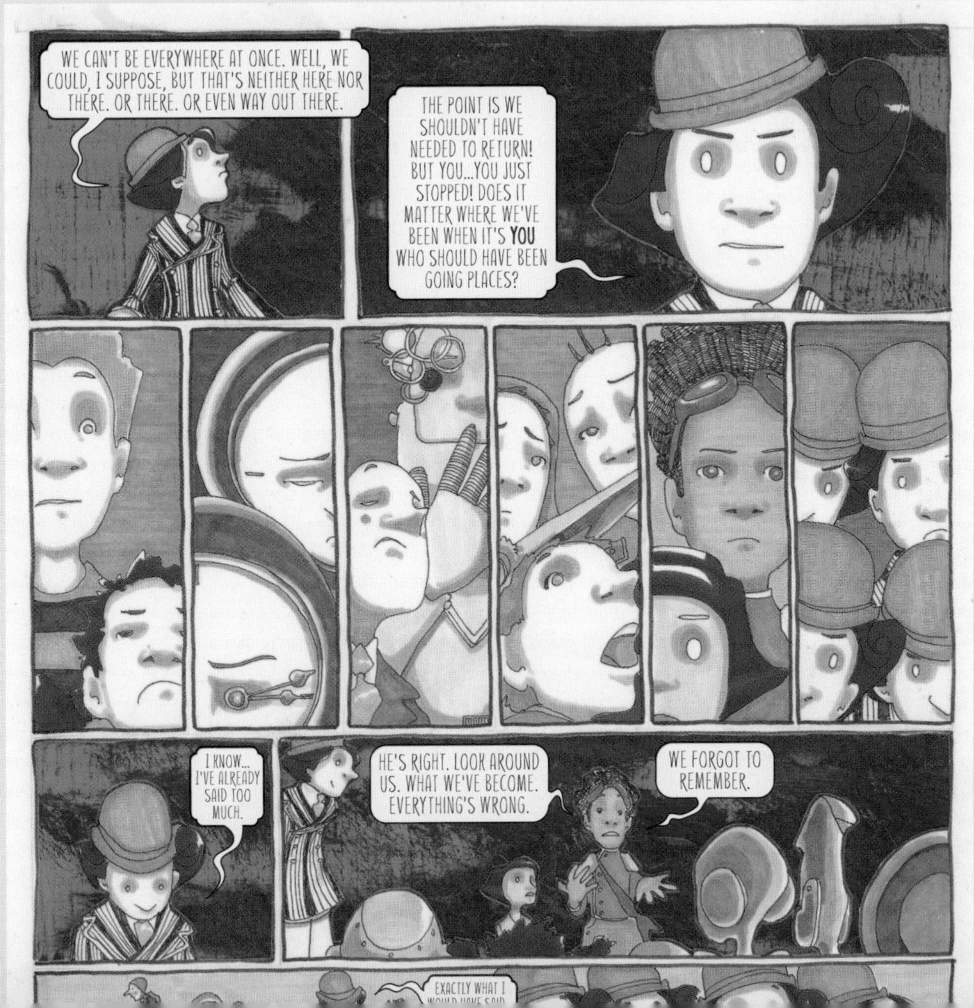
WE CAN'T BE EVERYWHERE AT ONCE. WELL, WE COULD, I SUPPOSE, BUT THAT'S NEITHER HERE NOR THERE. OR THERE. OR EVEN WAY OUT THERE.
THE POINT IS WE SHOULDN'T HAVE NEEDED TO RETURN! BUT YOU...YOU JUST STOPPED! DOES IT MATTER WHERE WE'VE BEEN WHEN IT'S YOU WHO SHOULD HAVE BEEN GOING PLACES?
I KNOW... I'VE ALREADY SAID TOO MUCH.
HE'S RIGHT. LOOK AROUND US. WHAT WE'VE BECOME. EVERYTHING'S WRONG.
WE FORGOT TO REMEMBER.
EXACTLY WHAT I

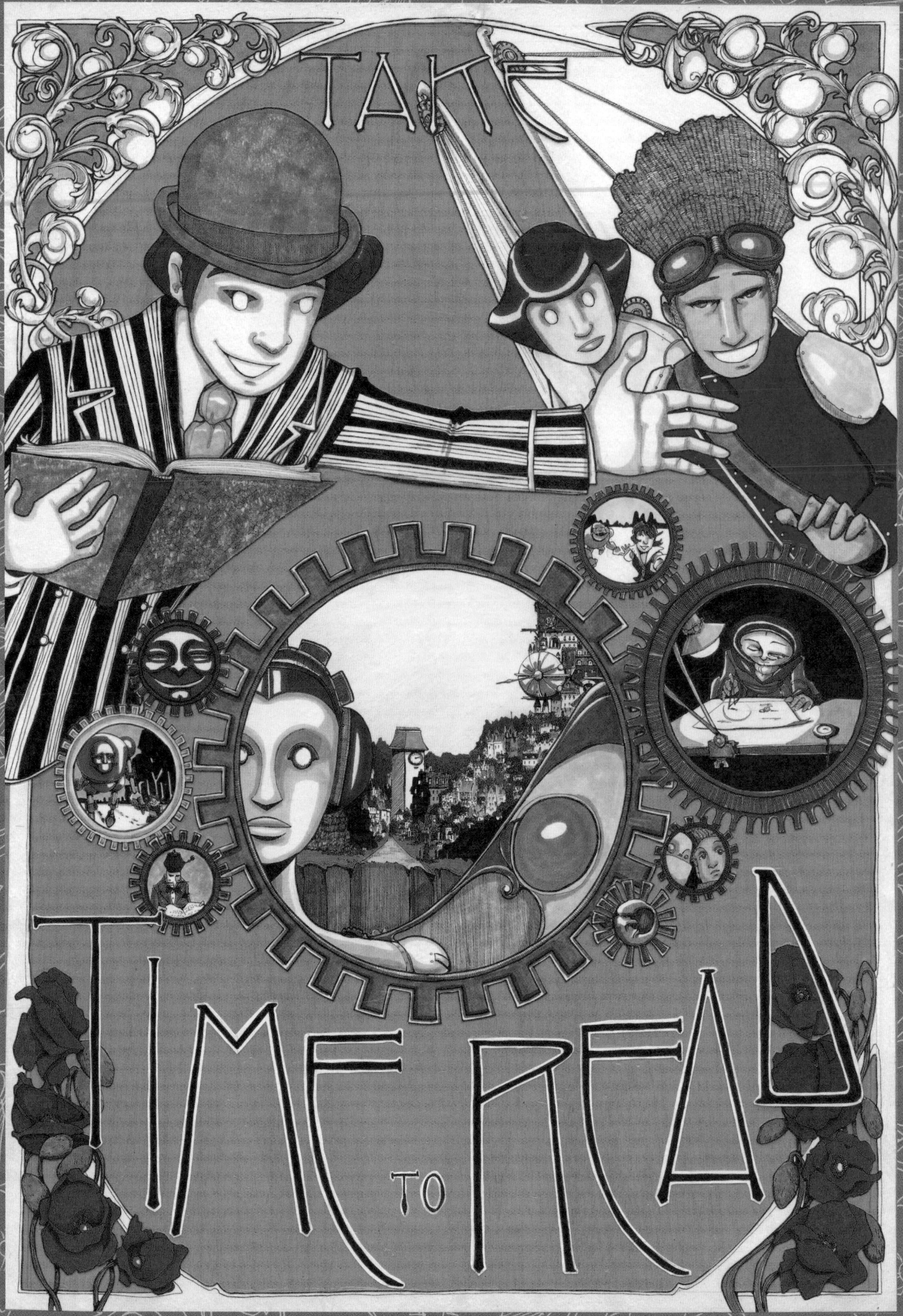

TAKE
TIME TO READ

DAPPER MEN IN AMERICA'S LIBRARIES

I grew up in a bookish family. My dad was a professor and physicist; my mom was a teacher and nurse. Mom didn't care much for TV, and though video games weren't really a thing back then, I'm sure she would have disapproved of them too. Mom did approve of playing outside and reading books, so our weekly treat was a trip to the library. Libraries were magic. Even today, the smell of rows and rows of books gives me a thrill of joy. With my library card, I traveled the known universe and beyond, sitting high in a tree branch or curled up in my room.

We got the call in early 2011 that *Return of the Dapper Men* had been nominated for the prestigious YALSA list, "Great Graphic Novels for Teens". Jim and I were invited to the American Library Association's Midwinter Conference, and their big event that summer as well. I knew many of the people and libraries there — not personally, but with an intimacy unique to book-lovers: through their library collections. For the better part of two decades, I worked by day as a book wholesaler, purchasing books from publishers to supply libraries just like these.

In my office for that job, I loved to hang book-centric artwork: advertising posters made by publishers for bookstores to display, and especially posters produced by the ALA which encouraged patrons to READ. In an ALA poster, a famous Star Trek actor might be reading a copy of Huxley's *Brave New World* accompanied by a statement of what reading had meant to him. Or Spider-Man might be reading a comic book while dangling head-down from his web. They were beautiful and enticing, and such a wonderful way to celebrate reading. That year, at the 2011 conference, we met ALA's Tina Coleman and were asked if we might want to make one of those posters — and a bookmark! — for *Return of the Dapper Men*. We were thrilled!

I went home to work up the designs. As with everything Dapper, the design process was collaborative, with much back-and-forth between Jim and me. We knew immediately that we wanted the artwork for both the bookmark and the poster to keep the Art Nouveau sensibility, and for the medium to be decoupage, just as it had been in the book. The bookmark was to be a triptych: three repeating gears framing our three main characters, Zoe, 41, and Ayden, on a simple background. Oddly enough, the bookmark was the first time I digitally lettered anything. Pretty simple stuff, but a milestone, nonetheless. The poster was more complex.

We decided that I should hand-letter the poster in decoupage. I have a not-so-secret fascination with type, and a year earlier I had created an art project that would eventually be published as *The Wonderland Alphabet*. Laying out a phrase on a poster, however, was a very different thing. For example, I had to go big. The original art is on a two-foot by four-foot piece of wood. Because we wanted to frame the piece in an intricate border, that meant that in order for the border to look seamless, I had to get creative. I worked with large pieces of heavy watercolor paper — difficult to cut and destructive to delicate pen nibs — but still they weren't quite large enough. So I disguised the seams. In the end, the piece showcased 41 reading to Ayden and Zoe. Below them, a series of gears framed glimpses into the story itself, and our text admonished "Time to Read"—a hint at the second book in the series. We had plans even then.

Our posters and bookmarks for *Return of the Dapper Men* can still be found on the ALA Graphics website. And it still gives me a wonderful thrill to think that our book is in a library. I'm so happy that the young — and the young at heart — can find our Dapper Men there and dream of Anorev.

—JANET LEE, FEBRUARY 2017

ABOUT THE AUTHORS

JIM McCANN is an award-winning writer of stage, television, and comic books. Before he could write, he found himself swept away by fairy tales in books and movies. He lived in Nashville, TN, but spent most of his time in galaxies far, far away. He wrote his first short story at the age of ten and hasn't looked back. Eventually he moved to the fairy tale city of New York where he fulfilled a childhood dream and life-long goal—working for Marvel Comics—where he stayed for six years before leaping off the sidewalk's end into the land of full-time writing. Anorev, the land in *Return of the Dapper Men*, is the biggest world he's ever visited and hopes everyone feels welcome to take their shoes off and escape to whenever they want.

When **JANET LEE** was a child, she couldn't decide if she wanted to be a singer, an actor, a writer, or an artist. She stopped acting after high school. She stopped singing after studying opera. She got a degree in British literature from a near-ivy-league college and worked for more than a decade in the book industry, but she never wrote a novel. Through it all she never stopped drawing and making things and telling stories with her art. In time, she showed her artwork in galleries around her hometown of Nashville and was acclaimed by local critics. One day, her friend Jim McCann called to ask Janet if she would illustrate a wonderful book called *Return of the Dapper Men*—which she had always wanted to do even before she knew the question. And she did!

NEXT

TIME CHANGES EVERYTHING

Time cannot show favor or weep. Time can slow to allow you to savor moments, and can help old wounds heal. But most of all, it lets you know when you have to move on...

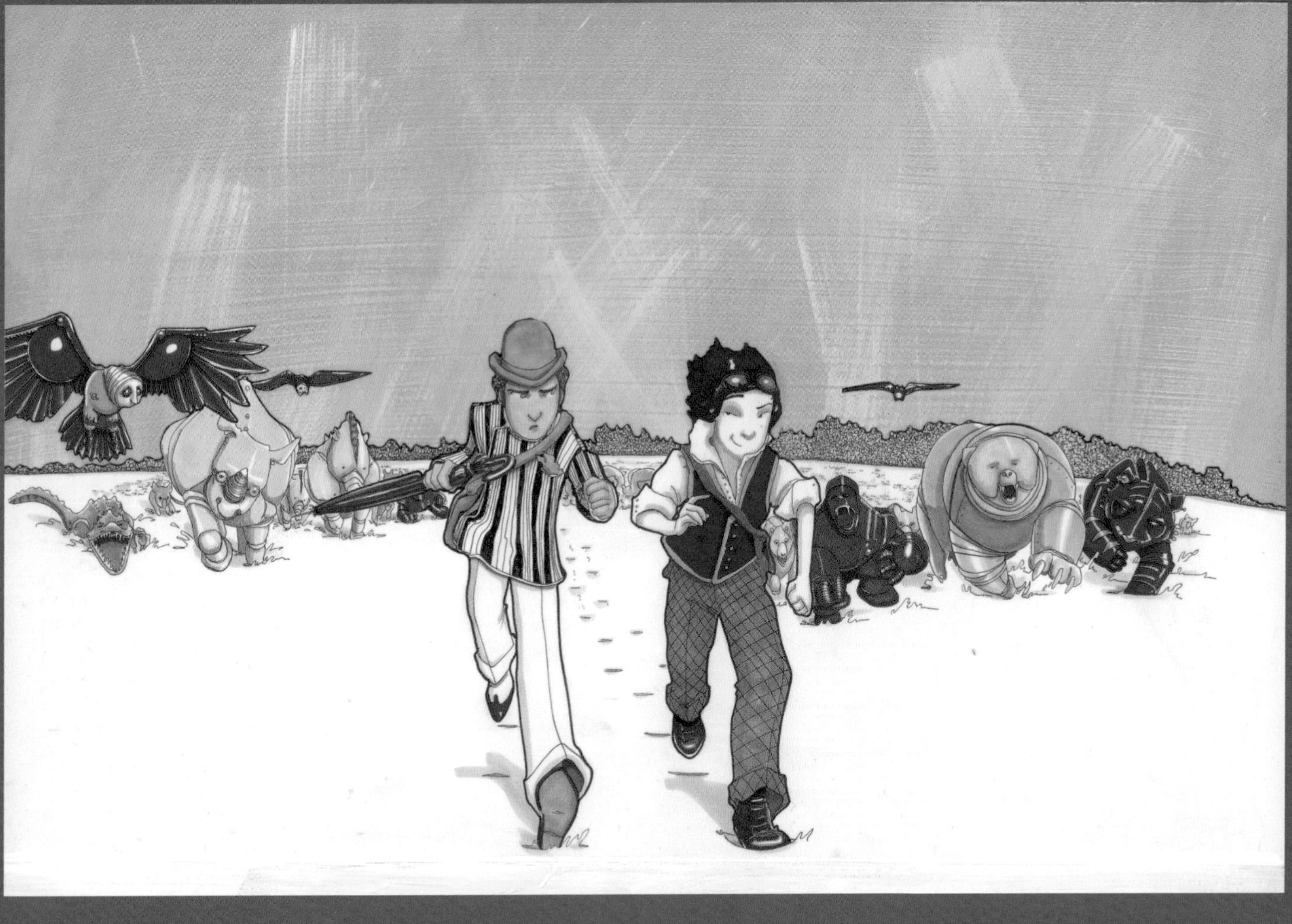

TIME OF THE DAPPER MEN

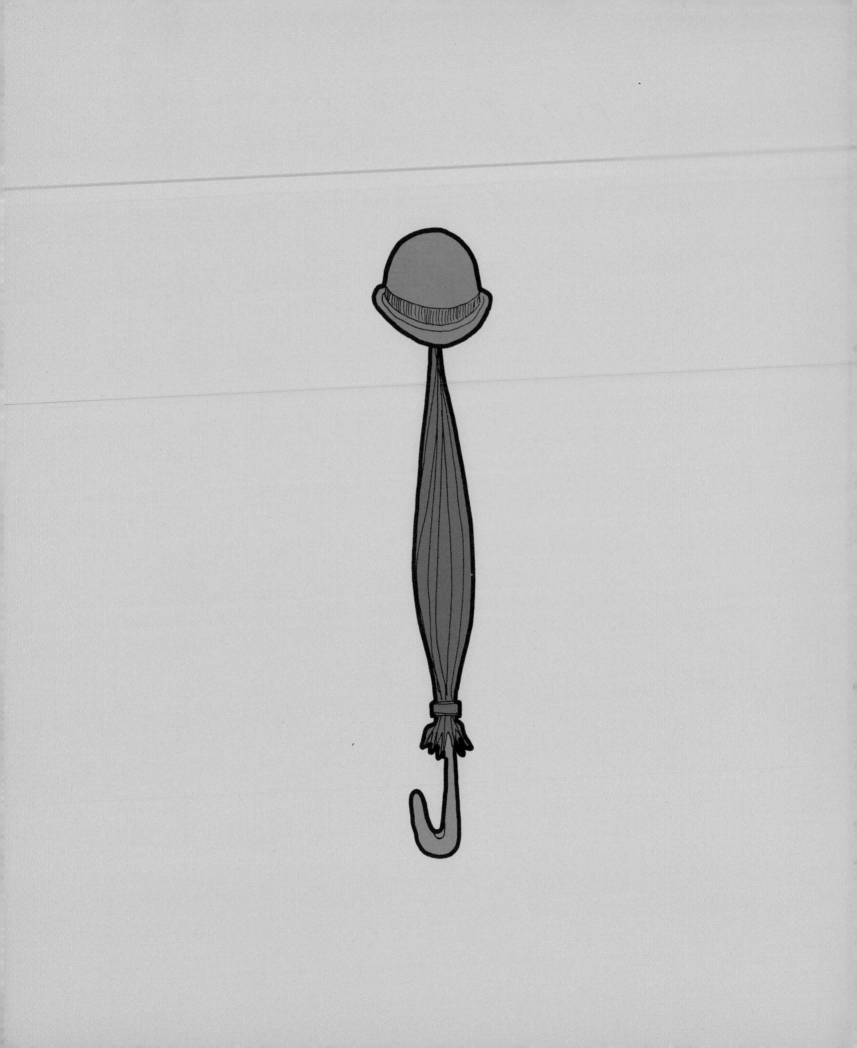

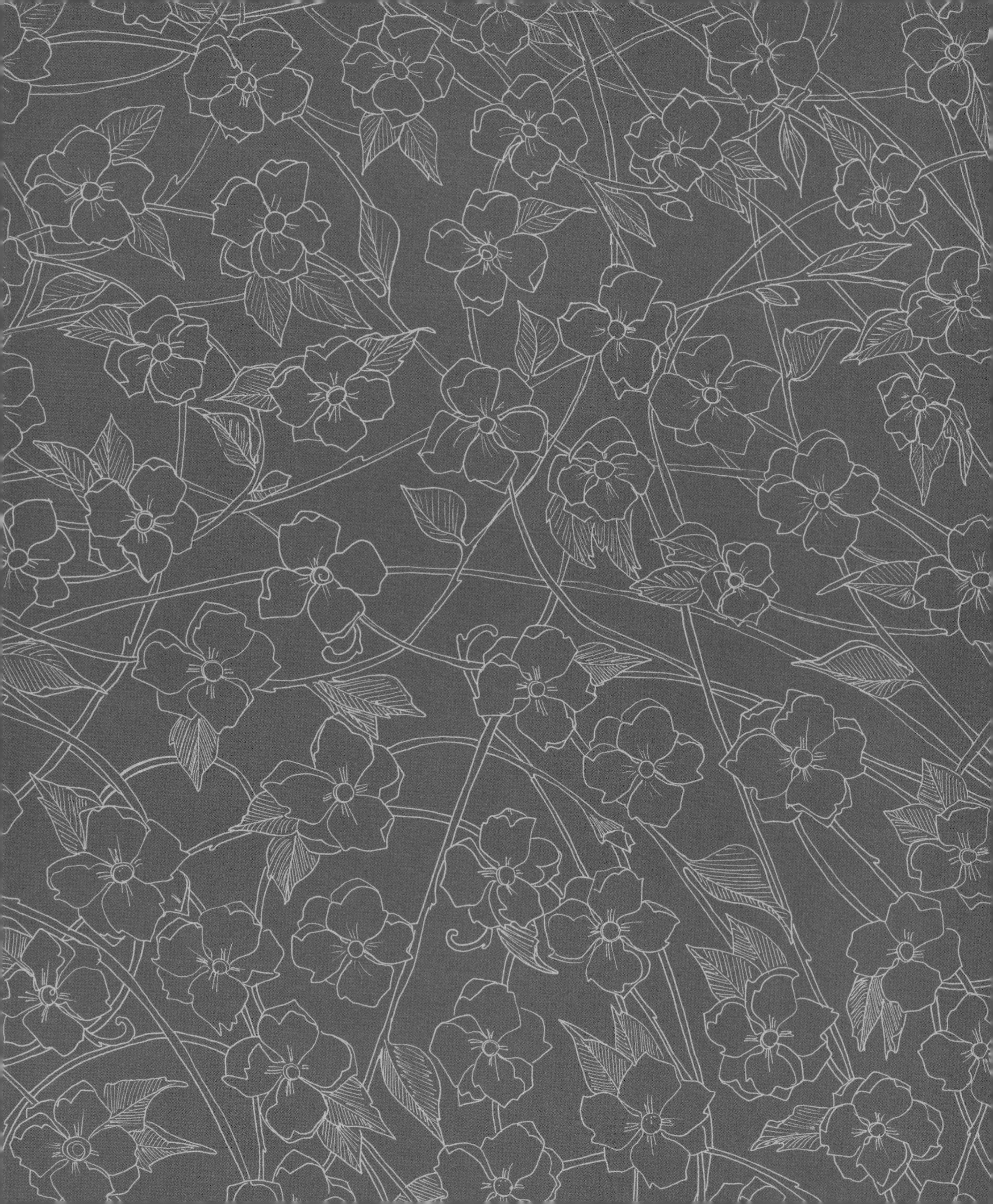

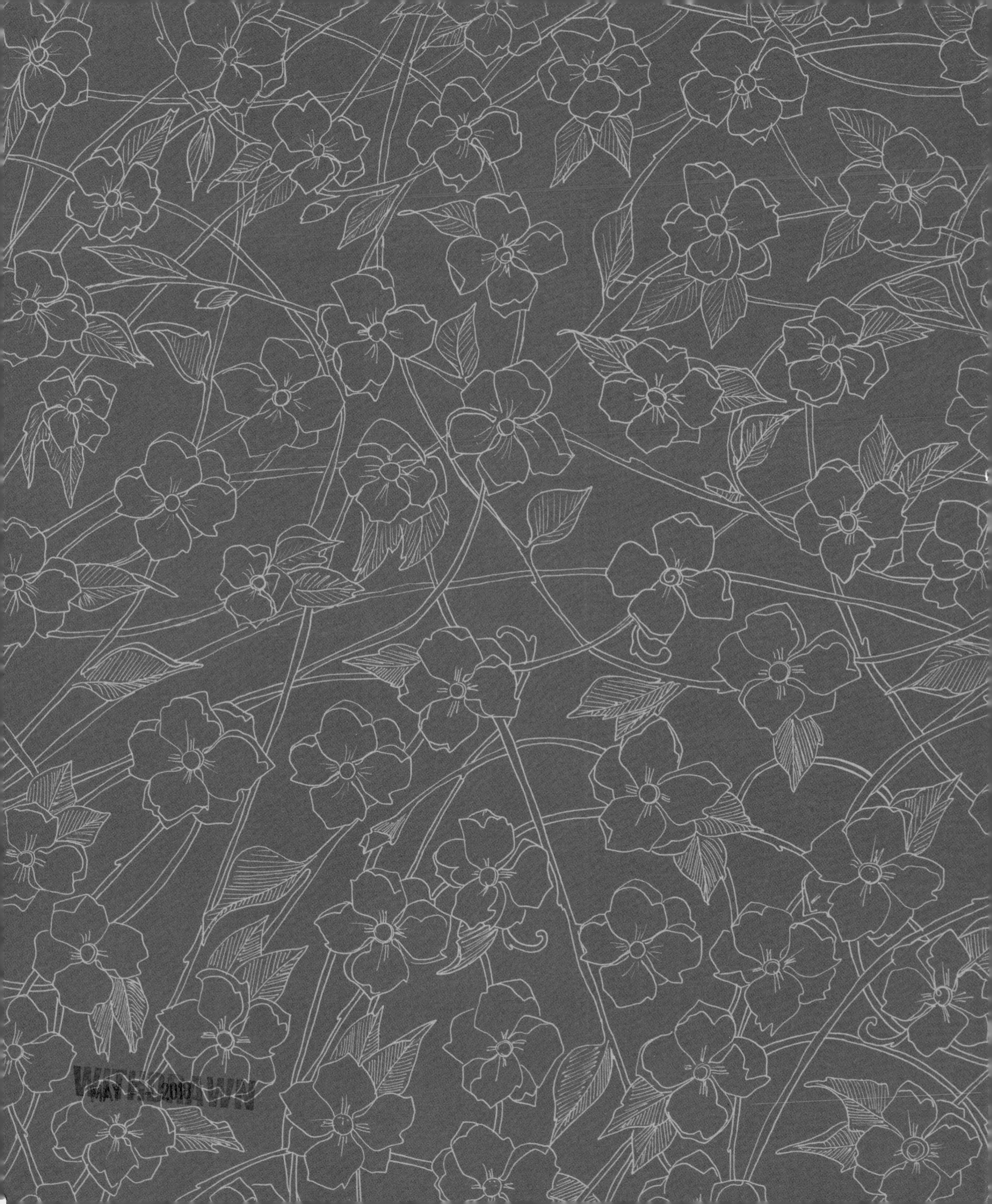